WALKING THRU

ANGIE PELPHREY

Dr. Singer

3:45

1:30 leave

TABLE OF CONTENTS

PROLOGUE

As I entered the gates, shackled and handcuffed, I could only wonder, "How did I get here"? I'm locked up in the Ohio Reformatory for Women in Marysville. A few weeks prior I was at my daughter's ball game cheering in the crowd. Now, I'm a prisoner, an inmate, a felon. State property on this "Farm".

I began social drinking at parties at the early age of 14 and my drinking progressed tremendously within the next year. I drank to fit in. I drank to be popular, to be in the "In" crowd. I drank because I thought people would like me more. I drank because I didn't love myself and the more I drank, the more I could numb the pain.

I loved to play sports and I loved to win, but when I played, winning was never good enough. I was never good enough. I received the award for most valuable player, but that wasn't good enough. I searched to be good enough, to be loved enough, and to be anyone else, other than myself. I only drank on the weekends so I thought that I didn't have a problem, even though I couldn't even remember what had happened most of those weekends. By the time I was 15½, I was a full blown alcoholic. The blackouts were every weekend along with driving drunk and putting me and my community at risk.

I headed out with my friends to another weekend bash and I can remember stopping to buy wine coolers. I drank all four in the car before we got to my friend's house. When we got back to her house, I was already buzzed but I decided that I needed more liquor if I was going to be able to party like everyone else. I drank more and more and more until I passed out. Suddenly, I awoke, dazed and confused, to a teenage boy raping me. I tried to push him away, but I was so drunk that I couldn't move. My arms and legs felt like they were a hundred pounds apiece. "No, no, please stop", I yelled! He slowly got up, looked at me, opened the door, and walked out. I never saw him again but the image of him has been embedded in my mind for the last twenty years. Fear and shame tormented my mind day and night. I held onto the shame, guilt and the secret of my rape for the next twenty years. I held onto the secret because I thought it was my fault. I thought if I had not been drunk again then he wouldn't have raped me. After the rape, I became very promiscuous. I thought that if I slept with the right boy then he would be the one who really loved me. I thought that as long as they told me that they loved me then that was all I needed. I didn't need self respect or self worth, I just needed for someone to see me, for someone to tell me that they loved me. My parents were very loving people but that just wasn't good enough. They hugged me, kissed me and told me they loved me every day of my life, but still it wasn't good enough. It's never good enough when you don't love yourself.

At the age of 16 my parents admitted me into treatment in Columbus, Ohio for thirty days. I can remember thinking, "How could they do this to me"? I'm only 16 years old and now I have to leave my high school and be labeled an alcoholic. I just wanted to have fun like everyone else. I just wanted to party. I just wanted for someone to love me. I only drank on the weekends like my friends. But I was slowly killing myself and my family and I just wasn't ready to admit it. After rehab, I thought that I was doing really well because I wasn't drinking every weekend like I used to, but after about 6 months I went right back full force.

After high school I received a scholarship to Ohio Dominican College for volleyball and softball. After the first few months in college, my drinking became so bad that I was failing classes and quit the softball team and lost my scholarship. I continued playing volleyball, but I couldn't seem to get to practice on time and I was always hung over from the night before. My coach looked at me one day and said, "Angie, you are good enough to play for Ohio State, what's going on with you"? My self-esteem was so low and

2

I really didn't even know who I was. My college years which should have been wonderful were turning out to be a disaster.

After two years of college, I met my husband Barry and only after 3 months of dating, I was pregnant. We were married 2 months later and on September 25, 1990 I delivered our first daughter, Kayla. My life changed tremendously. I always wanted to be a wife and mother and my dreams were coming true. When I didn't feel loved, I knew that my daughter would love me, because I was always told that kids had unconditional love.

Life was still difficult but I stopped drinking the moment I found out that I was pregnant. I never drank again. I was without a job, my husband moved us from Columbus to Minford, Ohio and I hated it. Barry was traveling in his sales job and I was in a new town with no friends or family. So I went back to college in the nursing program. I remained sober through it all. I became pregnant with our second daughter, Tori, and worked hard to finish college. I received my nursing degree as an RN and started looking for work. My first job was in a doctor's office, where I stayed for about a year and then was hired at another local pediatric office. He was a Christian doctor with a love for people and I knew that this was where God wanted me to be.

In 1995 on my way to Catholic Church with my two daughters, and pregnant with our third daughter, God spoke to me, for what I thought was the first time. I turned the car around and headed back over the hill and ended up at Rubyville Community Church, where I gave my heart to the Lord. At that time I really didn't know what had happened, but I did know that I felt different inside. We were both working good jobs, we had two beautiful daughters with one on the way, and we were now living for the Lord. I never thought that I could be so happy. Barry was called to preach about a year after getting saved and he began to travel as an evangelist.

In October 1995, I delivered our third daughter, Aleah. I loved my family and our new way of life. At the age of 30, I was in Myrtle Beach with my family and I got a pain in my hip. Over the next few days, the pain had moved to all of my joints. When we got home, I went to the doctor where he diagnosed me with fibromyalgia. The doctor said that there really wasn't much that he could do, other than for me to maintain an exercise program. After several months the pain was so bad that I decided to try another doctor, who in turn, prescribed 80 Lortabs a month. After the first month on the lortab, the pain increased tremendously. (I didn't know until after I was clean that pain pills made fibromyalgia symptoms worse) I returned back to him for my monthly visit and he changed my prescription to percocet and gave me over 100 pills a month. After the second month, I couldn't go a few hours without a pill. I was a full-blown drug addict.

This went on for about three years. I would become bedridden without the pills. So, when I started to withdraw, I would have my husband take me to the emergency room to stop the pain. I started going to other doctors to make sure that I would never run out of pills. My life was so chaotic at this time; most of which I have trouble remembering. I was always late for everything, I couldn't do the housework without pills and I wasn't there for my husband and children. I couldn't understand how this happened. How did I get this bad? I couldn't stop. Many times I thought that death was my only option. If I just ran my van into a tree and die, then my family won't have to live like this. I thought that my husband and children would be much better off without a drug addict for a wife and mother.

How could I tell anyone that I had a problem when I was supposed to be a Christian? Christians can't become drug addicts, so I must be a horrible person. The shame and the guilt were so overwhelming that I didn't even want to leave my home. I didn't want anyone to see me like this. I pushed my family and friends away, and most of all God. My husband was the pastor of our church and I was a closet user. I stopped reading my Bible and praying, because the pills came first. I can remember a time when my husband held up a picture of my children and a pain pill and he said, "You decide which one you want the most?" I couldn't do that because the most important thing in my life at that time was the pills. I loved my family so much, but the pills had control over my mind, body and soul.

In 2003 I was working at a local hospital and was nine months clean of drugs. I thought that I could go right back to work as a nurse as long as I wasn't dispensing pain pills to patients. I was so wrong. Being around the pills, knowing that they were there and seeing them every day was too much for an addict to take. I had quit on my own, but I was just a "dry" drug addict who didn't use pills any longer. I still didn't love myself and I still didn't know who I was. The only thing that I knew was that I wanted true freedom from the pills. After some time at the hospital, I began manipulating ways to take pills from patients. I went to their home to steal their pills. I couldn't believe that I could do something like that. I was a nurse, a caregiver and a woman that loved to help people, but the drugs were bigger than any of that. I couldn't live without them. After a while, I was turned into the police for stealing pills and on November 23, 2004 I was arrested.

I stood before the judge, my family, friends and God, and was sentenced to 2 years in the Ohio Reformatory for Women. My family began to weep. My children were so scared and confused, wondering how they were going to make it without their mom for the next two years. My husband, who was always able to help me and take care of me, was unable to fix this. He was unable to free me from this addiction or this prison that I was headed to. He felt like a failure, but to me he was my "hero". He stood by me never giving up hope.

The guards escorted me back to the Scioto County Jail

where I awaited my transfer to prison. While in jail, my life changed forever. I met women that were just like me; they were mothers, grandmothers, aunts and friends. These women had a hurt inside of them and a void that was missing in their lives; again they were just like me. The void was Jesus. The void was filled with drugs, alcohol, sex, gambling and anything they could fill it with. They were human beings that made bad choices. While in jail, I thought that my purpose was to help them but in turn they helped me. They taught me what humility was. They taught me what real life was all about. They taught me that I was no different than the prostitutes in Portsmouth or the drug dealers on the streets. You see, I thought that I was different. I thought that I was better than them but they taught me that I was just the same. They taught me that bad things happen to good people and some people have just had to go farther down in life than others. They taught me the true meaning of life and they opened my eyes to the reality of this chaotic world.

In jail we were up every day around 5:00 a.m. for breakfast which was difficult for me because I was not a morning person. As each day passed it got easier and easier to get up. I was beginning to find a reason to live, a reason to get up every day, and a reason to keep fighting, and it came through God's Word. I began reading my bible for hours at a time, and time was something you have a lot of when you're locked up.

After about a month, I was sent to the Ohio Reformatory for Women, the farm, hell on earth. As they escorted us from the police car, shackled and handcuffed, we were taken to a cement room with a bench. We were told not to move. I sat there quietly awaiting our next move. A female guard handed us a gown, a pair of flip flops, a piece of soap and lice shampoo and told us to go into the shower. We had two minutes to wash. No brush to brush our hair nor a hand towel to dry off on. We were then taken to get our picture taken to get our I.D. made. I can remember thinking to myself, "Do I smile or just sit stone faced?" So

I decided not to smile because there was nothing to smile about. I was handed my I.D. with my name and my number on it, 59691.

From then on I was just a number without a name. The guard called my number out, after sitting in reception for over 5 hours, and she told me to follow one of the inmates. This particular inmate had just told us that she was in prison for a life sentence. No chance of ever going home. No chance of ever seeing outside of these walls. She would eventually die behind this razor wired fence. As I followed her, she said "Just walk straight ahead toward that building, and by the way, welcome to hell." Welcome to Hell, what's that supposed to mean? My mind raced and I could feel my heart beating outside of my chest. As I got closer to the building, I could barely see the name of the building I was about to enter and as I approached the door, it read Hale. I thought to myself, "she didn't say 'Welcome to Hell', she said 'Welcome to Hale'". Then, I opened the door to what seemed to be hell on earth.

A CHANGE OF HEART

Sixty-nine assault charges and multiple convictions, she was known for carrying a .38 with her at all times. She has broken the legs, arms and noses of men and women who have gotten in her way. She's done multiple jail sentences and now prison, with her 1st number. I first met this woman at my county jail. I was immediately warned to stay out of her path. "She's mean and angry, and will fight you in a second." So for the 23 days I spent in jail with her, I knew to keep my distance. I never went anywhere close to her. But God had a different plan, He sent me to prison; to the same prison and same dorm that she was in. When I saw her at "Hale" for the first time, she came right up to me and spoke. She was so friendly, I couldn't believe it was her. There was something so different about her. She smiled all the time. She was so friendly and one day spoke of her change of heart and soul. She had been saved. Her heart of anger turned to love. Her thoughts of fear turned to faith. She was truly a different woman. When I talked to her about the change in her life, she just kept saying, "God! It was all God, because I wouldn't have changed for anyone else." She said, "Many people wanted me to change and even tried to help me to change, but I just couldn't do it." She murdered her husband. She had been physically and mentally abused and just felt like she wasn't worthy enough for God to save her. Today, as I sit in this prison with Kim, we speak daily of our 'Jesus.' We go to church together, pray together and now share a true friendship together, between two sisters in Christ. God is willing and waiting to save a heart like hers. I love you, Kim.

A CHILD'S LOVE TURNED TRAGIC

A man was murdered; her father. He was viciously attacked and killed by her mother. She is a young 17-year old I met today in "New Cottage." This is a cottage at the prison that houses juveniles who are 21 years old and younger. One afternoon this girl had received a phone call and on the other end of the line she heard her mother say, "Get here quick, you have to help me -- I just killed your father!" Not knowing what to do the young girl soon arrived home with her new husband of two months. They found her father dead in the bedroom. Her mother had viciously murdered him. "I can't go to prison. I can't leave you children behind!" her mother cried. "You have to help me get rid of the body. If you love me you'll do it. You don't want to see your mother go to prison, do you?"
"I loved my mom with all my heart," said the young girl. I couldn't stand for her to go to prison so we helped her. My new husband and I set fire to my parents' home to destroy the evidence. I had to. They were going to take my mom away if I didn't do something. My mom needed me. My mom begged me. I had to do it for my mom.
It is now four months later and this young girl sits in the Ohio Reformatory for Women serving 25 years to life. Her mother is serving a life sentence in another cottage and her new husband is at a men's prison serving 25 years to life. She lost everyone she ever loved in one day, never to see any of them again, no one to visit, no one to write to her. She loved her mother so much that she gave up her own future for her. This is an unconditional love that's not always understood. The love of a child; used and manipulated to protect her mother's own selfish interests. God's love is a safe love. His love is a kind love, not a manipulating love. I pray that one day she may know true love: the true, unconditional and forgiving love of my Savior Jesus.

A DASH TOWARD DEATH

One of our Tapestry sisters made a dash toward death. She was found last week shot in the head, her body sliced into pieces, and left on the side of the road. She thought that she had gotten all that she needed at the Tapestry Program, but death was what she received. Today a friend of mine decided that she was leaving the Tapestry Program. She said, "I've already got all that I need to stay clean". She has been a drug addict for about fifteen years and she thought that four months in recovery was all that she needed. Today she read the obituary of her friend. She was on a dash towards death, right along with her friend. Running is all that both of them had ever known. Today our Tapestry family took a stand for her. One at a time each sister stood to her feet begging and pleading for her not to leave; begging and pleading for her to choose life over death; to stop running for once in her life, and to stand still and let God move. Today she chose to live. Today she chose to stop running away from her past and to run towards her recovery. I love you, my Tapestry sister.

A GENTLE WAVE OF LOVE

As I sit at night and look out my window, I can clearly see into the window across from me. I watch a woman in an orange outfit sitting at her window. She does the same thing every night. She props both arms up under her chin, and gazes out past the bars into the deep blue skies. We can see each other through the glass and we give a little wave as the lights dim down, and we head off to our bunks to go to sleep. We have so much in common, but living two different lives.   We are both inmates but I will be free soon, and she will live her life here on this farm as a death row inmate.   She will eventually die here, only known as a murderer. I   see her as more.   I see her as a friend.   A friend that I can never speak to, I can only give a wave to her as a gesture of kindness.   She is a person with a horrible past but a person that needs our love and the love of Jesus down in her heart.   I want so much to tell her about the love of Christ and the freedom that she can have in this prison, but I can't.   It is forbidden for anyone to speak to her.   She must live her life as an outcast just as a lot of us have.   But I pray each day that God will allow someone to reach her, to touch her heart, to save her soul, and to free her from the bondage of sin.   Until then, I'll give a gentle and kind wave letting her know that there is someone out here who cares.

A HEART CONDITION

Man's actions are simply a reflection of what is in his heart. So, therefore, man's heart must change if his actions are to change.   When man's heart and life are changed, then his behavior will change.   For many years, the system has attempted to punish man's actions without addressing the root of the problem and the attitudes within the heart. Real change must come from the heart.   Imprisoning can't change a mans heart, so we must rehabilitate him to change his behavior and in turn, change his heart.   The only hope they have is through Jesus Christ.   Here at Marysville we don't have the means to do this.   We are without a chaplain, just like so many other prisons in Ohio.   Officers, as well as inmates, face severe problems each and every day and are in desperate need of the hope of Jesus Christ.   God desires us to change our heart and lives. So, go out and share the gospel with the brokenhearted. Heal the broken hearts by mending them with the Gospel of Jesus Christ. For, when the heart is changed, so are the behaviors.

A JOURNEY THROUGH GRIEF

I'm stuck in my own grief: the loss of my drugs, and now the loss of myself. I feel empty, dead inside. I feel frozen in time, unable to move on. I feel buried alive, unable to get out. I feel trapped in a burning room, unable to find a way of escape. I'm underwater, unable to breathe or see the light. No way of escape! I feel dead, numb inside. I'm running and running, but no place to go. I'm on a spiral spin, spinning faster and faster, round and round. Falling, faster and faster, but never hitting bottom. There's anger, fear, sadness and overwhelming fatigue. These feelings are very common to the women that I converse with daily. Their lives have been shredded by feelings of overwhelming grief. They have felt that there was no place to turn. No one to turn to, and no end to the madness. They sleep just to escape their world of confusion. Today it's time to wake up. Today it's time to end the journey called grief. Let God help you. Seek His love. Seek His wisdom and accept His guidance. Grief is a passion, but we can meet it, beat it, endure it, and come out as victors through Jesus Christ, our tour guide.

13

A LITTLE BIT OF HOPE

I was sitting on my bunk just before the four o'clock count when a woman came toward me. She had just come in from outside; no coat, no hat, no gloves and shivering from the cold. I had seen her before, out in the recreation room and in the yard, but never really had a conversation with her. She stood about 5'10", 250 lbs., and her head was shaved. She wasn't the most beautiful woman I've seen, but she really didn't seem to care what people thought of her. She was known not to shower, or even to brush her teeth. Here in prison you can really get persecuted for that. Well, she approached my bed and said, "Could you help me?" I said, "Sure, what can I do for you?" She began telling me that when she went to work today at the Chow Hall, someone stole all she had; her coat, sweatshirt and gloves. On a cold winter day like today warmth meant everything. She said, "I've been sick for days and now and I don't have anything to keep me warm." So I handed her my sweatshirt and told her that it might help her a little. For the first time since she's been here I saw a little hope in her eyes. The shirt might not have fit her too well, and yes in my mind I thought back to her hygiene problem, but God told me it was okay. That it was okay to give a little hope to someone in place of a lost dirty jacket.

A LITTLE GIRL'S DREAM

There she was, a little girl, who always seemed to live in the shadows. She used to wish so hard for just one friend to play with her. She wanted a mom who would hold her and hug her, and let her sit on her lap. She dreamed of being the popular one, with lots of friends and parents who would smile and laugh with her, people who would sometimes listen to what she wanted to say. She wanted to know that she was a smart girl. But as much as she wanted these things, she knew better, because she was bad. Most people were scared of her, and didn't like her. Her biggest dream was to grow up and be an airline stewardess. She wanted to fly all over the world. Just fly away. Fly to a place where she could have lots of friends in faraway places. When she told her mom, her mom said, "A stewardess is nothing but a waitress in the air." Her dream ended. Her mom told her she could be a waitress, right here on the ground, because that's all she'd ever be. She never dreamed again.

A PLACE CALLED HOME

I dream of a place, not so far away, a place that I call home; a place where I'm free to feel loved. A place where family is love, strength and friendship. Today I can only dream because today home is not an option. Prison is my home today, but I do have the freedom to dream. To dream of rocking my baby girl, Aleah, to sleep, tossing ball with Tori, and having girl talk with Kayla. I dream of taking a walk and maybe even running to wherever I dream to go. I dream of flying a kite on a warm sunny day or walking on the beach hand in hand with my one true love, my husband. I dream of home beyond these prison walls; bubble baths, diet coke and sleeping in my own bed. I dream of a place not so far away. A place I call home: heaven. I dream of walking hand in hand on the streets of gold with my Jesus, soaking my feet in the river of joy, feasting at the Lord's table never to be hungry again. Rocking my baby boy who's been rocked by my Jesus for 10 years now. I dream of having my grandmother hold me one more time, stroke my hair and kiss my forehead. I dream of a place not so far away. I dream of a place that I call home.

A PRISONER IN MY OWN HOME

If you ever leave me, you fat and lazy woman, I'll kill you. No one wants you but me, and I must be stupid to want you. You think that you're beautiful, but you're nothing. Every day as Luanne would wake up for work her keys would be missing, tires slashed or even her car windows busted out. She had a good, well paying job that resulted in her making more money than her husband. In turn it made him feel less than a man. He would do all that he could to prevent her from going to work. Eventually, she was fired. She lived as a prisoner in her own home. He always told her that if she left him, he would hurt her and she would never see her children again. She couldn't let anyone see her bruises or scars, because if she did then she knew that the next time would be worse. So for fifteen years she stayed with him living as a prisoner in her own home. She never realized that for all of those years that she stayed with him that she was hurting her children the most, even though they weren't physically beaten like her. For years she thought that she was protecting them.

A 'SIGN OF LOVE'

I met a young twenty-two year old the other day that is doing a two and a half year sentence for burglary. She proceeded to tell me about the night she was arrested and how when she arrived at jail the women wouldn't even speak to her (because of her crime). She has been an addict for over 5 years and she came from a family where her father encouraged her addiction. He is an alcoholic addict who showed his daughter that the only way to have "real fun" was by using. So that's what she did. As the years went by she fell so deep into her addiction that it led her to crime. She and her co-defendant began robbing churches. Stereo systems, sound equipment and literally anything else they could find to pawn to support their habit. The last church they robbed was the church where her son had just performed in the Easter program. She went inside the church, walked up on the stage and she immediately felt sick. All she could see was her son up on the stage saying his little piece for the program. She began to cry hysterically so she and her co-defendant decided they should leave. As they left the church and began to pull away she saw a phrase hanging under the church sign. It read, "Today is Sunday, but Monday brings a new day." Even as high as she was from all the drugs, she knew that she had to change, and that Monday would be a new day for her. That was the beginning of the rest of her life. On Monday she was arrested and sent to prison to prepare for her new future. Yesterday she opened a Bible (that she had kited from the Chaplain) for the very 1st time in her life and she opened it up to Mark 1:14-15. "Now after that John was put in prison. Jesus came into Galilee, preaching the gospel of the Kingdom of God and saying, 'the time is fulfilled and the Kingdom of God is at hand: repent ye, and believe the gospel.'" God has blessed her with a second chance at life, and I know that one day very soon, she'll give her heart and soul to Him.

A VANITY AFFAIR

"Control! Power! Status! I want it all, the money, the attention, the T.V. shows, all of it." After seeing herself on Maury Povich, the only thing she said was, "What color was the coat I had on?" She wanted him dead. Was it anger from a bad marriage, or was it the insurance money? Was it the abuse as a child; the molestation, or the pain? It was power, control and a desire to live a life of vanity. Always wanting more and more until one day it backfired. She was sentenced to nine years in prison. No money, no home, no family. What's left? Nothing. Many times I have talked with women here in prison who are here because they just wanted more. More & more & more, never able to get enough. Money, sex, drugs, whatever it may be, but never, ever enough. Today she lives her life in a cold prison cell. She met the undercover cop in a hotel room. "Shoot him, but don't let him suffer." Eyes cold...no emotion...staring deep into his eyes—blank, nothing there. Why? I asked myself that many times. How could you kill your own husband for money? Money, that eventually will be gone one day. Many people live their lives only for money: to make more money every day, and for what? Material things? It's all vanity. But where is Jesus in a life of vanity? Nowhere. Think about it.

18

ADDICTION WILL STEAL ALL THAT YOU HAVE AND LOVE

Addiction is like a thief in the night: so quick, so subtle. Not even realizing that you've been robbed, one day you wake up and all that you have and love is gone. Addiction robbed me of many things. Most of all it robbed me of my family; time with my girls. It robbed me of my freedom; free to tuck my kids in bed, free to walk barefoot in the grass, free to curl up on the couch and watch a movie. Addiction can and will rob you of your life. It can take your life in the blink of an eye. One day you're on your way to church with your husband and kids, the next day you're on your way to prison shackled and handcuffed. Addiction cannot take your heart, your desire to live, your desire to do what's right. Addiction cannot take your Jesus away. While your addiction had you hostage, Jesus was waiting patiently with the keys in His hand. Don't let addiction rob you of your life.

ALL IN THE NAME OF LOVE

Hi, my name is Angie and I am a recovering addict, wife, mother and nurse. But today I am first an addict, because I know that if at any time I should forget I could slip right back into my past. I was lost, lonely, sick and miserable. I was suffering so deep inside, that today I know that I never want to forget that pain. I am not that person today. I don't have to live in the past or live the past anymore. I don't have to be ashamed of me today. I don't have to be ashamed of my past or my life today. I have finally come to the realization that wherever I am or wherever I may be,

19

that God is with me. I am one of His children and today I have a purpose and plan. I couldn't have done it without you. You are my people and my family. You are the ones that took me in and loved me for me. You are the ones that loved me when I couldn't love myself. You were the ones who loved me back to health and sanity. Yes, it was you who helped to restore my soul and you gave me my life back. It was all because of a four letter word, LOVE. I love you, New Beginnings, my people, and my family.

ALLOW YOUR MESS TO BECOME YOUR MESSAGE

We have to allow God to take us through our difficult times in life and let Him work in us so our mess can become our message. We have to begin to realize that the difficult things that we have endured in our past helps to prepare us for God's blessings in our future. For many years I have looked at my past as just one big mess. Rape at 15, rehab at 16, addiction and prison as an adult. I was never able to hang on to friends because I was always fearful that I would be judged. I could never let anyone get close enough for fear of rejection. It took me many years and many months in prison to realize that my mess had a message. The pain that I endured as a teenager can be used to keep another child from making the same mistakes. It can help them to work through the pain and fears that they face as a child, to show them that they can make it no matter how messy their life had become. We all make mistakes and some are just messier than others but through it all there is a message. So share your pain with someone else. Share your past no matter how messy it may be because your mess can be a message for someone else. Trust in the Lord and spread His message.

20

ALWAYS LOOK AHEAD

When I look back on years gone by, I see the error of my ways.
But let me not build monuments-to senseless, empty Godless days.
By looking back I waste today-and add to my own sorrow.
While sifting through my deep regrets, I'll also miss tomorrow.
So, let me use the lessons learned-that old mistakes are not to dread.
They're but a stepping stone to teach us that we should always look ahead.
The God who gave me past and present in Holy Scriptures hast said,
That He will guide my every footstep, if I but trust and look ahead.

AN ETERNITY WITHOUT A RAZOR WIRED FENCE

I've been in the Tapestry Program now for two weeks. We are getting ready for the annual talent show that's held every year in front of the alumni, staff and companies that help fund the program. I looked over some of the skits that were being done and to my surprise one of them was the "Praise Dance Team". I couldn't believe it! They were just like the raquad dancers at my church. They turned the tape on and it was the exact same song that the kids at my church danced to, I can only imagine. So I signed up immediately. I felt as though I had a little piece of home right here with me in prison. Well, we began practicing and the moves were much harder than I expected. But as we began again and I raised my hands to the sky, I opened my eyes only to see a razor wired fence right outside the barred windows. Immediately, I felt something stirring inside me. The moves became reality. I can only imagine what it will be like. Not beyond these prison walls but in eternity in heaven with my Jesus. An eternity in heaven with no more pain, no more fear, and no more prison. An eternity in heaven with peace in my heart and Jesus in my soul.

AN OPEN DOOR TO THE DEVIL

On a nice summer evening as we went to sit outside, we accidentally left the back door open. When we came back into the house, we had flies and mosquitoes everywhere. If I hadn't left the door open, they might not have ever gotten in. This goes the same for the devil. If you try to keep all of the doors closed behind you, then the devil has less of a chance to get in. Yes, there are many times that he slips right on through a small hole in the screen or a crack in the door, but if we have our doors checked and mended then he is less likely to get in. Many times I have allowed the devil to slip in and to slip right through the door without being seen. But believe me once he gets in, you'll know that he is there. The only thing to do is to get him out. How, you may ask? The answer is through prayer, meditation and scripture. I had to have the word of God hidden in my heart and ready at all times.   I had to have it on hand for those times when the devil slipped in. This was my home, not his.   There are many times in all of our lives that we fall back on reading and praying, and this is one of the greatest ways for the devil to sneak up on us. So, be prepared at all times.   Always be on guard and if he does try to slip in, then let him know that this is your home and he is not welcome.   As for me and my house,   we will serve the Lord.

AND BECAUSE THEY HAD NO ROOT, THEY WITHERED AWAY

- Matthew 13:6

Because I had no root, I began to wither away.   Like the parable of the four soils, I too began to wither away, as the seeds did.   I was planted on a good foundation.   I was in church, saved and living life to the fullest, but I was not deeply rooted.   I was like the seed, tossed onto the stony ground.   Not much earth was beneath me, so I didn't have much room to grow.   There was no depth to the earth so when the sun came up the seeds were scorched and withered away because they weren't deeply rooted.   I was that seed.   I lived the life as a Christian should but I had no root to myself.   I fell among the thorns.   The thorn of addiction had a hold on me and it choked me until I couldn't bear it any longer.   The addiction took the soul of my seed and placed it among the fowls of the earth that were ready and waiting to get me.   God picked me back up and placed me on fertile ground in the deepness of His soul. He planted me and watered me with His love.   He shines a ray of hope down upon me every day.   I am rooted today in

His love. I am growing and prospering from the root up. I am on good, solid ground now. I am bringing forth fruit and turning this prison into a vineyard of hope.

AND LET US RUN THE RACE WITH COURAGE, THE RACE THAT IS SET BEFORE US

In every race that I have run, there has always been a starting gate and a finish line. Some races that I have run have had hurdles in them. Some hurdles I leaped across with no problem. Other hurdles I tripped and fell. Eventually I got the courage to try again. As with any race, your eyes must always be set on the finish line. When at any time your focus begins to sway, then so does your balance. You begin to focus on the other runners and where they are in the race. You turn back to see what they are doing and where they are. You look to the crowd of people on the sidelines, focusing not on the finish line, but on your surroundings around you. As with our relationship with Jesus, we begin to stumble and sometimes fall when we look away from Him. We need to run to Christ and not away. We need to stop focusing on ourselves and start focusing on Him. Suffering is the training ground for Christian maturity. It develops patience and makes our final victory sweet. Just as Christ did not give up, neither should we. We must run the race and run it with courage.

ANGELS ALL AROUND US

I think that my bunkie must be part cat, because she has been granted nine lives. What I mean by that is that she has had nine DUI's and she has lived through every one of them without killing herself or someone else. She has had multiple wrecks, gone over bridges, and has come out of every one of them with only scratches. God had to have had his many angels watching over her. I am so glad that God gave me the privilege to meet her because she has been one of my greatest inspirations here in jail. She was gloriously saved two weeks ago and ever since then she has been a totally different person. I can see a glow about her face, especially when she is reading her Bible. She is a now a warrior for God instead of a warrior of the streets. She no longer has to fear for her life on the streets because she knows that God has saved her from that life. God saved her from her past and all of her bad choices. She now knows that she has a purpose in life and that her purpose is to spread the Good News of Jesus Christ to the broken hearted.

ANGRY AT GOD

Get me a beer, little nigress, and hurry up! Don't make me come in there. My daddy would pat me on the back and call me his little bastard. I thought for many years that this was love. He would beat us with his belt and leave imprints on our skin. I hated him for what he did, but I hated him worse for the way he treated my mommy. I had to get away from him so I ran away at the age of fourteen. I was married by the time I was sixteen and had a son. He was my everything. I took him to see his daddy for a weekend visit and on Sunday I returned to pick him up. "Bye daddy", he said, as he began coughing. His dad told me that he was starting to get a cold and that he had given him some aspirin for his fever. We loaded up in the car, and I held him on my lap so he could sleep. When I awoke from the car trip, I tried to pick up my son but he became limp. I turned him over and his eyes were rolled back in his head and he was foaming at the mouth. He had no pulse. His heart had stopped beating. My baby boy, my love, my angel, had died in my arms of Reye Syndrome from the aspirin given to him by his father. God took my son away. The preacher told me that if I were a better mother then God wouldn't have taken him from me. So, in turn, I hated God for taking my son. God took the only thing in my life that I have ever loved. God was punishing me. I knew that He was mad at me because I was a drug addict. This is the true story of a friend of mine in the Tapestry Program. She was so angry at God for taking her son and living her life on the words of "man". Those words lead her to self-destruction. We must always think and pray before we speak. Love our brothers and sisters, and show them God's love through our own actions. God is love.

ARE YOU A CAMEL OR A DEER?

When you think about camels out in the hot desert sand, you never dream that they can go for months living day to day without a drink or even a swallow of water. Deer pant for it daily thirsting for it. Seeking and searching for that one swallow just to quench their thirst. Which are we, the camel or the deer? All too often we imitate the hardy camel, going for weeks and months without a real swallow of living water. We need to become as deer, daily panting for God as our deepest desire. We need to thirst for the intimacy of God. For years I lived as the hardy camel. Being content where I was, out in the hot desert. But today I live as the deer, using this prison to soak up all of God's living water. I live as a sponge, ready and willing to quench my thirst. I strive for the intimacy with my Jesus, never wanting to thirst again. I go from cottage to cottage seeking and searching for hurting people, thirsting women who desire to drink of living water. So live as a deer today. Quench your thirst through the intimacy of a relationship with Jesus Christ.

ARE YOU READY TO PAY THE PRICE FOR WISDOM?

Solomon wrote in Ecclesiastes that even though he had great wisdom, it could not offer the satisfaction that he was seeking. I pray for wisdom daily here in prison, because I seek to provide guidance, not only for myself, but for others around me. The more I begin to understand, the more pain and difficulty I experience, the more I know. The more imperfection I see around me and the more I begin to observe, the more evil around me becomes evident. Today I am ready to think more, feel more, question more, and to even hurt more. Today I no longer chase the wind, fight the wind, or try to stop the wind. Today I know that I cannot catch the wind and keep hold of it. Good feelings are only temporary. We can't grab on to them and hold them until the next day. Good feelings will eventually pass by. I seek wisdom today and am willing to accept whatever comes with it. Today I realize that it is better to be wise than to be foolish. I know that wisdom does not guarantee eternal life. It is eternal life that I strive for but wisdom I do desire. I desire wisdom to increase my knowledge of what God has to offer, my knowledge necessary to fight the devil off with the word of God; to hold scripture in my heart, as the armor of God, and fight against the evil in this prison. Today, I am ready to pay the price for wisdom.

AUSTIN'S HOUSE

A four year old, brown eyed little girl runs into the house from playing outside and she says to her mother excitedly, "Mommy can we go to Austin's house today?" Her mother answered softly, "Not today honey, now run outside and play". Her mother drops to her knees, weeping, uncontrollably. Today her mother sits in prison, wishing that she would have visited Austin's House one last time. Austin died one year ago today. It might be four more years before she can go back and see Austin's grave, as she did so many times before. After Austin's drowning, his mother found cocaine as a replacement to numb the pain of his tragic death. Each time she talks to her little girl on the phone she asks the same question over and over again, "Mommy, when you come home, can we go to Austin's house?" Austin's house is a grave. The day of his burial, her daughter said to her, "Mommy this is Austin's house now." Her mother answered by saying, "Yes, this is Austin's house now, but today he's not home. He's in heaven with Jesus." So, don't put off what you can do today, for you never know what tomorrow may bring.

BARBIE, THE PLASTIC CHILD

Barbie is my bunkmate and friend at the Ohio Reformatory for Women in Marysville. Over the last few weeks I haven't seen Barbie's expressions change much. Today I asked her to tell me how she ended up here. Tears welled up in her eyes as she began to tell me of a past that no child should ever have to go through. Barbie was kidnapped by her father at the age of 3. Her mother lived in Columbus, Ohio and her father lived in Oklahoma City. Due to a bad marital relationship, Barbie's father thought that it was best for her to be with him and his new wife. For Barbie this was the beginning of a nightmare that never seemed to end. Barbie told me of the many times that she would cry for her mother and her father would tell her that her mommy just didn't want her anymore. Those words stuck with her for many years. My mommy just didn't want me anymore. Her childhood became a whirlwind of abuse, anger and fear. Love wasn't even a word that Barbie could comprehend. A hug or a kiss was not what she received at bed time, but a beating with brass knuckles or a verbal attack that hit so hard that she never saw it coming. Over the years Barbie withdrew from her friends and family. She learned to take care of herself. She learned to just live to make it until the next day. She became as a doll, made of plastic, unable to hold it, rock it or love it. She became as plastic like the Barbie doll, the only Barbie she has ever known.

BATTERED ANGEL

While sleeping one night I had a dream, it left a tale to tell. I dreamed that I saw an angel and she wasn't looking well. Her body was bruised and battered. Her wings were ripped and torn. I saw that she could barely walk. She was tired, weary and worn. I walked over to her and said, "Angel, how can this be?" As she looked back and tried to smile, she said these words to me... "I'm your guardian angel, quite a job you see. You've lived a very hard life, with this you must agree. You've broken laws and hearts, this life you've lived so recklessly. Don't you see what you have done to me? I've often had to pay the bill; these bruises are from shielding you. Each day I do my best still... My wings you see are ripped and torn, a noble badge I bear. So many times I've shielded you, though you were unaware. If only you would embrace life, choose to do well on your own. It would end the pain and suffering and you'd know that you're not alone. I'll always be there to watch over you until my strength doth fail; as for just when that will be? Only time will tell." When I awoke I thought about what my guardian angel said, and how much she seemed to care. Then I looked around my prison cell, and my heart sank in despair; as I sat there and wondered, I asked myself, "Why didn't I even try?" The air rushed by as from broken wings and I thought I heard an angel cry. - Author Unknown

As I sit quietly in this prison cell I hear many angels cry. These are cries from women that have been saved either before or after their arrival here. They cry for what they have done. They cry for what they have become. They cry wondering about their future and their children's futures. I cry for them as they weep. My heart wants to fix it all for them. Some are so battered and bruised that I can only pray for them. Learn from the cries of angels around you. The ones with broken wings and broken promises, that thinks that they're unable to fly. Cry out to your Jesus and what he has given you, blessings and eternal

30

life; a hope that angels can't even comprehend.

BE MY MASTER TODAY

Lord, be my Master today; and go with me where'er I go.
Guard my lips each word I say; and let my light to others show.
Lord, be my Master today; and let Thy will be mine,
for You know what is best for me, and the hills that I must climb.
You know the burdens that I must bear, and the joys to come my way.
So give me the wisdom to accept it all, and be my master today.
Lord, be my Master today, and let me be your child.
Send your angels to encircle me as I travel each weary mile.
Let me follow You, Lord, and not go any faster than Your footsteps will lead me . . . Today, Lord, be my Master.

BE PREPARED TO FIGHT

I have been in the Tapestry Program now for almost five months and I have seen more women from the Scioto County area than the Cleveland area. Right now our cottage holds 80 women and 12 are from Scioto County. The counselors told us one day that they have seen more women from Scioto County then any other county in Ohio. Most all were drug related charges. This is so sad to me,

31

because some of these women I met in jail, before I came to prison. We all seem to say the same thing, I can't believe that you're here? We are everyday ordinary women with everyday, ordinary problems, but we chose to use to numb the pain. Why? I know for myself that I never intended to become an addict, let alone a felon. It happened and here I am. We're mothers, daughters, grandmothers, aunts and even your next door neighbors. The only difference is that we became addicts. I don't think any of us ever said as a child, "I want to grow up to be an addict or a convicted felon." We made bad choices and big mistakes, but we are not mistakes. We are survivors. Being in prison and seeing women from my hometown has given me more reason to fight--not only for my life, but for their lives too. I have a dream, and that dream will one day come true. My dream is to become a Christian Counselor and to share my story with others all over the world. To let them know that everyday ordinary people can become addicts. Addiction can take over your life so you must be prepared to fight. You must be prepared to fight for your life, your children, your husband and your dreams. The devil is ready and waiting, so be prepared. Live for God. Live His word and know that you are not alone. Please pray for the Scioto County area that maybe one day we will be free from this drug war.

BEAT DOWN

Today I watched through the bars of my window as one inmate brutally beat another prisoner. There was nothing I could do. As much as I wanted to be down there and drag her off of the other prisoner, I just couldn't. I had to sit and watch as she beat her to the ground, kicking and hitting her repeatedly until finally the guards yelled for her to get down on the ground and to put her hands behind her back. They arrested her for assault and took her to the hole. As I watched through the window, I also saw three to four hundred women watching this girl get beaten. I wanted to scream, "Help her! What are you doing just sitting there and watching?" Some were laughing, some were screaming, "Get her, hit her again!" This event took me back to the death of Christ; the beatings, mockings, scorners. They just sat and watched. Some laughed, some yelled, "Crucify Him!" But there was nothing that could have stopped it. Today I thank the Lord for His love that took the beatings and pain for me, for you, for us all. Today I thank you Jesus for loving me enough to die for a sinner like me.

BEAT THE STREETS

How can one beat the streets and win? How can one beat the streets of homelessness, prostitution, and drug dealing? How can one live the streets and not have to live on them? These are questions asked by women who live they're lives on the streets. They feel like they will never get off the streets because they're not worthy enough. They've lived too long on the streets of hell instead on the streets of gold. One can walk these streets without giving themselves up to the streets. Who wants to walk the crooked path when they can walk the straight and narrow path? A lot of women face fears of not being able to make it, not being able to clean themselves up and get off those streets. They almost start to feel content with the streets they walk on daily. God doesn't want us to live this way. Walking from street to street but going nowhere. He has a better place for us. He has a set of directions for us to follow that will take us to the streets of gold. God can remove you from these streets and help you beat them. You can receive peace on the streets wherever you live through Jesus Christ our Lord. You must read the directions carefully and follow the right path, the straight and narrow. It will lead you to the streets of gold. You can win! You can beat the streets.

BEAT UP, BUT NOT BEAT DOWN

She was 12 years old when she ran away for the first time. She had been physically, mentally and sexually abused in her own home. She had been beat up so many times, that she couldn't even remember a day when it didn't happen. She climbed out of her bedroom window and ran as fast as she could. She didn't know where she was running to, but she knew where she was running from. She was 12 years old and living on the streets of Columbus; no food, no shelter, and no one to love her. As she was walking the streets, she turned and saw a large Cadillac pull up beside her. A 35 year old man, in a suit and tie, was walking toward her. He introduced himself and asked her if she was hungry. She was so scared, but so hungry. So, she left with him. He gave her everything that she had ever wanted and needed, except what she desired and that was love. But, to her, he loved her because he treated her like a princess. Within two weeks, she became his lady. It didn't take long for him to start abusing her. He had her forging checks, prostituting, and boosting for his addiction. The beatings came regularly, especially if the money wasn't coming in. She couldn't leave him because he loved her. So she thought. Ten years later, she sits here in prison for forgery for the man that said he loved her. For 10 years she worked as his slave, trying to earn his love. Today she is a strong and beautiful woman. Today she realized that she could and did survive. She is a survivor and she has not been beat down, but beat up. The trials of life can beat you down so badly, but you must never let them beat you down.

BECAUSE HE LIVES,
I CAN FACE TOMORROW

I don't know how many times over the last few days that I had to say that to myself, "Because He lives, I can face tomorrow." I never thought that I would ever end up in jail, let alone in jail with a woman who would cut your throat for staring at her. I had to learn the tricks of the street to survive. I had to show these women that even though I was a Christian I was still able to hold my own. I had to be able to read my Bible and take the slack for speaking about Jesus. There were many times when anger would arise in me, when Jesus' name was spoken in vain. One girl said, "I don't want to hear anymore about that Jesus stuff." I had to rely on God for protection and for guidance. I had to ask God daily to help me to witness to these girls without offending them. Well, God is good! He allowed me to witness to these women and for a friend of mine, Jamie Backenhaster to come back to our unit to witness also. For her to come all the way back to our unit was a miracle. The biggest miracle was that 6 women were saved, 3 prostitutes and 3 drug addicts. I had to have faith like I've never had before. Now, I can truly begin to live, because he lives in me and I know that whatever cometh my way, I can face tomorrow.

BEHIND THE CURTAINS
FOR THE LAST TIME

She's backstage just waiting for the curtains to open. She's prepared and studied for her part for months. The makeup artists have been working on her for hours. She's in her costume ready to walk out onstage. The crowd is waiting. The lights are dimmed and she's just waiting for her cue. She's waiting to walk out from behind the darkness of the curtains and into the spotlight. The excitement has built up inside of her. She's eagerly waiting and finally the curtains are drawn. She steps out and walks onto the stage and the applause begins. Who is she? Who is this woman in the costume? Listen to her, she knows every line. You wonder how long it took her to prepare for a part like that. It's just a part, a role that she has prepared for. She's in shoes that don't fit and a costume that's a little too big. But it's time! It's her time to shine. It's time to get out of those clothes and makeup and into her real garments. It's her time to step out from behind the scenes and into the spotlight. It's time for you and me to be the leading lady. Many of us have been hidden in the dark behind the scenes for way too long. We've had dark pasts that have kept us from stepping out into the light. We've been beaten, raped, abused and even lost in a society of sin. It's our time now, ladies. It's our night to shine. Step up and take those mismatched shoes off and put on your own shoes. Take the limits off and go with it. It's our time to step up and tell our story. It's our time to step up and be God's lady. It's time for us to shine like we've never shown before. It's our time to step out of the shadows of our past and into the light of our future. Let Jesus be your light. Take that step to change your life from darkness to light.

BLEEDING INTERNALLY

On this day Jesus was moved with compassion. He was bleeding internally (spiritually) over the brutal murder of John the Baptist. Jesus had considered John as one of the greatest men who had ever been born, and to Jesus, John was a friend. The news filled Jesus with overwhelming grief. Jesus was in pain. Day after day in terrible pain Jesus poured out His love for all of us. Jesus withdrew by boat to a deserted place to be by Himself. He needed time to pray and to be healed. The crowds followed. They wanted and needed Jesus, who was Himself wounded and bleeding internally, to heal them. So, Jesus worked miracles with loaves and fishes to feed them and to heal them physically. Jesus did not dwell on his grief. He soon returned to the ministry He came to do. There have been many times that I felt I was bleeding to death internally and overcome with grief while being here in this prison. So, I too, like the crowd, ran to where Jesus was for Him to heal my bleeding, wounded heart. I fell on my knees in my cell and prayed for healing. I embraced the cross and Jesus healed my bleeding heart. He fed me with His love and raised me up with His touch. Jesus can heal your pain. Jesus can feed your soul. Allow Him to help you. Allow Him to heal you. Allow Him to love you.

BLESS THIS MESS

I'm sure that all of us have prayed for something in our lives that really wasn't what we needed but what we wanted. We have all been in situations that we got ourselves into that we prayed for Jesus to get us out of. Our motives were to get ourselves out and not to be blessed.

This time is different. I can't say that in the beginning of my trial for theft of drugs that I didn't want Jesus to just fix it and take it away. But now I am asking God to bless this mess. Help me Jesus to do your will and not mine. Help me Jesus to be a witness for you in this prison. Bless me Lord with the words to say to minister to these hurting women. Please Jesus, bless this mess. I know that I have made a mess out of my life for the past couple of years, but I know that God will bless me with strength to endure this race. I have been running from my addiction way too long. I have been running from the fears of my past way too long. I am ready to pay the consequences that were sentenced to me by the judge and to receive a blessing everyday that I have to serve. I know that God has a plan, because there have been eight women saved in the county jail with me and two women saved here in Marysville. One was a prostitute and crack addict and the other girl is a murderer. God has truly blessed me with the life I have. There are not too many people that God has truly blessed to be able to witness to some of the hardest criminals in Ohio. But God blessed me, and He blessed my mess.

BLESSED BY A COOKIE

It's a normal day here in prison. We get up, go to morning meeting, then we have 'groups' all day. I've been blessed to be in a recovery program here at Marysville, so I don't have to be out with GC (General Population). Today ended up being a blessed day; blessed by a cookie. Not just any cookie, but a cookie given to each and every inmate: a cookie that was made with love. Every cookie prayed over. Every cookie blessed by the hands that made it. I got a knock at the door and another inmate said, "Here's your cookies from God." I thought about not eating it, just sitting and looking at it, remembering where it came from. But it was chocolate chip, my favorite, so I ate it. I'll always remember how much that one chocolate chip cookie meant to me. Today I was blessed, not by the actual cookie, but by the hands that made them. Thank you Jesus for the small blessings in life.

BLESSED BY THE BEST

I've been in prison now almost five months. I've known for a long time that God had a plan for me. At first I thought the plan was to come to prison and lead many women to the Lord. I realized that He had a bigger and better plan. His plan begins with me. I had to heal myself from the inside out. I had to start on me first before I could help others. God showed me that I had to work through my feelings and emotions, to work through my fears and pain, before I could ever help anyone else. God is so good. Today I've committed to put me first, to realize that I am unique and that it's okay to fall, as long as you get back up. God has truly blessed me at this prison, for today I know that I would never be the person that I've always wanted to be if I hadn't traveled this lone difficult road. Today I feel that I have emotions and I'm learning to deal with them through God's help. I'm learning to share my hurts and wants with other women so they can help me. I've learned that I don't always have to try to fix others, or help guide others, when I haven't done that with myself first. Today I am growing. Today I am who I am only because I've been blessed by the Best.

BREAK INTO PRISON

There are three types of inmates in prison. Those who are not changed and don't want to be changed. Those who are not changed, but desperately want to be, and there are those who have changed and want to stay that way. There are thousands of men, women and children behind bars who are hurting and have no hope. Prison is a dark place, and the only light most of them ever see is the light and hope of the gospel that other Christians bring into the prison. Thousands of inmates have never really heard the truth of the gospel, and as Christian disciples we are obligated to bring them the message of hope and salvation. Jesus said to His disciples, "The harvest truly is plenteous, but the laborers are few," Matthew-9:37. Being a Christian is more than hymn singing, hand clapping and social activities. Christians are to be Christ-like, to carry the love of Christ into the darkest holes that nobody else cares to enter. We have a responsibility to others that are hurting. Our responsibility is to take and share the gospel to every lost person within our reach. We, as prisoners, are no different than you are in the free world. We all have come short of the glory of God. Prisoners have broken the laws of the state, but ALL of us have violated the laws of God. "For all have sinned and come short of the glory of God." (Romans 3:23) There is no greater place for a Christian's light to shine its brightest than in a prison of darkness and brokenhearted people.

BUT GOD REMEMBERED NOAH

There are many times that I would struggle in my heart to understand why I am here, or why I had to go through this trial. When I read in the Bible, "But God remembered Noah", I realized that the Lord knows where I am at all times. He knows how much I can handle and how much I have left inside me to fight. Before Noah ran out of his food resources and provisions for his family and the animals, God remembered Him. God wants us to hold onto His word. He knows that I am still weak in many areas, but He takes and opens doors for me to continue to grow. He brings people into this prison to help and guide me on this troublesome path called life. He shows me in His word that I am a strong and beautiful woman. He is showing me that I can overcome, because He remembered me. He brought me to this prison for me to grow and to help guide other women to Him. He needed to show me once again that I must rely on Him at all times, not just in time of need, but in the good times too. God will never forsake us. He knows exactly where we are and He won't forget. If you too are sitting behind prison walls, or locked in a prison within yourself, know that you are not alone. He is with you and He does remember you.

BY THE GRACE OF GOD, I...

I have been justified, completely forgiven and made righteous. I have received the Spirit of God in my life that I may know the things freely given to me by God. I have been bought with a price, I am not my own. I belong to God. I have been established, anointed, and sealed by God in Christ. I have been saved by grace and faith. I have been crucified with Christ and it is no longer I who live, but Christ who lives in me. I have been blessed with every spiritual blessing. I have been chosen in Christ before the foundation of the world to be holy and without blame before Him. I was predestined. I have been redeemed, forgiven, and am a recipient of His lavish grace. I have been delivered from the domain of darkness and transferred to the kingdom of Christ. Christ himself is in me. I have been firmly rooted in Christ and am now being built up in Him. I have been made complete in Christ. I have been given a spirit of power, love and self-discipline. I am saved, chosen for His holy work. I will rise to meet the Lord in the air and live with Him forever. I have been given exceedingly great and precious promises by God. I am His. I am in Christ, and He has freed me from this prison within my own heart.

CAPTIVES SET FREE

She didn't know that there was a God who could love someone like her. Someone that had committed armed robbery and attempted murder to support her drug habit; a habit that had held her captive since she was 10 years old. She didn't believe that anything or anyone could heal her of the feelings of hopelessness at being robbed of her freedom. She hung onto the street life here in prison as long as she could. Then one day, seven years later, something changed. She had gone to church and even praise-danced on Sundays for three years, but she just didn't feel anything inside. Then she heard the words that would change her life forever. "I'm free in this prison, even though I'm serving life, and you can be too." Even though she knew that J.M. was free, she still believed that her life was hopeless. She had felt for years that God was angry with her and that He could never love someone like her. That night she prayed for the first time in seven years, "God, if you're there, please help me and forgive me." The next morning was a different day. She woke up with hope and no desire for drugs. Her anger had disappeared and she felt free for the first time in this prison. Today, after 8 years, she was called to the C.O.'s desk to receive the news that she was going home. "God is real and He does love me," she said. Thank you Jesus for loving someone that couldn't even love herself.

CHANGE

As you walk inside the gate with two armed guards, you're taken through a metal detector, then another, then another. Then you walk through a huge metal door, that's slammed shut and locked behind you. The farther I went inside, the more locked doors were left behind me. How will I ever make it? Will I ever get out of here? It's all about change! It's all about committing to change your life. As you walk through one door and you take the first step in changing your life, the door closes behind you and another one opens. The next door opens and you close that door behind you. The farther you go and the longer you stay committed, the more it becomes a part of who you are and who you are becoming. We are all prisoners and we all have walls and doors that lock behind us. My prison is an actual place, but your prison may be virtual, created in your mind. As I walked through the door on my new journey in life, I committed to change. I am free in this prison. There is no turning back now. I choose to keep the doors locked behind me, and to carry the keys of freedom in my heart. Freedom is a choice! Which door will you choose?

CHILD-LIKE FAITH

God sent a message through three beautiful little girls. The devil has fought me so hard these last few weeks, telling me that I haven't done anything in this prison since I got here. He told me that I deserve to stay in prison for eighteen more months because I haven't done anything to work on myself while I was here. I had a visit with my family. I was so beaten down by what the devil had been feeding me. My daughters looked at me and my oldest daughter Kayla said, "Mom, you've got to stop worrying, God has everything under control. We need you and want you home with us, but if it's God's will, you'll be home. If not, then God needs you more in prison, than we need you at home." Tears filled my eyes and my heart wept with joy. I then realized through the strength, wisdom and faith of a 14 year old little girl, what I had allowed the devil to do to my heart and mind. Not only had I grown in strength, wisdom and faith, but God had strengthened my children also. This trial has made my family so strong. This trial has given us a greater love for ourselves and others. A kind of love that Jesus intended for ALL to have; for us to trust Jesus like we've never trusted him before and to turn our will and our lives over to him. God's will not ours. So whatever tomorrow may bring for me in this prison, it will be ok, because today God opened my eyes through a child's eyes. He gave me child-like faith through the faith of a little girl. Thank you, Kayla, Tori and Aleah for your strength and courage. Thank you for your encouraging words and your unconditional love that gets me through from day to day.

CHILDREN RAISING CHILDREN

"When I was four years old I had to change my little brother's diapers. By the age of six I was babysitting; changing diapers, feeding and running around the house after him. I can remember a time when my little brother accidentally dropped a plate and it broke. When my step-dad got home he decided since I was the babysitter that I should be the one punished. So at age 9, I was whipped and beaten with an electrical cord. I can remember my punishments well because they were so often and so brutal; kneeling on bottle caps, beans or rice, standing on one foot in a corner with my nose to the wall. If my foot dropped at any time, then I would be beaten. I had to take the beatings for my kids. My kids were my brothers and sisters, all 7 of them. I raised them. I took care of them." These are the words of a friend of mine here at Tapestry. Her childhood was taken away never to be returned. She raised them the best way she knew how. Today she sits in prison with an eleven year sentence for a drive-by shooting and a high-speed chase. She has served eight years and has just turned thirty-two years old. She dreams of the day she will be reunited with her family. Today she can only dream, because for her, dreams are all she has. Children aren't meant to raise children. But God loved her enough to save her at this prison, and today she is a praise dancer for her Jesus. Today she allows Jesus to raise her, raise her from her life of sin into an eternity with Him.

CHRISTMAS "TIME"

Today is December 27th, 2004. I am imprisoned in the Marysville Penitentiary for Women. Due to my addiction, I spent my first Christmas ever away from my family. When I awoke Christmas Day, my heart was heavy. I was unsure whether to laugh or cry. I wanted so much to be home with my family, but I knew it wasn't possible. So, I had to seek out Jesus behind bars and ask for my heart to be lifted. As the day went on and I was able to speak to my family, Jesus granted a peace within my heart. I took what began as an emotionally trying day and turned it into a joyous and peaceful one. I was able to enjoy the birth of Jesus and to praise Him for that beautiful day. Never in my 35 years of life have I been able to enjoy Jesus' birthday like I did 2 days ago. I was able to sit and reflect on the love that He has given me. I was able to see what family and true love was all about. Jesus' gift to me this Christmas was Time. Time for me to seek His face like I've never been able to do before. Time to reflect on what family really is. Time to enjoy life like I've never done before. This Christmas Jesus gave me the perfect gift, the gift of   Time with Him.

CLIMBING OVER

A couple of years ago we went to the Smoky Mountains. It was so beautiful. The only way to get up and down the mountains to see the view was to walk. So, we drove up the mountain as far as we could go and then we got out walking the narrow path. The path went this way and that way, curving up and then down again. At the end of the path was the very top of the mountain. We stood at the top of the mountain and looked at the beautiful scenery. The clouds that hovered over the mountain were like a soft blanket wrapped securely around a new born babe. Once we were done enjoying the view, we knew that we had to turn around and go back down. It took so much energy just getting up the mountain, how would we ever make it back down? A thought entered my mind, "what if we could have just gone through the mountain?" It would have been so much easier. But what about the view? We would have never gotten to see its beauty. We would have never gotten to see what was on the other side. We would have never been able to say that we made it to the top. True, it would have been so much easier and less strenuous, but what about the view? So many times we want the easy way out when it is the hard path that God intended for us. We have so many mountains in our lives that we want to just drive through, but Jesus put them in out path for a reason. That reason is to help us to grow emotionally and spiritually and to show us that He is there to help us to the top of the mountain to see the view more clearly. He wants us to see the beauty that He has waiting for us on the other side.

COLORS OF THE RAINBOW

The colors of the rainbow are so bright and beautiful. They were made by Jesus to put color into all of our lives. There are so many beautiful colors of the rainbow, but when they are put all together they make the colors of the world; black, white, brown, yellow and more. When the rain comes down and the rainbow begins to fade, all of the colors begin to fade into each other. They blend together to make up the beautiful colors of this world. Here at Marysville, I have met all the colors of the world. I have met the most beautiful people here. They have made mistakes in their past, just like all of us have. It doesn't matter what color we are, our status, ethnicity, or who we are, we are all human and we all our God's children. We all have a past and our past does not define who we are. A lot of these women here see color and not the heart. They see with their flesh only, just like so many others in this world. But, I have learned to see only with my heart. When you see with your heart you don't see color, you see love. A love that only Jesus can give you. So, every time you see a rainbow think of Jesus love. Think of the many hurting women in this prison that need your love and the love of Jesus Christ.

COMES THE DAWN

After a while you learn the subtle difference between holding a hand and chaining a soul. You learn that love doesn't mean leaning and company doesn't mean security. You begin to learn that kisses aren't contracts and presents aren't promises. You begin to accept your defeats with your head up and your eyes open with the grace of a grown-up, not like the grief of a child. You learn to build all your roads on today because tomorrow's ground is too uncertain. Plans and futures have a way of falling down in mid-flight. After a while you learn that every time the sun shines, it can burn you if you get too much. So you plant your own garden and decorate your own soul instead of waiting for someone to bring you flowers. You learn that you really can endure, that you really are strong, and you really do have worth. And you learn and learn... with every good-bye you learn.
With every good-bye we learn. We learn from the good-byes of fear, doubt, insecurities, loves, anger, and much more. Learn from your past and what your future has for you: a

fresh flower, a sun shine, a beautiful child's face. This is my future and I am blessed and have all this to look forward to. You can hold the same future for you if you can just say good-bye to your past. Give your sins to God because he holds the keys to your future.

COUNTED EVEN AS WE SLEEP

I awaken every morning to a loud horn that blows at 4:00 a.m. It's count time. Sometimes I don't even hear it because I'm so used to it. The officer unlocks our doors, comes into our rooms and counts us as we sleep. Many of us don't even realize that we've been counted because we're counted 5 times a day. This made me think of how Jesus counts his flock every day, no matter where we are, and even if we're asleep. He knows our whereabouts at all times. If we're sleeping in our beds, in a prison cell or even under a bridge, He counts us, every one of us. But Jesus' count time is different. He counts us because He loves us. He counts us because He doesn't want any of us to ever stray from His flock. So remember as you sit in your cell during count time, that there's another count going on; a count from a Man that loves you for just being you.

COURAGE TO FACE THE ROAD

All of us in our lives have taken many roads that have led to many different places. We have walked the road of fear, pain, love, hate, and destruction. We have walked roads that have lead some of us to near death. All of us, every one of us, have taken one of these roads, probably more than one. What roads have you driven down? Where did your road take you? Where did you take the road to? All of us have pasts. We have had broken promises, abusive pasts, and even rocky roads that took us to the lowest point in our lives that we've ever been. Some of us had the courage to turn around and come back. Some of us learned that the road we took was a dead end street. A road that had no addresses on it. A road that had no reason for ever being. Many times I have taken roads that have lead me to wonderful places, like love, friendship, and faith. This time I took a road that lead to the Ohio Pen for Women. A road that I am going to now ask directions on how to get back. I have asked my Lord Jesus to give me the faith and courage to get back home. I am going to a place of no return. I am going to walk down a road that only the chosen get to take. I am going to walk streets of gold. I now have the courage to overcome. I now have the courage, strength, and peace to take a road of no turning back. I am on Jesus' path... the road to eternity.

CRAVE HIM

Being a recovering addict, I know what it feels like to have cravings. Your palms get sweaty, knots grow in your stomach and your mind starts racing, but the physical craving only last for 7 seconds. After 7 seconds it becomes a mental craving. You allow your thoughts to become actions. You now are thinking of what you can do to stop it. You either react to it and find the drug or you can act on it and do all you can to fight it. It's the same way with seeking Jesus. You have two choices. You can choose to act or react. You can crave Jesus in all that you do or say; crave His word, His love and His friendship or you can fight it and run. As with addiction, the craving will continue to come for a period of time, but eventually they will stop, just as Jesus does with us. He'll knock at your door at only so many times, and eventually after no answer, He will leave. Don't let Jesus get away. Crave Him. Crave His love.

Crave all that you can, because eventually this world will overtake your life, and you will end up living your life without any hope – Jesus.

DADDY'S DEATH

Why did he have to die? He was so young, the father of a beautiful young girl. He had everything going for him until the day he found out his wife was having an affair. He felt that he had nothing more to live for. The only thing he knew to do was to end it all -- commit suicide. He drove to his wife's place of employment, walked in to where she was, and shot himself. It was over. His daughter is incarcerated with me at Marysville. Two weeks before his death, he was reading his Bible, praying, witnessing, and more. For some reason he felt like his life should end. For many years his daughter has blamed God for this tragedy. The day she found out about his death, she cried out to God in pain, "Why did you have to take my daddy?" Finally six years later, God spoke to her in a small still voice and told her, "I am your daddy. I did not take your father from you, that was his choice. I wanted life for him, not death." Ever since that day she has had peace, a peace that she didn't have before. Understanding her father's reasoning is still a mystery to her, but understanding that the Lord never left him or forsaken him has given her an answer that she's wanted for years.   She is finally able to open her Bible again and pray for God to heal her pain.

DAY OF SENTENCING

I remember waking up on Tuesday, Dec. 7th 2004, knowing that at 1:45pm, I had to go to my court hearing.   The only thing I could think of was being shackled by my hands and feet walking to the courtroom in front of friends, family and especially my children.   The thought of going to court on my dad's and brother's birthday was heart grieving.   I waited until 1:30 and the cell door opened.   Tammy, the deputy, walked me up to the front where the male deputies were and before I got to the front Captain Hall stopped me. He told me good luck and then he told me that his father had been saved at our old church.   I asked him who his dad was and he yelled, "Hey dad, come here a minute."   He walked over around to us.   He was around 70 years old. Dave introduced me and told him who I was.   He said, "Before you go how about a prayer?"   He took me to an empty room and asked another deputy to come in and pray with me.   After the prayer, I was taken to the front where I was cuffed and shackled.   I had thought many times what it would be like but I never imaged how humiliating it would be.   I thought and prayed that day to not humiliate any of my family by walking out in front of everyone, but when I got out of the elevator, there were thirty people there.   It was an unbelievable sight.   I couldn't help but to cry.   I was able to stop and see almost half of them until they told me it was time to go inside.   All thirty followed right behind me into the courtroom, and right behind them was the woman I took the pills from and the lady I used to work with. I hated it. We sat and sat for well over an hour, trying to smile and be strong when all along my heart was pounding inside. I ached to hold my husband and children. At around 3:30 pm my lawyer finally came in and told us there was a continuation. She said that they were waiting on Pike County's response, but that they were going to give me 30 days in Marysville Maximum Prison and six months in Cincinnati. Anger arose towards my lawyer and I thought to myself, we have to fire her. She's not doing her job. Then she spoke up and said to my husband, "It's out of my hands now, she did it and she will have to pay for it." I know I can make it, but I just pray that my family doesn't fall apart. I don't worry one bit about myself. I just can't imagine what it's going to be like for my children to have to face their peers. What have I done to my beautiful family? I had it all and lost it all in one minute. As I walked out of the courtroom I couldn't even lift my head. My mother was crying, trying to smile that smile that says you're going to be okay. My girls were crying, but they still gave me the I love you and I miss you sign. My oldest daughter Kayla was crying hysterically. I looked back one more time and saw my baby Kayla peeking around the corner, mouthing the words "I love you mom." My heart sunk. How amazing God is to allow me to be their mother. I mouthed the words, "I love you too," and gave a wave back to her. I assured her everything was going to be okay. Then I walked back to the elevator and back to my floor. As I returned back to my cell, there were women from Pike County having church. As I walked through, one lady took my hand and squeezed it. I knew then, that she too would be praying. I returned to my cell and received hug after hug. They cheered me up the best they knew how. I received a letter from Barry that made everything okay. I knew then that as long as they were with me and behind me, everything would be just fine.........

DEATH BEHIND PRISON WALLS

I'm 36 years old and have only had to experience the death of a loved one twice in my life. To experience death behind prison walls is indescribable. I got word from the correctional officer at 10:30 p.m. last night that I had to go to the captain's office, and I knew that there were only 2 reasons a person goes there: either you're in big trouble or there's a death in the family. So immediately, I knew someone had died. The captain told me, ever so kindly, that my grandmother had just passed away. I could not believe it. I never dreamed that after only being here 3 months that she could be gone. Many things passed in my mind. Who would hold my girls and tell them it would be okay? Who would be the strong one for my husband as he goes to preach her funeral? Were her last thoughts of me going to be seeing me being shackled, and handcuffed? The shame and guilt were overpowering. The captain said that he could arrange for me to go to the viewing, but it would be a separate viewing, for me only, shackled, handcuffed, and escorted by 2 armed guards. I just couldn't do that to her. I couldn't shame her in that manner. I needed her to know that I would meet her in Heaven one day. Then I realized that somehow, she already knew this. Somehow, she knew how much I loved her and my Jesus. So if for any reason you have to go through death behind prison walls, make sure you are just as ready to go to Heaven as your loved one is, and know that even if you are behind prison walls, God loves and cares for you just the same.

DEATH BY OVERDOSE

Little Johnny, Sarah and Joey died yesterday when their daddy took a lethal overdose. Their hearts were torn apart, ripped in two, when their mommy walked into their rooms last night to tell them that their daddy would never be coming home again. Their burials will be held at the park where their daddy used to take them every Sunday before his addiction; over by the swings where the children loved being pushed on a bright sunny day. They are to be remembered for their strong will, which they carried for their father, their strong desire to help their daddy find his way home after being gone on a binge for the last 10 days, and for the many nights that they were found on their knees, praying for their father's safety. They were praying to God that He would protect their daddy one last time. Flowers can be left next to the old oak tree, directly underneath the tree house that was never finished. To all who will attend, please bring a small piece of your heart to help mend the children's broken hearts, to help put them back together piece by piece, one day at a time. The children would like to thank all who will attend their funerals. They would like you to know that if you would like to talk, they can be found on their knees praying for all of those other daddies and mommies who won't be coming home tonight.

DEATH ROW

Four years alone in a dark, cold, cement room with only one small window to see out of. Meals brought to her three times a day, no T.V., no communication with the outside world other than through the correctional officers who brought the meals. No cards, no phone calls, not even a kind word. Then one day as one of the inmates was walking outside past the death row window she heard these words, "Don't give up, God loves you." Four years without communication from the outside world and these were the first words she heard. Ever since that day, various inmates would pass by and say the same thing, "Don't give up, God loves you, and so do we. You can do it." Then one day, word was sent to her that she was going back to court to try for a revoke on her sentence in order to get life in prison. That day she knew that God truly loved her. She wasn't alone. For four years she felt so alone; like no one cared or loved her. Then He spoke to her, "Sharon, I'm here, and I love you. I've been here the whole time, but you just wouldn't answer me. I will give you life here on this earth to spread the Good News to others so they may have eternal life." Sharon got a life sentence; life in prison for thirty-four years and eternal life in Heaven with me. Sharon has now been in prison for twenty-two years and has helped lead many women to the Lord. God gave her life back to her, so she could help give life back to others.

DECORATE YOUR OWN GARDEN, DON'T WAIT FOR SOMEONE TO BRING YOU FLOWERS

My husband Barry would stop by Big Bear Grocery Store about once every two weeks to buy me roses. After so long the workers would say to him, "Boy, you sure are in the doghouse a lot sir." He replied, "No I'm not in the doghouse, this is the way I keep myself out." Every time I would see him come my heart would putter and I would blush like a teenage girl. It really wasn't the roses that brought me joy, it was just the thought of him taking time out to bring me something so beautiful for no reason. As time went on, our lives got busier and the flowers would come less and less. It wasn't that he didn't care. It was because our lives had become so overwhelmed with church, friends, children and much, much more. So, after a while I would stop by the store on my own and pick me up some flowers or a potted plant. I enjoyed the flowers because they reminded me of Barry. Not many times, but occasionally I did have to decorate my own garden. I would sometimes go and buy them twice a week just to encourage my heart. I loved decorating my home with flowers. The aroma reminded me of my husband. Sometimes in our lives we need to take special thoughts for ourselves. We need to decorate our own garden and not wait for someone else to bring you flowers. You are worth every flower that you buy for yourself. Take time for yourself. Be good to yourself. Buy yourself a rose every day. You're worth it.

DESTROYING STATE PROPERTY

The sun is shining. It's about 75 degrees outside, and there's just enough breeze blowing to smell the scent of summer coming. I gathered up my books, my iced tea and my notebook for a nice relaxing day out in the prison yard. I sat outside for hours just soaking up the sun. I was remembering home and all that I am missing. Thinking of the past, of the many summers I spent outside with my kids. Then one of the correctional officers came by and yelled to all of us to put our sleeves down. He said, "There's no soaking up the sun here. It's destruction of State Property." Another girl told me about her friend who was sunburned last summer. She was taken to the captain's office and given a ticket for Destruction of State Property. I couldn't believe what I was hearing. We're considered a piece of property. Just like the benches that sit outside. Just like the lock box that holds my life's possessions in it. To this prison we are nothing but a piece of State Property. Then I thought of Jesus and what we mean to Him. We may be State Property to this prison, but to Jesus we are His children, His flock and His everything.

DISOBEDIENCE OF A DIRECT ORDER

I had never heard that once you were sent to prison you could still receive a ticket. You can receive a ticket for smoking in the bathroom, talking to certain people in population, not making your bed or for disobeying a direct order. I can remember disobeying my parents many times as a child. When I was given a direct order, I knew that if I didn't obey it I would receive punishment. Once you've received the ticket, then you receive your punishment. The ticket is like a warning that in just a little time your punishment will be coming. This reminds me of the judgment day. Jesus has given us many verbal warnings. He has written us many tickets in our lifetime, but on judgment day there won't be any tickets given out. It will be a judgment. If you don't obey His direct order of salvation, then you will be sentenced to eternity in hell. No more warnings, no more slaps on the wrist, but a death sentence is given. Sometimes Jesus sends us so many warnings that one day He stops giving them to you. Don't sit back and wait to heed them. Get in the front of the line and sign up to be on the winning side. Obey the direct order from God and Jesus will tear up every ticket you've ever received and throw them out. Obey His calling today, and you'll no longer have to live on death row.

DON'T ADD GUILT TO HIS SACRIFICE

Have you ever been judged or criticized for your sins? Do you feel shamed by religious people in your community? There is no reason to feel the shame and guilt anymore, if you have asked Jesus to forgive you of your sins. You are forgiven of your sins no matter what anyone else says or does. Jesus was our sacrifice for our sins. He died on the old rugged cross for you and me. We have an Advocate, and it is Jesus. There is no reason to continue overwhelming yourself with the shame and guilt of your past when Jesus sacrificed His life for your sins. We don't have to punish ourselves for our sins, if they're forgiven. Jesus doesn't accept pay backs. He only wants your love and desire to serve Him. Joyce Meyers once said, "Jesus did not die so we could have religion. He died so we could have an intimate relationship with Him." So, today make the guilt and shame a part of your past, not your future.

DON'T CHOOSE BARABBAS

Barabbas or Jesus, whom do you choose? You are faced with a choice today, a choice that was given many, many years ago. Will you choose to have the tangible force of human power or salvation that is freely offered by the Son of God? At the feast, the governor wanted to release a prisoner. He gave them a choice, and they chose

Barabbas. They chose a murderer, a sinful man, over a perfect, loving and complete man, Jesus. They chose hell over an eternity in Heaven. They chose death over life. Today we have the same choice. We are freely given salvation, but we must ask for it. As the thief hung on the cross beside Jesus, he chose to live. He chose Jesus over Barabbas. The thief died on an old rugged cross, but he lives in Eternity with Jesus today. Without Jesus in your life, you have no true life at all. For many years I chose Barabbas, but today my life is filled with Jesus. Jesus is here with me in this prison and I live today with many Barabbas. But with Jesus you too can change. You too can be free in your prison, whether it's in your heart or mind, or if it's your home for today, here on this earth. Choose Jesus because He has chosen you.

DON'T LOOK BACK

The Bible tells us in Genesis of a man in Sodom. Lot ran to Sodom and Gomorrah with his family to live a life of wealth and comfort. He lived contently in a life of sin. Not willing to seek God's will. God sent sudden destruction to the city, due to the unwillingness to love God like they loved themselves. God told Lot to take his family, escape for their lives and not look back. God was giving them a new life. God was offering them something that they never had before, a life of freedom. As they began to flee the city, Lot's wife stopped and looked back. She looked back at what she was leaving behind, a life of wealth and comfort. What she couldn't see was that God was trying to offer her more, a life of freedom and eternal life with Him. Lot's wife looked back and was turned into a pillar of salt, frozen, unable to move. I believe Jesus allowed her vision to be free, free to see exactly what her eternity would be, a life of burning fire.   God told her not to look back for that reason. He told her not to look back at her past, but to look toward her future.   God wanted her to turn from an eternity in hell.   I have learned not to look back.   Jesus has set my vision on something else, Him.   He has shown me how to live for Him and not myself.   The past is the past and my future is eternal life in Heaven with Him.   I have nothing to look back at, but I have much to look forward to.   Don't look back; keep your eyes on Him.

DON'T LOOK UP AT THE DEVIL, LOOK DOWN ON HIM

We must keep from falling into the trap of Satan.   We must speak out loud to the devil.   We must tell him daily of our deliverance by the Lord.   When we're feeling down and defeated, we must look up.   Look up to Jesus and know that Satan is below you, under your feet.   Trapped, only until you let him in.   Quote Psalm 91, "I will say of the Lord, He is my refuge and my fortress; my God; in Him will I trust.   Surely he shall deliver, ME".   Hold onto that Psalm.   Carry it with you everywhere you go.   When we speak the Word of God to ourselves, our spirit hears it. The more we hear it, the more we grow, and the more we grow, the easier it is to look up.   Look up to Jesus and look down on him, the devil.   The word is sharper than a two edged sword, but we must use it to defeat the devil.   Don't let Satan defeat you when you can keep him down with the Word of God.

DON'T TAKE YOUR LIFE FOR GRANTED

Taking your shoes off and walking in the grass. Running, really fast, through the park with your kids. Singing in the choir, so soft, but so proud. Going to Wal-Mart, trying to beat the crowd. Walking along the beach, hand in hand; buying an ice cream, from the ice cream stand. Playing in the rain, splashing in the puddles. Holding your daughter, when she just wants to cuddle. A kiss goodnight, as you tuck your kids in bed. Watching a sunset; yellow, orange and red. Going to the mailbox to get that special card, from the one you love so deep, so hard. Flying a kite, on a bright sunny day. Watching the flowers bloom, in the month of May. Don't take life for granted, for life is all you've got. Focus on what you have, and not what you have not.

DON'T WORRY ABOUT CRIMINALS BECAUSE THEY WILL GET WHAT THEY DESERVE

On the last day of Jesus' life, He was taken from a cell on death row, marched up a hill where He was spat upon, ridiculed, mocked and beaten. As the crown of thorns was placed upon His head, He stood with blood dripping from His brow. Nails were driven into His hands and feet, and He was left to hang on the cross and die. Jesus died just as much for the men, women and children in this prison as He did for you. As Christians, we are to reach out to those in prison, regardless of why they are here. Many men in the Bible spent time in prison because of their faith. So, what if God said, "Don't worry about the prisoners, because they're getting what they deserve." Who do you think would have written the New Testament if God didn't love Paul, the prisoner? The only answer for sin and crime is found in the hope offered through Jesus Christ. Christ told His followers; "Go ye into all the world, and preach the gospel to every creature" (Mark 16:15). The harvest is ripe and plenteous, so where are the laborers?

DON'T WORRY
GOD ISN'T MAD AT YOU

When I became a Christian, the first thing that I thought was; What if I make a mistake? Will God be mad at me? I thought that He was going to punish me by making me sick or strike one of my children with a horrible disease. Then, it would be my fault because I sinned. He had every right to punish me. I sinned and now my children had to pay for my mistake. I couldn't believe it when my husband told me that God wasn't mad at me, and that He wouldn't punish me like that. I was so shocked. How could God be that forgiving? How could someone love me that much? When all I feel like I do is make mistake after mistake. My husband told me that sin had no control over me, and that I was in control. I had the control to stop myself in any situation that was leading me to sin. God wasn't mad at me because He loves me just the way that I am. He died on the cross for my sins and yours. That doesn't mean that it's okay to keep repeating the same sins. If we truly ask for forgiveness and mean it from the heart then God will forgive us. God loves us just the way we are. When God forgives us of our sins, our sins are thrown away, never to be remembered. Remember, God doesn't hold grudges and he is not mad at us when we sin.   God has unconditional love.   God is unconditional love.

DOWN ON THE FARM

Life on a farm is hard work.   You wake up with the sun coming up every morning.   You clean stalls, milk the cows and feed the animals.   Some animals fly free on the farm, but some, most remain caged up day and night.   The farm, here at Marysville is somewhat similar to a farm in the country.   Some correctional officers see us as caged animals just waiting to kick you one more time.   Some feel that we don't deserve to ever fly free and even some women remain as caged animals by their own choice.   They choose to do the same crimes and cause the same pain that they did when they were free.   They put off such a foul odor. The stench of fear and anger lingers behind them everywhere they walk.   Even as the bars are opened for them to go outside, they remain as a caged animal.   They hunt their prey.   They see themselves as nothing but an animal.   They have let themselves sink so far down on this farm that they feel they can never get up.   They awake in the morning with the attitude of a stubborn mule and go to bed with the anger of a wild boar; but to me they are someone.   To God they are everything.   They haven't gone too far to turn back.   They still have time to fly free on this farm.   They must be willing to step out of the gate.   They must be willing to let God wash the stench off.   They must have the desire to be human again.   God wants to clean us up and set us free; but we must be willing.   Animals don't realize that they are caged up.   They don't know any other life because that is their life.   We must see the difference. We must show others that there is more to this farm than being caged up.   We can be free on this farm if we just let

God into our cage.   We must be willing to walk through the walls of fear and doubt and allow God to lift us up and out of the shame of the past.   We are not animals; we are God's children.

DREAMS FROZEN IN TIME

Time is a word that has a different meaning to me than it does to other people. Time for me means family, friends, smelling a flower, even holding a newborn baby.   Time for me is standing still.   My dreams that I had for myself are stuck, unmovable in time.   I dreamed of being the best nurse ever.   I dreamed of raising my children in a strong Christian home, but now those dreams seem frozen, frozen in time.   But are they?   As I sit in jail and have nothing to do, my mind seems to race from my past to my future. I begin to wonder if time is standing still.   No, I am finally able to see that time for me is still moving, even though it seems very slow.   As long as God is moving inside of me, so is time.   God has a plan for me, but it's all in his time, not mine.   God has shown me that time is very important. Time is Barry, Kayla, Tori and Aleah.   Time is all that I have to spread God's word to all of those who think they have more than enough time.   Time is love, forgiveness, friendship and freedom.   Time for me seems like it's all I have now.   I get to spend most of it with Jesus.   Time is Jesus Christ and he never stops moving.

FROM DRUG LORD
TO CHILD OF THE KING

Many months ago God allowed us the privilege to bring a man to our Safe Haven Home at our church. He was ready to be free from his addiction. For many years Shawn's family had been known as the biggest drug dealers in Scioto County. Well, for us, this was a privilege to bring him into our church and help him with his addiction. Most of all we wanted to help lead him to the Lord. Drugs were a huge part of Shawn's life. The dealing, manipulation, and use of the drugs were how he survived from day to day. When drugs are the most important thing in your life, church isn't even close to being on the top ten list. For Shawn God was what he had been searching for all of his life, but he just was never given the opportunity or the word of God. Shawn was saved the 1st week after his admission into our home. This time Shawn found what he was searching for, but in the back of his mind he knew that to fulfill God's will, he couldn't go home to his family. Unlike most that come to our home, Shawn dreaded going home. The others worked hard just to get their families back. The love that Shawn had for his family was so strong, but now the love that he has for himself, God and his church had to come first in his life. Shawn is now able to make 1hr visits about once a week with his family, anything more is too overwhelming. Shawn finally found his Safe Haven and that is with Jesus Christ as his Savior.

DYING FOR ATTENTION

Can you see me? I'm over here. Hey, look this way. I'm the one who helped her. I'm the one who takes care of her. I'm the only one who keeps her safe. I'm the only one who is there for her when she is sick and she's always sick. My daughter has cancer and she's dying. You can see what the chemo has done to her. The dark circles and her hair; her hair is all gone. The teachers raised a lot of money for her, but it will never be enough. It will never bring her back when she's gone. These are the words of a sick young lady, here in prison. For two years, she shaved her 5 year old daughter's head every night when she would fall asleep. She told her that she was dying of cancer. She told her family, friends and her daughter's school teachers that she had cancer and that she was dying. But it was her mother with the problem. The mother was dying for attention. She suffers from Munchausen by proxy, a disorder that causes the parent to harm their child in many ways, to seek attention from other people. To be held higher in society for being that strong mother who took care of her sick and dying child. But, to act as if your child was dying from day to day, minute to minute, was truly killing her inside. Attention and love for the wrong reasons will always cause a little piece of your soul to die every day. Seek only for Jesus' love. Let Him love you. Don't let yourself die for attention, but live for Jesus and His love.

EMERGENCY COUNT

"On your bunks, no talking." "Get out of the yard." Correctional officers running from everywhere. Whistles blowing. The siren goes off. The captain makes a call to assure count has begun. "Someone's missing." "Who is it?" "Where could she have gone?" "Emergency!" "Emergency!" "Move it ladies." "Run, run to your bunks." Everyone frantically searching to make sure their bunkies are in their beds. Searching up and down the bays looking for their friends. "Who could it be?" "Did she really escape?" "How could she have gotten over the razor wired fence?" "Could she have climbed over?" "Could she have ridden out in an unmarked vehicle?" Just like here, at the Marysville Penitentiary, Jesus is searching. Searching for that one lost sheep. You've heard the sirens. You've heard the whistles blowing, but you kept running. Running to a place you think is freedom. When all it is, is a razor wired fence. There's no way out. No way of escape. Only pain and sorrow. Deep cuts from the razors that leave you with scars for the rest of your life. Stop running! Listen for the whistle. Listen for His call.

ENTERTAINING ANGELS UNAWARE

Brotherly love; what is it? It is real love toward others. It is kindness to strangers. It is sympathy for those who are in prison (in bondage), whether in their minds or hearts. Those held in bondage because they have been mistreated. Satisfaction for what you have and not what you don't have. People entertain angels everyday without even realizing it. Abraham, Gideon and Manoah are three men who entertained angels unaware. People think that because of other's pasts or present mistakes that they cannot be suitable to sit in our church pews. Don't think and look at what they did, look at what they can be, because they too deserve God's love. They could be that one angel, waiting to be entertained and loved by you. You may have entertained angels unaware. You too may never realize what a smile or a kind word can do for a hurting person. Real love toward others is loving someone without even knowing them; loving them for who they can be; loving them for who you can help them to be. You never know who you are entertaining in your home, work or church. So, show real love today- the love of God, because there are angels waiting for you to show them true love, God's love.

EVEN SMALL LIES AND LITTLE WRONG DOINGS HAVE SERIOUS RESULTS

A few days ago we got a new bunkie in our ten person dorm. The other 9 of us have been in the same room for the last 2 months. Since we've been in here, we've never had a problem with our belongings. By that I mean that we've never had a problem with stealing. We all share together and help each other out when another sister is in need. Well, the last few days have been different for us, because several of our items have come up missing. We soon realized that the new girl was taking our things. Even though it was small things she took; like coffee, cigarettes and food, it could have brought on serious results. My way of dealing with her was to speak to her, but my other bunkie's way of dealing with it was to physically hurt her. Her small lies and little wrong doings were going to have serious results if she didn't change her ways. We have to begin to realize that what may seem small to one person may be very big to someone else, especially in prison. Many women in prison live off state pay and they live from day to day, from pay to pay. We must realize that sin is sin. No matter how big or how small you think it is, it always has a serious penalty before God. Don't risk your eternity with Jesus on the small vanities of life. Do the right thing, because the wrong thing may cause you serious consequences.

EVEN THOUGH A PRISONER

Even though Paul was a prisoner and on house arrest, he was free to have visitors and write letters. So, Paul did just that. He wrote to teach others how to nurture and maintain unity in the church. He spoke to visitors, witnessing to them, and sending them out to share the Good News of the gospel, even though he was a prisoner. Paul could not go out into the churches, but he wanted to circulate the Gospel any way that he could, even though he was a prisoner. Just as Paul, I too, am a prisoner. I also am free to circulate the Gospel. I too write letters, stories of my life and speak to other prisoners here to circulate the Gospel. Even though I am a prisoner, I too am free to spread the Good News. I too, was chosen by God, as was Paul, and was freely given my salvation. I was not saved because I deserve it, but because God graciously and freely gave it. God saved me, according to His plan. My life, as was Paul's was predestined. My life was planned and marked out beforehand by God. Even though I am a prisoner, I have the freedom to tell others what God has done for me. As with Paul, I too am on a missionary trip, sent by God to first and foremost, free myself and others from the prison that holds us captive. The prison of addiction and the prison of sin will destroy you if you allow it. Even though I am a prisoner....

FAILURE IS AN EVENT, NOT A PERSON

You just don't know all that I've done. These were the words of a 41 year old widow and mother of two. Back in 1991 her husband Tony was killed by friendly fire in the Dessert Storm War. The day he died is the day her life was changed forever. We had it all; a wonderful marriage, wonderful children and a beautiful home. We might not have had much material wise, but that didn't matter because love held us together. When Tony died, a huge part of me died with him. As the years passed by she eventually married again, but this time to a verbally and physically abusive man. The only way she knew to cope with the abuse was turn to pills. The pills helped me for a while, but after so long the pain was too hard to handle. She turned to crack cocaine for her pain. She could cope for a while, but when the arguments and beatings got worse, so did her addiction. From all the beatings, she in turn ended up in jail for her enraged anger and intoxication. Her life, she thought was falling apart. She failed her family, her children and even herself. How did all of this happen? How did her life turn upside down? She thought she had it all together, but in fact she was falling apart. Just as quick as her life fell apart, she accepted Jesus into her heart as her Savior. After morning church service in jail, she came to me and said, "You know, while we were here in service, I really wanted to get saved." I had known from the moment I woke up that morning that

71

God was touching my heart. So, as I went through the Romans road and we began praying, she asked Jesus to come into her heart. Her failures had turned into complete freedom, even though she was still behind bars. Lisa was saved December 11th, 2004.

FAILURE TO APPEAR

Being in jail now for over three months, I've gotten to know a lot about the Judicial System. Failure to appear in court is one of the biggest reasons that these women are in here. When these women are picked up on a charge, they are given a court date. Once they're released they head right back to the streets for their drugs and they can't even tell you what day it is, let alone, when their court day is. So, when they're walking the streets, the police officers drive up next to them and pick them up on a warrant for failure to appear. Otherwise, all they had to do was make an appearance, but they just didn't show up. The first few days I was here I thought to myself, "Oh Lord, where are you?" I thought surely Jesus won't fail to appear too. But it was me that had failed to appear. All I had to do was look for him. I was the one that was hiding from God. I was the one who made the decision to walk away, actually run away. So, the next time you're looking for Jesus and you think to yourself, Jesus where are you? It's you that went the other way. It's you that failed to appear.

FAITH VERSUS FEAR

Matthew 10:16: "Behold, I send you forth as sheep in the midst of wolves: Be ye therefore wise as serpents and harmless as doves."

The day I walked into the Scioto County jail I felt like a little sheep in the midst of raging wolves. These women were out for themselves and themselves only. As God sent me into that jail, so did God send them. I knew what I had to do, but I didn't know how to do it. I've never been around women like this with such hard core attitudes, anger and wolf like features. I knew I had to come across without fear, but wise as a serpent. So I just started out by telling them about my addiction and why I was there and within seconds, half of them were crying right along with me. I learned a great lesson that 1st night in jail and that was that God has it all under control and I just have to have the faith that He will protect me. He not only protected me, but He softened hearts of hard core criminal women that might not have ever been softened otherwise. Remember, we are sheep and we must be ready to go anywhere at any time. Fear not for the Lord is with thee.

FAKE IT 'TIL YOU MAKE IT!

While in jail, I've had to learn many skills. I had to learn to do my hair without any hair products. I had to use jail house toothpaste which is made out of a clear gel. I used it as hair gel to style my hair. The girls used rolled toilet tissue for curlers along with the jail house glue (toothpaste). For my eye liner I used hot pencil lead. We had to adjust to many new things to get through the day. I saw many fights. Some were real, but a lot were fake. They would fake a fight to get the guards back and then they would have a runner go get their cigarettes that were waiting for them. They would say "keep faking it, keep faking it she's almost there!" Well, the same thing happens with faith. I've heard many times the saying, 'Just fake it till you make it'. What they mean by that is eventually you'll give in and accept the Lord; until then, just fake it. The good Lord doesn't work like that. The Lord doesn't want a fake heart; He wants a true and sincere heart. I am so thankful that there is no more faking in my life. My heart is clean and clear, and I truly believe the Lord is proud.

FALLEN ANGELS

Mothers, Daughters, Aunts and even Grandmothers have fallen from the disease of addiction. They were born as Angels, but have turned into concrete fallen Angels. The disease of addiction, low self esteem, physical abuse and much more have overtaken their lives. It turns their minds into concrete, only being able to focus straight ahead. They are unable to see the future, only able to see the past. Destruction, anger, and shame held above their heads, but too high up and unable to reach it. The only way to fly high now is to take pills for their shame and guilt. No goals, no hobbies only drugs. No hope, no dreams, only nightmares. Why? The answer is sin. Sin is the host of all evil and the devil will do all he can to make you fall. He makes you fall hard. He makes you unable to think about getting up, and unable to see clearly. He makes you think that the only way out is death. A death that will lead you straight to hell. Hell to these women is better than hell on earth.   Why?   Fallen Angels? Why? Sin!

FATAL ATTRACTION

Most of us have dated someone in our lives who we just didn't seem to have compatibility with. We argued a lot over silly things and the relationship just wasn't what God wanted or what we needed. For me, relationships in high school always seemed to be wrong because I was always attracted to someone for a fatally wrong reason. I wanted and sought attention. As popular as I was, I still didn't feel like that was enough. Many of us are attracted to things that can be fatal to our health. I know diabetics that love sweets, but they know that if they eat too much it can eventually be fatal to their health. For some reason, they still do it anyway. If you love old cars, you don't wait out on a four lane high way until you see one coming, because you will get hit. Many of these women at Marysville have fatal attractions. Throughout their lives they have been in abusive marriages that are due to a fatal attraction to that mate. They grew up in an abusive home and then turned around and grew an attraction to a man that was just abusive. They turn to drugs or alcohol to ease the pain. They become attracted to a world of sin and destruction. To some of them, it is contentment. When I first started taking pain pills for my fibromyalgia, I didn't have an attraction to them.   I just wanted the pain to stop, but after a while, I began having a fatal attraction to them. Wherever they were, I was there too. I stalked them. I watched them day and night, never to be without them. In the end, the addiction overtook my life and the results were nearly fatal.   I ended up here, at the Marysville Penitentiary. Don't let yourself live with fatal attractions. Put your trust in Jesus so he can stop the fatal attraction

75

and turn your life into something wonderful. Live for Jesus because he died for you.

FEELINGS OF PEACE,
IN A PLACE OF TURMOIL

Trapped in a lonely dark prison. It's a place where you desperately search for happiness, hope and love. How can you be lonely when you're with thousands of women? You search for a way to break out, not out of prison, but out of the fear and loneliness that's hidden deep within your heart. Help me not to withdrawal emotionally, because God gave me a responsibility when he sent me here. He sent me here for a purpose. His purpose was for me to find peace within my own heart first, then to show that peace and God's love to the ones that are trapped in sin. When you have a heart filled with bitterness and anger, you have to let your heart succumb to turmoil, not peace. The danger and bitterness only tightens and secures yourself to sin. As you sustain the anger and resentment toward your abuser, you remain a victim and still have a special bond with your abuser. That bond is sin and it will imprison your life until you receive peace from Jesus. You must be willing to break the bond with your abuser. You must be willing to stand alone in a room of hundreds of women. You will not be lonely anymore. You cannot be lonely or without peace with Jesus on your side. Don't stay trapped in the lonely dark prison. You must break free. Break free from the bonds of sin that cause the turmoil in your heart and mind. You can be locked up in prison and still be free.

FIELD OF DREAMS

As I look outside my window through the bars that hold me in, I see a field of dreams shattered and torn.

Hundreds of women that sat as children dreaming of what one day they would become. Doctors, lawyers, nurses and teachers; hopes and dreams never fulfilled. Alcohol and drugs overtook their lives and now hold them hostage in this prison. The yard is a field of lost hope and shattered dreams. Women scarred from their pasts. Hearts broken and bodies bruised. Families torn apart by a pill or by a drink. Lives lost into this deep world of sin.

This chaotic society that we live in, otherwise known as life. A field of dreamers in this place called Tapestry.

Dreams that were hidden deep within their hearts, yearning to one day become reality. These women are dreamers for what they will one day become, not for what they used to be. This field of dreams is full of life.

Full of broken-hearted women with big hopes, big dreams, and a faith that they'll one day soon grow up to be what they always dreamed of being.

Tapestry is full of dreamers, women with a desire that one day their dreams become reality.

FOR THE CHILDREN

Drugs and death go hand in hand. Stealing, manipulating, and conniving anyone and everyone you can. My bunkie's husband is headed to the Lucasville Penitentiary for murder. A death sentence by lethal injection. A drug deal gone bad. A man is murdered. Cornell and his two accomplices waited for the man to bring them his money

77

and when he didn't have it he was shot execution style. To remove the body they duct taped him, then decapitated him and cut him into pieces. To get rid of the body they burnt it. The only way to identify him was his teeth. The worst part is that Cornell has two beautiful children and now both parents taken from them due to drugs. My bunkie is here for dealing drugs and her ex-husband is sentenced for murder. Two children left behind to pick up the pieces. What went wrong? How could this happen? Five years ago they were so happy -- a home, car, money and love. Today they've lost it all; but it's the children who have to pay. It's their two precious boys that remain at home to suffer. God moved here at the Marysville Pen when Kym gave her heart to the Lord. She has changed her heart and her life. She's able to return home to her boys to make a fresh start. Her children will soon have their mother back; a new and improved mother. A mother with a hope and joy that she's never had before. Even though her life was filled with drugs, death and more, she now has a life filled with the Holy Spirit that she can take home to her precious boys.

FORGIVE THEM FATHER FOR THEY KNOW NOT WHAT THEY DO

"It's all I know," she said to me. "Screaming, hitting, stabbing and even trying to kill each other--my dad beating my mom, my dad beating my brother and my dad beating me! We had to protect my mom or he would have killed her. It's all I know. There was no god when I grew up. My father was god in our home. I never heard about God. I just never knew. We didn't get up on Sunday mornings and go to church. We got up on Sunday mornings listening to the screams of my mom. Listening as he took her head and beat it into the wall. We just never knew. I didn't go out and play with friends. I got up and did the dishes. Not just the dishes we ate off of for dinner, but he made me wash every dish in the cabinet. If I didn't, then I got beat. I got hit upside the head with beer bottles. I got chased with axes. I got stabbed by my own father. I just didn't know."

She sits here today in the Ohio Reformatory for Women because she 'just didn't know.' That's the only life she knew until God saved her life by sending her to prison. God saved her from the prison and hell of the world outside these walls. She prays today for her father. She prays, "Father, forgive him, for he knows not what he did." God gloriously saved Chris from not only eternal life in hell, but he saved her from hell on earth.

FREEDOM IS AN ATTITUDE,
NOT A LOCATION

A friend of mine, J.M., gave a topic group today on 'change'. She has been on this farm now for 12 years, and she is serving a 15 year to life sentence for murder. Within these last twelve years she has had to make a complete turn around in her life. She has fought the fight of addiction and won. She has been forgiven by her family members and she has turned her life over to Jesus. In her topic group, she asked us if we were doing 'time' or 'life'. She explained 'time' as just waiting on the day of your release, parole or judicial. 'Life' was described as doing your time by making improvements in your life so that you don't ever have to come back here again. Today, she is doing 'life'. Not her actual life sentence, but a life of freedom behind these walls. She's made a change in her life that has

79

opened her eyes to a new way of living in this prison. For many years she lived day to day, waiting on word from the parole board. Yes, she does want to go home and she does want to be free, but for the first time in her life, she realized that her freedom was her attitude and not her location. One of her most famous quotes is 'Freedom is a state of mind'. Today, whether she serves 50 more years, or life sentence, she is free.

FREEDOM RINGS,
JUST ANSWER THE CALL

I've been in trouble since I've been eleven years old. I can remember watching my brother getting his crack cocaine ready. He would have it all set up, and then he would pull up his sleeve, take a needle and inject it into his arm. Then one day I thought, I might want to try it. So, I did and I loved it. I wasn't sure how I was going to get the money to buy it, so I stole for it. When that wasn't enough I hit the ho-stro, and sold myself for it. I had to, I just couldn't stop. I just wanted to be like my brother, cool. I hit the block by the time I was thirteen and I ended up in Juvie Hall for thirty days. It was all happening so fast and I liked it. The fast life, that is. By the time I had my first child I had been in Juvie Hall, arrested over 40 times and in prison for the third time. It just became a lifestyle for me. It was like I was locked up in a cage and I couldn't get out. I could see freedom, but I couldn't get the lock open. Today, I sit in a prison cell for the 5th time. I had to leave my three children and my people from (216) back in Cleveland again. I'm writing about my bunkie, Ms. Smith. She is so beautiful and kind, but to herself she sees nothing. She's institutionalized even when she is out of prison. She says that she just can't stop. "I can't find freedom anywhere." Today I had the opportunity to speak with her about true freedom. I shared with her about my freedom, my freedom of sins. Today, March 1, 2005, my Bunkie remains enslaved to her addiction, but I pray the one day she will answer the call to freedom.

FROM SCANDALOUS
TO SERENITY

All my mom ever gave me was a drug, and all I ever wanted from her was a hug and an 'I love you'. These were the words from a 25 year old mother of two and another on the way, who was picked up on the streets for petty theft. She came into jail a few days ago after choosing drugs over her family. Her husband came to her and asked her to make a choice. The choice was to give up her drugs or give up her family. At this time in her life, the drugs had overcome her body and her mind. She told her husband that she couldn't make the choice, and his response was, "You just did." Her life on the streets was surrounded by scandals and schemes. She would and could talk her way into $1,500 at a time from men on the streets. Once the money was gone, so was she. She said that all she had to do was promise them the world, and they would agree to give her what she wanted.

The world was never what they received, what they received was a scandal and a scheme. She would say, if I just had a mother who loved me and not her drug, then I probably wouldn't be here today. Now, after spending time in prison and in jail, she now wants serenity instead of scandal. She said that when she gets out that she is going to find her kids and hug them and tell them how much she loves them. I never wanted the world, I just wanted to be loved.

Judges 16:18 – "And when Delilah saw that he had told her all his heart, she sent and called for the Lords of the Philistines saying, come up this once, for he hath showed me all of his heart. Then the Lords of the Philistines came up unto her and brought money in their hand."

Tabitha Cade Bellomy was saved December 11th, 2004.

FROM THE GARDEN
TO THE WILDERNESS

The garden was a place of paradise, where Adam and Eve walked together naked and unashamed. It was a place without sin, fear, shadows, or disorder. Love abounded until sin entered in. In one split second, paradise turned into wilderness. Temptation led Eve to offer Adam to eat of the forbidden fruit. Their lives changed forever, never to be the same again. Now a shadow hung over the garden. Fear and doubt became part of their daily routine. God created man in His own image to be like Him, not to be Him. Many of us have led good Christian lives, living in a form of paradise on this earth. But we all have temptations of desire and lust that we must not give in to. However, we are human, we are flesh. My flesh is what led me from paradise into the wilderness. By His grace God brought me out of the wilderness. He took away my fears and doubts and gave me the strength to witness for Him in this prison. Don't give-in to temptation or the devil and his demons can and will lead you from the garden into the wilderness.

FROM THE ROOTS UP

Early summer time you go into your well tilled garden, and get out all of your seeds to plant to make a great harvest for yourself. First, you till the garden and get out all of the rocks. Then you take your seed and sprinkle them out onto the ground, into a small hole that was made especially for that one seed. Once the seed is placed gently into its hole, you cover it up with the well fertilized dirt. Once the seed has been planted it must be watered to begin its growth process. Then the sun comes up in the morning and the rays begin to shine down upon the seed to begin the growth process. This process is just like the growth process for all of us. When we give our heart to the Lord, we must begin a growth process. We first need to get ourselves in a well fertilized area around other Christians, which I consider the church. Then, we need to get out all of the rocks in our lives that make us stumble. Some of my rocks were addiction, low self-esteem and a rape when I was a teenager. We are planted as a small seed in a big world. Once we are planted we must begin the watering process, which is praying and reading our Bible. As the sun shines down on the seed to grow, our Son shines on us to help us to grow. One ray gives us strength, the next courage, and the next is faith. The more you allow the Son to shine His rays on you the bigger and stronger you will be.

FROM WALKING DOWN STREETS OF GOLD TO LIVING ON THE STREETS OF THE GHETTO

How can one's life change so drastically? She was married to a preacher's son, four children, a good home and a Christian. Singing in a Church to tricking on the street. Sleeping in a nice warm bed to sleeping in abandoned warehouses. She bathed with garden hoses in restaurant bathrooms and baby pools. She was lost in a world of sin and destruction. Her life began so pure and free and then what seemed like an instant, she went from the jail to the penitentiary. Staci came from the Hamilton County Jail to the Marysville Prison for prostitution and crack cocaine. Most, if not all of the time, they both go hand in hand. They trick for money to buy crack. They sell themselves for drugs. These women are lost in a world of addiction. Staci ended up losing what meant the most to her in life, her family. Due to her addiction her husband left her. He placed her clothes outside in bags and her children were gone, never to be seen again. It's been about a year now and she weeps at the sound of their names. She lost it all for drugs. Staci might not have her family back, but she can have the one she lost many years ago, Jesus. Jesus never left her side during her pain and trials. He stood by and wept for her, patiently waiting for her to return to Him.

FROZEN IN TIME

She was locked up for 23 years; she was frozen in time. She never saw the outside of these walls for two decades. She's never been to Wal-Mart to shop for Christmas toys.

She's never run a car through a powered car wash. She's never been able to get ice chips from her refrigerator without using ice trays. She's never been shopping at the new malls. She's never ridden in a new SUV. She's been frozen in time, never to do any of these simple things. She's here for life. She's grown accustomed to having nothing. She wakes up every morning at the same time. She walks to the chow hall in line two and she works in the laundry room every single day. She's frozen in time at the Marysville Pen for Women. If you ask her if those things matter to her, her answer would be, NO! She's not concerned with the latest fashions because she has to wear a uniform twenty-four hours a day. She's not concerned with the newest vehicles, because she will never drive again. Her only concern now is where she will spend her eternity when she dies here in prison. Her only concern is spreading His word to those who aren't frozen in time. Her concern now is for others to die into eternity instead of others dying at the hand of herself. She's found Jesus while frozen in time. She's found her way, when her way before was a life of sin. Now she's living her life for Jesus. She might be doing time but she's not letting time do her.

FULFILLING GOD'S PLAN

Today, as I sit behind these prison walls I can see God's plan coming together. For many years I knew that God had a plan for me, but I had too much shame and guilt from my past holding me back. But, today I am set free. God is taking me on a path, His path, toward my dream. To help others fight and beat their addictions. God has put me in a place where I can learn about every drug imaginable. There are women from every race and ethnicity; women from the ghetto, streets and even women from the richest

families in Ohio.   There are lawyers, doctors, Sunday
school teachers and more; women with pasts from physical
abuse to mental abuse, violent crimes to petty theft.   There
are women from all walks of life.   I am using this
experience as a school.   A learning experience to soak in
everything I can, before this journey here in prison ends.   I
will fulfill His plan.   I will walk and talk with Jesus in every
way and manner that I can at this prison.   I will use every
way possible to bring God's word into this prison and to
give these women an opportunity to find the only way to
true freedom.   Freedom through Jesus Christ.   Today, I
will fulfill His plan.

FULL COVERAGE

As a prisoner sits in front of the judge as he slams his gavel
down, saying "Your pardon has been granted," the prisoner
is ecstatic.   But the prisoner knows that he has no chances
left, because his pardon only applies to his past.   It has no
affect on some future misconduct.   If he breaks the law
again, he'll go right back to prison.   As a Christian and a
prisoner myself, I am so blessed to have full coverage.
When God wrote out my check of righteousness, I
immediately became fully covered.   I may stumble and fall
in my future, but the man-made-judge here cannot rob me
of my robe of righteousness.   He can not take away my
future, my eternal home.   He cannot take away my inner
freedom-my freedom for living for my Jesus.   My Jesus
paid a debt that I could never repay.   He washed my sins
away.   I am now pardoned from my past.   Sin is a debt
that must be paid and justification is that gift of God's
righteousness that cancelled my debt and pardoned my
sinful life.   Today, I am fully covered.   Are you?

GET OVER THE WILDERNESS MENTALITY

Thoughts of your future are always affected by your past. Ernest Hemingway once said, "Life breaks us all, and afterward many are strong at the broken places." But not all are made strong-- many stay broken. When your car breaks down, the first thing you do is get the broken piece fixed. Why? Because you use it many times a day. It's a necessity to you. So why is it so hard to fix our broken hearts and our broken pasts? Why do we continue to remain in the wilderness? John 6:12 says, "Gather up the fragments that remain, that nothing be lost." If we want to get out of the wilderness of our past, we must pick up the shattered fragments and move on. We must rise again. We must let go of what lies behind and press on, because looking back gives much opportunity for return. We must know where we came from to know where we are going. Jesus knew where He came from and where He was going. We must continue to hope, believe and be positive about what our future holds, or we will continue to remain a part of the wilderness. So use your past to affect your future. Don't remain in the wilderness mentality.

GETTING TO THE ROOT

When I was a child, the best trees to climb were my neighbors' apple trees. I loved to climb all the way to the top, but getting down was sometimes a problem. The limbs on the trees weren't quite as sturdy as the lower limbs. So, I knew when I got closer to the top that I needed to hang on tight. I loved climbing higher and higher and picking the apples that were at the top of the tree. I would climb back down and sit at the foot of the tree and eat the apples I had picked. The apple tree reminds me of my life. Unless I pick off the fruits, which is the sin in my life, I'll never know what kind of tree it is.

Once you pick the fruits off, you must get to the root. The root is where the heart is. The root is where the problem starts. It's a heart problem, not a head problem. It's a sin problem, not a self problem. You must get to the root if you want to get to the top of the tree, the cross.

GHETTO: IT DOESN'T MATTER WHERE YOU CAME FROM, JUST WHERE YOU'RE GOING!

Ghetto? What does ghetto mean to me? Well, it's living in poverty, living in circumstances. Circumstances that you were born into. Circumstances that were beyond your control. Living without food for days. Walking almost everywhere you need to go because you don't have enough money to buy a car, let alone buy yourself a happy meal. Living in conditions that you probably never thought you'd have to live in. But, does it really matter where you came from? Does your past really matter? The only thing that matters is where you're spending your future and eternity. Don't dwell on the past or past conditions. God doesn't see the dirt that has stained your past. The dirt that stained your skin, the flesh, the heart & salvation. God only wants our present time. He only wants you to spend eternity with him. So live for Eternity.

GOD BLESS MYRIAH SKYE

Myriah Skye turned six months old just the other day. The last time her mommy called home to check on her, she was beginning to crawl around in her playpen, laughing and cooing. Shelly hadn't seen her daughter in over four months, but the love she had for her was amazing. Myriah's picture hung right beside my bed so her mommy could tell her goodnight every evening before the lights went out. When we awoke today, Shelly was awakened by an officer telling her that she needed to go to the captain's office to talk to an investigator. We all knew that whatever had happened that it couldn't be good. She was escorted into the office and they told her to sit down. She said, "It's my father isn't it, he's been sick? Is he okay?" The woman looked at her and said, "I'm sorry, but your daughter died last night." Shelly fell to the floor, screaming hysterically. How did she die? She was fine last night when I called home to check on her. What went wrong? Why wasn't I there with her? It's my fault. This never would have happened if I was there with her. Three days later, Shelly was in a cruiser, shackled and handcuffed, being escorted to her daughter's funeral. As she walked through the door she saw her husband sitting by the casket holding little Myriah, rocking her back and forth. He said, "I couldn't stand to see her lying in that casket all alone, so I thought I would hold her until you got here." Shelly spent thirty minutes with her daughter, with two armed guards watching her every move. After her thirty minutes were up, they told her it was time for her to leave. She kissed her daughter on the forehead and left her for the very last time. Myriah Skye died of SIDS, 2 months before her mother was to be released from prison. God used Myriah to save 13 other children's lives, when her parents donated her organs. But, one of those lives wasn't saved through organ donation. Shelly, Myriah's mother, got saved in prison the day after her funeral. Why did little Myriah have to die? That question I can't answer, but I can tell you that through her death, God gave eternal life to her mother. God Bless you, little Myriah Skye, I'll never forget that beautiful face.

GOD DON'T LIKE UGLY

I am sitting in the Marysville Penitentiary and I don't think I have ever been as angry as I am now. The girl beside me is in here for killing her four month old baby. If you think that's what has made me angry, you're wrong. What made me angry was the woman that just walked up to her and said, "So, how long did the judge give you for murdering your baby?" God doesn't like ugly, and that was ugly. The girl beside me has asked God for forgiveness and she is now a child of the King. She is saved no more or no less than you or I. She knows what she has done and she knows that God loves her. To me that woman that made the rude comment sinned just the same as Jeanette. I don't know if it was deliberate or accidental, but all I know is that now she's my sister in Christ. She is God's child. I know that no sin is larger or smaller than the other but, the way people talk to each other is wrong and just plain ugly and God doesn't like ugly. The hardest thing for me to understand is that the woman who said that to Jeanette told me she was a strong Christian and that she was able to express her own opinion. I pray that she is right, but God still doesn't like ugly and that is not what God wants out of us. God wants us, as Christians to help others, not hurt them.

GOD GIVEN CAMOUFLAGE SUITS

As the chameleon crawls deep into the green grass, its skin turns green to match its environment. As the chameleon goes back out onto the earth its color changes back to its original brown color to match God's given soil. The chameleon was given this mechanism for protection as it moves from place to place. Just like the chameleon, we change our colors and our attitudes to match the different environments that we place ourselves in. When I came into jail for the first time, my environment had definitely changed from the way I was used to living. I had never been around prostitutes, drug dealers, or felons. You are around people like me everyday. But, how do you know? People change to match their environment everyday. If you're around people with a foul mouth, then your vocabulary may eventually change to match the attitude of the person you are around, just like the chameleon. God didn't mean for us to be like or act like animals. He meant for us to be like and act like Him. When I came to jail, I made sure that the one thing that I would never change would be my love for Jesus Christ. No one can change my heart, my desire or my love for the one that gave me life and my salvation. I made up my mind that my colors and my attitudes, no matter where God sent me, would always remain the same. I will spread the Good News wherever I go, and I will not allow anyone to change my colors.

GOD IS MERCIFUL,
EVEN TO REBELS

I had the pleasure of meeting a woman today who calls herself 'The Rebel'. She has carried this name around with her for over 20 years now. Her life on the streets was hard and fast. She lived from day to day, figuring out ways to hustle people. She didn't know there was a different life ahead of her. She didn't know of God's grace and mercy. She only knew of pain and suffering. Day to day she fought, stole and drugged. She hated people. She hated everyone, including herself. If someone stepped into her path, she knocked them out of her way. She said, "They deserved what they got." Then one day, 24 years ago, Sharon deserved what she got. She had gone too far this time. She was no longer a rebel, but a murderer. She killed a man during a robbery and was sentenced to death row. But after 4 years of living life on death row, God showed his mercy. She asked Jesus for forgiveness of her sins and He gloriously saved her. 'The Rebel' was now a Christian. She had never felt so loved in all her life. She found more love in her death row cell than she had had in her whole 26 years of life. God was merciful. God overturned her death row sentence and gave her life in prison. She now has 10 more years, but to Sharon life is now a blessing. She speaks to women every weekend at the 'Hale Cottage'. She shares her story of life as a rebel changed to a Christian. God is merciful, even to the Rebel.

GOD IS REALLY BETTER TO US
THAN WE ARE TO OURSELVES

While growing up as an athletic, tomboyish little girl, I had my share of bumps and bruises. I played in the mud, climbed trees (even fell from a few), but most of all I loved playing sports. I played volleyball all the way up to college. I played the 'setter' position for four years in high school and two years in college. Being the setter was hard work because I was the one who had to make the perfect pass to the 'spiker.' That was the one who had to pound it over to the other side, but this meant that I had to go to the ball wherever it might be. I jumped into the bleachers, dove under chairs and rolled into walls just to get that ball. Granted, it was a lot of fun then, but today at 35 years old it has caused me a lot of pain. I have back pain, arthritis, and a lot of knee pain due to diving as a teenager. At that time in my life, thinking about arthritis as an adult or knee pain when I grew old was not even a thought. I knew that all of the diving was hurting me because the doctors told me so. But all I wanted was to be the best: to do what I wanted to do no matter the cost. Many times in our lives we treat ourselves worse than we treat others. God is better to us than we are to ourselves. Why is this? Why don't we take care of ourselves? We can't rely on any one else to do it for us. We must take control, and look at what we're doing to ourselves, because whatever we do to ourselves affects the future we hold for our kids and grandchildren. Treat yourself with love and respect, because you deserve it.

GOD RESPONDS TO FAITH
EVEN IN THE MIDST OF FAILURE

Probably the hardest thing for me right now is patience. There isn't anything harder for me to do than to wait, whether I am expecting something good or something bad. One way I have tried to cope with the waiting here in prison is to help God with His plan, to help get His plan into action before He's ready for it to begin. Sarah was one in the Bible that tried this same approach. Sarah devised her own plan. She figured she was too old for God to bless her with a child, so she thought the only way to give Abraham a son was through another woman. Her plan worked, at first, but eventually Sarah regretted her plan. She thought that since God hadn't blessed her with a child yet that she would never be able to bear a child. She had waited 90 years when God told her she would have a child, and she laughed. Not just because of a lack of faith in God, but because of the doubt that she had placed on herself. However, through her trials and her failures she learned faith. God responded to her faith and blessed her with a child. Many times I have shown doubt, not necessarily due to a lack of faith in God, but my own doubt. I put words into my mind because I doubt myself, not God. Sitting here in prison has been the hardest trial I have ever faced, but I know today that through my faith, God will restore me.

GOD SOMETIMES ACCOMPLISHES HIS WILL IN UNEXPECTED WAYS

Each morning a priest was to enter the Holy Place of the temple and burn incense. Lots were cast to decide who would enter this sacred room, and one day the lot fell to Zachariah, not by chance, but by God. It was a once in a lifetime opportunity. Zachariah, while at the altar burning incense, was praying for a son. God answered his prayer in his own way and own time. Zachariah's wife was barren, so God worked in an unexpected way in an impossible situation. An angel appeared to him and told him his wife was to have a child. Zachariah had his doubts, due to his age. So God prevented Zachariah from speaking until the promise became reality. But Zachariah was a faithful servant. God ever so quietly came on the scene. Zachariah doubted but was willing to obey. Prison for me today was very unexpected, but it was God's will. I had my doubts, but due to my faith, I will accomplish God's will in an unexpected way. Many of us have events in our lives that are truly unexpected. We must remember that this is all a part of God's will. We must do our part by obeying God's word, and in the end, God will ever so quietly come on the scene to accomplish His will in our lives.

GOD'S FINGERPRINTS

Have you ever thought about what it feels like when the hand of God touches you? When He heals your child of a dreadful disease? When he touches you with his gentle hands as you cry yourself to sleep? He leaves His precious fingerprints all over you like a stain, never to be released.

As He carried the old rugged cross, to die for our sins, He left His blood stained prints on the tree of life for you and me. Every morning as you bow your head in prayer, His prints are left upon your knees to remind you of His love. His prints are left on every child, no matter how rich or poor. His prints are left to give us strength when we think we can take no more. The Hand of God is so precious to me as I sit in this prison cell. As I pray for His hand to touch and guide me, His fingerprints remain. I can see His prints left on many women as His hand passes by. His love has guided them toward His saving power never to return to this prison again. God's prints aren't like the prints that most of us women in here know because His remain forever, by one simple touch.

GRADUATION DAY

Crime, hate, drug addiction, alcoholism, war, AIDS, environmental nightmares and even killer bees. Running on a treadmill, going faster and faster, but getting nowhere. But don't forget the babies, rainbows, shooting stars, hot fudge, Swiss cake rolls, the blue birds and even the Smokey Mountains. Earth is just a school; a place for all of us to learn. Some choose not to. They choose to only see and participate in the bad stuff. But some of us are doing all we can to learn what we need for our graduation day. We get to go home. We have something other than this earth to look forward to. We can sit in this prison and learn. We can grow from our mistakes, or we can just stay on the treadmill running toward nowhere. Just imagine, as you sit in your prison called life, no more pain, no suffering, no death, no illness, happiness all the time, seeing your loved ones once again, the beautiful colors, smells and sounds, and hanging out with God on a daily basis. Sitting on the riverside with your feet dangling in, talking with your Jesus. It's your choice as you sit in this prison, learn from your mistakes and graduate from this earth or continue running on the treadmill going nowhere.

HARD CORE CRIMINAL

They are hard-hearted, hard as a rock and unable to break through. You try to chisel your way in, but a blockade is placed up. There's no bridge to get across. The sign says: road closed, wrong way, danger, turn back. Hard core criminals, loving what they do, but hating themselves on the inside. Unable to show any true feelings. Beaten down by their pasts. Feeling like they have to prove something, but the only thing that they prove is that they are afraid. Afraid to let anyone in. Afraid of what they might actually find. A scared child, unable to break free from the past. Beaten down physically and mentally. Frozen in time with cement expressions. One day they will break. They have to break to open up their pasts. They would do anything for love and attention, but they can't let anyone know their true feelings. They think that they can't change. They feel unworthy. But, one day they have to. They have to open up for the first time in their lives. They hear a voice. But, who is calling them? It's Jesus trying to get in. Jesus is trying to knock, for you to open. Answer His call. Open the door. Jesus can and will heal your past. Jesus can make a hardcore criminal into a softhearted Christian. Answer Him today. Let Him love you. Let Jesus be your rock to stand on. Give Jesus you anger and pain. He wants to break those chains that are holding you captive in your past.

HARDENED HEARTS
ARE SOFTENED

In December 2004, I had the privilege of meeting a young, pregnant 22 year old girl in the Scioto County Jail. The day she was brought into our unit I knew from her appearance that she had had a rough life. As she began to speak every other word was a cuss word. She spoke of life on the streets and the consequences that went with it. The week before she was arrested she had jumped out of a car going 50 mph for safety of her life and that of her unborn child's life. She had been on the streets for 7 years now. She had been raped, beaten, thrown from cars and her life threatened. I wanted so badly to express to her the gospel of Jesus, but I had never met anyone like her so I didn't know how to approach her. Well, I didn't have to say anything to her, she came to me. She was lying in her bunk underneath me. She was crying and peaked out and said, "Hey mama tonight I want to be saved". So that night we read in Romans and she gave her heart to the Lord. God didn't stop there, because all the way in Florida her 15 yr old juvenile delinquent brother gave his heart to the Lord, the same night in juvy hall in Florida. I thank you Lord for allowing me to be there for her miraculous transformation.

December 9, 2004

HAVING JOY IN FORGIVENESS

Jesus shows us of the willingness to forgive as He hung on the old rugged cross. "Forgive them for they know not what they do." God forgave the thief as he hung on the cross and he was able to die into eternity with His Savior. Many of us have been hurt by someone else in our lives who have scarred us on the inside for years. Sin can and will eat at you day and night until you ask for forgiveness. Whether it's forgiveness of your sins or the tough act of forgiving someone else, either way you cannot and will not receive complete joy without forgiving yourself and others. First you must recognize your sinful tendencies. Then you must admit your sins to Jesus. You will receive peace and joy in your heart. Forgiving others is usually easier than forgiving yourself. Until you can love and forgive yourself you won't be able to truly forgive others that have hurt you. You will not be able to have that joy, deep down inside of you that you have always longed for. As you see your child forgive another child for something they had done to them, you can always see a peace about them. They have such forgiving hearts, so why can't we? That is why they can wake up every morning with a beautiful smile on their face. Have a forgiving heart, as a child does. Forgive yourself for your wrong doings. Jesus forgave me, so I know that He can and will forgive a sinner like you. Allow Jesus to give you the joy in forgiving yourself and others.

HE THIRSTS WHILE ON THE CROSS

John 19:28 – "After this Jesus knowing that all things were

now accomplished that the scripture might be fulfilled, saith, I thirst."

As Jesus knew that all things were accomplished, He said that He thirsts. Before He said it is finished, they filled a sponge with vinegar and put it to His mouth. But why did Jesus wait to say it was finished until after he had received the drink (vinegar)? Was He actually thirsting for a drink, or was He thirsty for something else? Have you ever been so thirsty that you could taste it in your mouth? You have a mountain dew in front of you, ready to drink and you know that once you get that first sip that it's going to quench your thirst. I believe Jesus was thirsty to see His Father. I believe He knew that all was ready for Him to return home and Jesus knew what home would be like. He thirsted to return to His heavenly home. All of us should have that thirst quenching desire to spend eternity in heaven with Jesus. He will quench your thirst, for you'll never have to thirst again.

HEALING THE CHILD WITHIN

I've been in the pen now for about four days. I have had the opportunity to meet many different women from different races and ethnicities. Nine out of ten of these women are still dealing with their troubled childhood. They have been raped, molested, beaten, and even forgotten by their very own parents. These women are dealing with open wounds from their past that have been seeping out causing overwhelming pain for more than twenty to thirty years. They have brought their childhood memories with them as they grew and matured into grown women. Wounds that have been unable to heal due to lack of peace through Jesus Christ our Lord. I am blessed not to have had a troubled childhood as a lot of these women, but I did go through a date rape at the age of fourteen years old. I have carried this event with me for more than twenty-one years now. It wasn't until about nine months ago that I was able to receive peace through this memory. For twenty-one years I had this secret deep within me, unable to heal the wound that caused me emotional pain and fear. I hid this secret inside of me thinking that if I never told anyone that it would go away. Due to this secret I grew more fearful of men each and every day. The man's face that did this to me now flashes through my memory multiple times a day. I was unable to get past that awful day. But, due to God's grace and guidance that He has so graciously blessed me with, I am now able to cope with my fears and have peace within my heart. I think that one day soon I will be able to forgive the man that caused my now healing wound. But until then, all I can do is pray for God's courage, peace, and healing within.

HEAVEN'S GROCERY STORE

I was walking down life's highway a long time ago
When I saw a sign that read, "Heavens Grocery Store"
As I got a little closer, the door came open wide
And when I came to myself, I was standing inside
I saw a host of angels-that were standing everywhere
One handed me a basket and said, "My child, shop with care"
Everything a Christian needed was in the grocery store
And all you couldn't carry, you could come back the next day for more
First I got some PATIENCE; LOVE was in the same row
Further down was UNDERSTANDING, you need that everywhere you go

101

I got a box or two of WISDOM, a bag or two of FAITH
I just couldn't miss the HOLY GHOST for he was all over
the place
I stopped to get some STRENGTH and COURAGE to help
me run this race
By then my basket was getting full, but I remembered I
needed some GRACE
I didn't forget my salvation, for SALVATION- that was free
So...I tried to get enough of that to save both you and me
Then I started up to counter to pay my grocery bill
For I thought I had everything to do my Masters will
As I went up the aisle, I saw PRAYER, and I just had to put
it in
For I knew when I stepped outside, I would run right into
sin
PEACE and JOY were plentiful; they were on the last shelf
SONGS and PRAISES were hanging near, so I just helped
myself
Then I said to the Angel, "Now how much do I owe"?
He just smiled and said, "Just take them wherever you go"
Again, I smiled at him and said, "How much do I really
owe?"
He smiled again and said, "My child, Jesus paid your bill a
long time ago

Author Unknown

HELPLESS BUT NOT HOPELESS

I may be helpless in this prison, but I am not hopeless.
The devil wants you to feel hopeless, wherever you may be.
He wants you to expect that doom and devastation is
headed your way. But, God wants you to be full of hope; to
expect good things in your life, no matter where you may

be. "Wait on the Lord; be of good courage; and He shall strengthen thine heart." (Psalm 27:14) Waiting is not easy, but God uses waiting to refresh, renew and teach us. I have to put my hope in God because I know that He loves me. The devil wants you to be hopeless, think hopeless, act hopeless and talk hopeless. But, Jesus is your hope. You may be helpless in your situation, but with Jesus, you'll never be hopeless. God has a plan for you and for me, but it's His timing, not ours. We must humble ourselves under the hand of God, to allow Him to fulfill His purpose and plan for us. I can truly say today that "I have been called out of the darkness and despair of hopelessness and into God's glorious light."

HIDDEN AWAY TREASURES

What is your treasure? What does a treasure mean to you? A treasure can be anything that holds great meaning in someone's life. A treasure can be a person, a home, or even a song. Being incarcerated with 287 women, I've been able to listen and learn what treasures really mean to some of them. One of their greatest hidden treasures is the song "Amazing Grace". I call this a hidden treasure because even though they sing that beautiful song, they still have Jesus hidden deep within their pasts. Many of these women grew up in strong Christian homes but chose a totally different future for themselves. It's a very scary thing for me to hear the words to "Amazing Grace" and then hear foul language and hatred all in the same breath. They're unable to see the words and the meaning behind them. They are hiding their pasts, unable to see what Jesus has for them in their futures. Cherish your treasure and don't keep it hidden away.

HIDDEN IN THE SHADOWS
OF HIS HAND

Our Lord and Savior; hidden from the eyes of the world.
When preparing and training, Moses, a great leader in the
Bible, hid in the desert for 40 years under the shadow of the
Almighty, in a secret place of preparation. Our God
developed a shepherd's heart in Moses, and taught him how
to live and survive in the wilderness. Our example, Jesus,
for 30 years was hidden in the shadows of the Almighty's
hand. After being hidden there for 30 years, he was finally
released into His ministry where for three and a half years
he prepared a place for me and for you. I, Angie Pelphrey,
a leader and servant of God, was hidden for 35 years in the
shadow of His hand. Preparing and training in the
wilderness, in the secret place of preparation. Called from
the womb before birth, my life's purpose already
determined, I was not predestined for failure, but for
sharing the gift of life with the fallen ones, to raise them
from the dead.

HIDING IN RELIGIOUS CLOTHES

Don't let the Spirit of Saul reign in your life. Saul was
anointed by God to be king. But first impressions can be

deceiving. Saul had created the visual image of a king by his appearance. He was chosen to be a leader, but that doesn't mean he was capable of doing it on his own. Saul was a good leader when he obeyed God. But he cut himself off from God. He was hiding in religious clothes. He was a moral man but not an honest man. The weaker Saul became, the more he hid behind his religious clothes. He showed religion all over on the outside, but on the inside he was growing farther and farther away from God. I have met many people who are dressed in religious clothes. They live good moral lives. When it comes to honesty the clothes don't mean a thing. We must realize that living morally right is pretty easy, but a truly Godly life (loving the unlovable, forgiving the unforgivable and choosing to live a life without fear of the lost) is a life with many ups and downs. It has many valleys and many pits. But we must remove the religious clothes and be honestly willing to have God's love, an honest love, a love that is not hidden.

HIDING THE GUILT THAT BELONGS TO THE ABUSER

If you have suffered abuse whether physical, sexual, or emotional, then your shame and guilt that you carry belongs to your abuser, not you, the victim. Don't keep your feelings buried inside. Don't let another's sin ruin your life. You must begin to learn how to survive. We all must be survivors whether or not we had abuse in our life or not. Many of these women at Marysville have had to go through an abusive past, whether it's physical, sexual, or emotional. A lot of them have let the abuser win, and that is the reason they are here. Many have had to live lives like David and Bathsheba. Was Bathsheba really to blame, or was she unaware of his gazing upon her? He was a King and a King at that time wasn't someone you would deny. He not only violated her, he killed her husband, got her pregnant, and then God allowed her child to die. When sin occurs like that it becomes like a whirlwind spinning and spinning until the earth shatters underneath you. But you can survive. You have to survive, because if you don't, the abuser wins. Don't let the abuse control your life. Talk to someone, a friend, family member or a counselor. Pray for those who are held under by their abusers. Do whatever you can to help that person and pray that God can restore their hope. You can be a survivor. You are a victor not a victim.

HIGH HEELS-HARD FALLS

I can remember as a child, going into my mother's room and getting into the shoes in her closet. I would always look for the high heels to put on and strut around in. The high heels made me feel all grown up. For a few moments, it made me into someone that I wasn't. But after just a few minutes the heels became very uncomfortable. I was stumbling around, tripping and falling. They just didn't quite fit like my little tennis shoes. It was so much easier walking around in my own shoes than it was walking in my mom's shoes. When I arrived at the Scioto and Ross County Jails, the first thing they did was give me an outfit and a pair of Bob Barker shoes. When I got myself changed and I put on the shoes, the first thing I thought of was how many different women had worn those shoes before me. Some had walked in those shoes for days, months and even years. None of us got a new pair. We had to wear the old, torn up ones. Those shoes have walked thieves, drug dealers, murderers, moms, dads, aunts, uncles and even children. They have stumbled, tripped, and even fallen while wearing these shoes. But a day will come when they are released. Released to go out and buy a new pair of shoes that have never been worn before. No more walking around in someone else's shoes. Now you can walk a different path. You can change your life, with Jesus as your Savior. So, take off the old shoes and put on the new. It's a much more comfortable walk of life.

HIS STILL SMALL VOICE

Can you hear it? He's talking to you. He's whispering your name. God is speaking to you. It's hard to imagine that the creator of all could or even would want to call you out by name personally. He keeps your name on His heart and lips. Listen closely to what He has to say. If you listen you will learn to hope again. One of the girls in my cell room asked me how I knew that it was God speaking to me, and not just my inner thoughts. How do I know that He even loves me? She said, "I'm in prison aren't I?" If He really loved us then we wouldn't be here in this awful place. I told her, "Lindsay, if God didn't truly love us, then we wouldn't be here in this prison, we would be dead and on our way to hell." There have been many times in our pasts that we should have been dead, but God spared our life. You are here for a purpose, but you must be willing to listen, to heed to His calling. God is giving you a wake up call. He is calling you, but you must pick up and answer. I told her about the love of God and she held my hands as we prayed together for God's forgiveness. Today, Lindsay lives her life for the Lord behind these prison walls and she said that she can finally hear God's still, small voice.

HOW DO YOU OVERCOME COVETOUSNESS OF YOUR OWN CHILD?

Doesn't she realize that she is killing her father and me? She has stolen almost everything we own, and she sells it for crack. I'm her mother and I can't walk away from her. I'm supposed to be the one that is always there for her. She needs me. Last week she broke into our home while my husband was gone (and as I sit here in prison) and she took our money, credit cards, and our checks to buy crack with. I can't let her go. God would never leave me and I'll never leave her. He loves me too much. I awoke today to one of my bunkmates crying hysterically. She said, "I can't take it anymore." She's going to kill herself if she doesn't stop. Her husband had to make the decision to have her arrested, and possibly spend time in prison, or to bail her out again. We talked with her for a good while and we told her what we thought she should do; love her but let her go. We all got up from our beds and she turned on her favorite T.V. program, Charles Stanley. It came on right after we spoke to her and gave our advice. The words of his titled sermon came across the screen and it said, "Let them go." He went on to say that coveting someone or something will take you away from the one you really need, Jesus. He went on to say that we were to disassociate ourselves from the ones or things that we are coveting, whether or not we think it is for the right reason. So, today Ms. S made the decision to love her daughter and let her go. Ms. S realized today that for her daughter to survive in this world of addiction, she must let her go. We must trust in God and not in ourselves. We must let some people go that we truly love (and even covet) to in turn save their life and your own.

I AM BLESSED

A few weeks ago on the day of my pre-trial at Pike County, I walked into the courtroom with two men and two women. As they walked us up to the front of the room to sit down, I noticed one of the men desperately searching around the room for someone. I turned to look around also, and saw my husband, my three daughters, my parents, in-laws and twenty-five church members scattered around the courthouse. The man said aloud, "Boy there's a lot of people here today." I answered back, "They're all here to support me." He immediately teared up and said, "My wife and son should be here anytime." Over the next few minutes he continued searching the room, awaiting the arrival of his family. Just before court began he saw her coming through the doors, hand in hand with his three year old son. He smiled immediately and raised his shackled hand to wave. The little boy yelled, "There's my daddy, Mommy, there he is." She quieted him down quickly and gave a half smile back to him. Immediately after his hearing, they allowed him to briefly hug his wife and son. He was so happy. At the moment his wife hugged him, she whispered in his ear, "I want a divorce." His head dropped in pain and tears began to flow. A few moments before, he was so happy, but within an instant his life had changed. I felt so terrible for him because I had never felt so blessed in all my life. Now, he had no one standing by his side and I had everything and everyone to stand beside me and hold me up. To hold me up when I can no longer stand and to pray for me when I can't pray for myself. I might be headed to prison, but they can't take away the freedom of love of a family. I am so blessed.

I AM NOT AN ACCIDENT

I am not an accident. My birth may not have been planned, but that doesn't mean that God didn't plan me. Some may have called me a mistake or a failure, but I have a purpose. My birth or my existence in this world didn't surprise God, because he expected it. I'm here in this prison, and alive, only because God wanted me here. He created me for a purpose and He will fulfill His purpose in me. God chose my race, gender, hair color and even the color of my eyes. I guess you could say I'm custom-made, as are you. He determined my natural abilities like sports, art, and the ability to make people happy because of my personality. God made me for a reason. He even chose my birth date and the day I will die to live out eternity with Him. Some people may be unplanned by their parents, but to God none of us are unplanned. We were not an accident, a coincidence nor a chance happening. We are alive only because God loved us and wanted to create us to fulfill His purpose.

I AM SIGNIFICANT IN GOD'S EYES

I am a chosen child of the King, I am loved. I am a walking testimony. I am the salt and light of the earth. I am the vine that is one of His many branches. I am called to do His will. I am beautiful. I am God's temple. I am a broken vessel mended by His workmanship. I am a bondage breaker. I am an over comer. I am anointed. I am forgiven. I am needed. I am complete in Christ. I am Christ's friend. I am redeemed. I am transformed. I am free from condemnation. I am alive in Him. I am His flower just waiting to bloom. I am a winner. I am appointed to do His work. I am the small hand in His big hand. I am a citizen of heaven. I am happy. I am blessed by His riches. I am His daughter. I am a mother. I am a wife. I am a friend. I am significant. I am a follower of Christ. I am a winner in the race of life. I am clothed in armor for the battle. I am washed by the blood of the lamb. I am covered by His gentle arms wrapped around me. I am significant. I am adopted by His grace. I am confident. I am born of evil and the evil one cannot touch me. I am united with the Lord and I am one in Spirit with Him. I am significant in God's eyes.

I COULDN'T DO ANYTHING, I WAS JUST A KID

She was raped by her step-father at the age of ten, only to be molested and continually raped for the next ten years. Her step-father threatened to beat her with a 2X4 if she told anyone what he did to her. She was so afraid to say anything. She was so afraid to be alone. She was so afraid that he would hurt her again. One day she got up the courage to tell her mother. "Mom, he hurt me. He touched me." But, her mother didn't believe her. When her step-dad got home, he beat her with a 2X4 with her pants down. She was hardly able to walk. She was bruised and bleeding. He mother tried to step in and fight him off of her, but she too, was stripped naked and beaten. I couldn't do anything, because I was just a kid. I couldn't stop him. I wanted to run away, but where would I go? I'm only twelve. Where would I live and how would I eat? Two days later he was arrested after her teacher contacted the police. She was unable to sit in her seat at school that day, so the teacher called her out in the hall to question her. Once he got to jail, her mother turned around and bailed him back out. She brought him home, only to have the pain and suffering start all over again. She couldn't handle it anymore, so she took off and ran away. She ran from her parents, the abuse and the police. She had to provide for herself, so she started stealing small things. Eventually, the thefts grew larger and larger, until she was caught at the age of fifteen and was placed into juvenile hall. She was afraid in the beginning, but then she realized that she didn't have to run anymore. She was safe there. She had food and shelter. She was afraid in her own home and now juvenile hall was her home and she loved it. I couldn't do anything, I was just a kid. Be not afraid for the Lord is with thee. No matter what this little girl went through, she now has a forgiving heart. She has a heart like I have never seen before, a heart of love. Please pray for her that she will accept Jesus Christ as her Savior, so He in turn can give her His forgiving love.

I DESERVE ALL THAT I GET

"He pulled me by my hair to the basement and locked the door behind him. He did not allow me to eat any food or water for the four days I was locked up. He would unlock the door and bring in crack. He waited for me to shoot up before he left. If I didn't do what he said, he would beat me. Occasionally he would come in and make me have sex with him, otherwise I was locked up by myself. He had two pit bulls stationed on the outside of the door if I tried to get out. I was a prisoner in my own home. After the four days he unlocked the door and let me out. I packed my things up and left him. I told him that I would never be back. But three days later I returned home to him. I had told myself that I could never make it without him. So, for 4 years I remained his prisoner." This is the life of a sister of mine in Tapestry. Her self-esteem had dropped so low that she started to believe that she deserved everything that she got from her husband. She believed that the life she was living was the best life that she would ever have. Today she is a prisoner in Marysville, but she is no longer a prisoner to herself or her husband. Allow God to love you as this sister has today. Without accepting the love that God had to offer, she would still be a prisoner to her low self-esteem, herself, and her husband. "Let Go and Let God."

I FOUGHT THE LAW, AND WON

I fought the law today, and won. A few weeks ago I received a ticket from a correctional officer at the visiting hall for (what she called) inappropriate behavior. My husband and I were stunned when the officer approached us and started screaming at us. She told me that I had disrespected the prison and her, by behaving inappropriately. This was all untrue, so I decided to fight the ticket and take it to the R.I.B. (Rules Infraction Board). It should have consisted of three sergeants and me. When I arrived, however, another Sergeant was sitting in. I was unsure who she was, but I was too nervous to think about anything but that ticket. The hearing began and I proceeded to tell my side of the story. Then I called three witnesses; two correctional officers and one inmate. As they began their testimony the butterflies went away. They told the truth and testified against the other officer. The truth set me free from that ticket and restored my dignity. After the hearing the Sergeant told me that an official apology would be made to my family and myself and that strict disciplinary action would be done with the correctional officer, Ms. Shaffner. So today I not only fought the law and won, but I fought a fear I've had for years. I had a fear of standing up for myself, no matter who got mad at me. Today I fought that fear and won.

I LIVED MY LIFE LIKE A VENDING MACHINE

For many years I lived my life pleasing others around me, seeking their approval. At times I wore so many masks that I couldn't even remember who I really was. I got to the point where I did not really know how I was supposed to act. I lived my life like a vending machine. People came up, pushed a button, and I gave them what they wanted. They pushed the button "super-mom," they got it. If they pushed the "kind, caring and considerate wife," they got it. If they wanted my attention, submission, or time, they got it. However, about 8 months ago God repaired the vending machine inside of me. He gave me myself back. He gave me my life back. He transformed me into who He wanted me to be. I once chose to live my life like a vending machine, but today, I push my own buttons. Today, I live for my God, and only my God. Today, I live to please Him and not this chaotic world.

I SEE WITH MY HEART, NOT WITH MY EYES

For many years I've seen people with my eyes and not my heart. I saw what they portrayed on the outside and not what was within. I could only focus on their demeanor, their tattoo, earrings and even their hair. But once God placed me behind these prison walls, He allowed me to see with my heart and not with my eyes. I began to see their fears and not their tattoo. I began to see their pain instead of their appearance. I began to see their hearts and not their crime. God allowed me to see these women for who they really are and not what they display. To see with your heart and not with your eyes is truly the meaning of Christianity. Today it is a part of my life that will help lead these women to the Lord. To shun a person for their appearance, their fears and even their past, is not what God intended for us. God tells us to help the broken hearted, as He did. God wants us to show His love to those that were never given the opportunity to know what true love was all about. So today, see others with your heart and not with your eyes.

I SHALL NOT BE MOVED

I am sturdy like a rock and unmovable. Standing still on the edge and still unable to make me fall. Shouting to the heavens, I shall not be moved. They can tease and mock me, but I shall stand. I will stand up for my Jesus. I am called the Preacher's wife, Jesus girl and more, but to me I am proud. I am all of these and I am a Christian. I am saved by the blood of the Lamb. They think that Jesus isn't in here with us in prison, but they don't know that I brought Him in here with me. He lives deep within my heart. I show Jesus not only by my voice, but my actions. They see me read and pray all day. Some frown, but most smile. They see Jesus living inside of me. They see Jesus all around me. I had a girl down the bay come to me yesterday and say, "I need you to talk to someone for me, because you're the only one I know that doesn't have that jailhouse religion. You walk the walk and talk the talk. You share Jesus with us in a special way." She said, "It's just so peaceful every time I am around you." It felt so good to hear that. I thought to myself, I shall not be moved. I can do this. I am not ashamed. Ask God to help you take a stand for Jesus. It's hard at school to stand up for Him. I know because I have three daughters that have been mocked and teased for taking a stand for Jesus. But they are strong, strong in their faith. It is so hard to be solid in this prison. It's tough, but with God all things are possible. I will make it. I will spread the Gospel to all that are here. I will stay strong, and I will remain as a rock. I shall not be moved.

I TOO WILL WIN THIS BATTLE

Great victory is what I am expecting. Deborah, a prophetess, fought the battle and won. Joshua overthrew kingdoms. Nehemiah ruled God's people well. Daniel was kept from harm in the lion's den. Shadrach, Meshach and Abednigo were kept from harm in the fiery furnace. Elijah escaped the swords of evil Queen Jezebel's henchmen. Hezekiah became strong after sickness. Gideon had great power in battle. A widow's son was brought back to life by the prophet Elisha. David fought Goliath in battle and won, only by the armor of God. I too will win this battle. I too am fighting a fight with Satan. I too will have great victory. Whether I leave this prison today or in another year, I will have won. I am a winner either way, if I go or if I stay, because I have the Lord on my side. This is not my home, I'm just passing through. Real victory is just ahead. Victory in Jesus is what I have today. This is the toughest battle I have ever faced, but I will overcome. By faith God will deliver me from this prison. By faith, God released me from the prison from within and granted me freedom. It's not about getting out of this prison; it's about the prison getting out of you. That is when true victory comes. I too have won this battle.

I WANTED THE WORLD TO STOP

I wanted the world to stop the day I went to prison. For some reason I thought it would. I hoped for time to stand still. I hoped for the seasons not to change. I hoped for the world to stand still. I couldn't imagine all that I was missing. The ball games, the good night kisses, the hugs and the long nights of playing outside with the kids. Then I called home. I heard the playing and the laughter in the background. They were having fun without me. How could that happen? Don't they love me? Don't they miss me? Don't they realize that I'm here, locked up in this prison? Then God showed me that time keeps moving on. Time has to go on, because as I grow in prison, they too must grow on the outside. The world can't stop, the time must move on. As much as I wanted for the world to stop, I had to realize what God has in store for all of us. God was giving us this time apart to grow and to learn all that we can. There's a time to laugh, and a time to cry, but today it's a time to live.

I WILL MAKE IT

I look through the bars, staring out my window. Hoping and dreaming, wishing upon a star, hanging on to faith, that one day I'll be set free. Dreaming of my future, of what someday I will be. To live without my fears, that used to cause me pain. To make it through the storm, as I stand out in the rain. To climb upon the mountain and make it to the top. I stumble and fall, but never will I stop. I strive to become that person, the one I used to be. I remember that person, for that person was me. I was a wife, a mother, a Christian and a nurse. But today I am myself, today I put me First. Today I am a number, a face without a name. So never forget this face, when I arrive into my fame.

I WILL SURVIVE

I was working the desk in the Rec Room one day and had the pleasure of meeting a young 22 year old girl. She was pregnant with twins and had been sentenced to six months here at Marysville for robbery. She told me that she had a 4th grade reading level and asked me to help her find cigarettes on the commissary sheet because she was unable to find it. She began telling me her story of how she ended up here. Both of her parents were addicted to crack and at the age of five she was taken away from them. She stayed in foster care until the age of sixteen when she ran away to the street, and that became her home. She didn't have book smarts but she did have street smarts. She said that she had learned how to survive, otherwise she would have died. She was reunited with her parents at the age of seventeen but she was only welcome as long as she had drugs to offer them. By the age of twenty she had been raped, stabbed, and was pregnant with her first child, a son. Her daughter was born fifteen months later and both were crack addicted babies at birth. Within two years both children were taken away from her and put up for adoption. Her son died at age two due to lung complications related to the crack addiction and her daughter was adopted. She spoke highly of her family because she said they had done the best they could for her and her brother. She said, "They loved me, but they were messed up just like me." She also said, "They just couldn't survive like me." Her dad had died three months prior of alcohol related illness and since then she hadn't seen anyone else in her family. Her brother is in the penitentiary for arson and in two months she will deliver her twins here at Marysville. She lived her life the only way she knew, whatever it took to survive. She had to steal for her food and drugs, and prostitute herself to survive the street. Living on the street was all she knew. I have thought about her quite a lot since our conversation and pray that she will learn how to truly live and not just survive. God wants us all to live for Him so that we can survive here on this earth. May God be with her as she returns to the street to survive the only way she knows how.

I WILL WORK A WORK IN YOURDAYS, WHICH YE WILL NOT BELIEVE

This was God's message to Habakkuk and to me. God has given me long-range plans and a purpose for this life, and in this prison; plans and purpose that I now know to be a blessing. God has blessed me with the opportunity to see life behind bars, life behind a razor blade fence that has no escape except through salvation. You cannot escape this prison, nor can you escape the sin and corruption here. You see it daily, you live with it daily. But I must work. I must believe that this is God's plan. I must believe that my purpose for being here is to guide others. At times during these horrible circumstances I am facing I wonder if God has forgotten me. Then I remember His plan, His purpose, and I know that the evil doers will be judged. Therefore I must work harder, for the time of judgment is coming soon. I must spread the good news, sometimes by my actions and not my words. I must bring hope to this prison and to the prisoners that cannot see it. Hope for me means going beyond these unpleasant daily experiences just to know and feel God's love and the joy that He has for me. I must rejoice in knowing the Lord. I must surround these women with God's love. I must fulfill God's plan and purpose for me and know that this work is for God's glory not mine.

Today is my second day in population. Anger and fear is what I awoke with this morning, but I shall go to bed with love and joy in my heart. I have poured out my heart to my Jesus and He will answer. He will continue to guide

120

me with His wisdom. I will go forth at His command. I will shine with joy, because I know that my Jesus is my strength. God has answered my prayers and given me hope. A quiet hope that has given me the strength for today to fulfill His plan and purpose. Thank you Eric Barker for your words of wisdom and encouragement that showed me God's plan and purpose.

I WISH I COULD HAVE WHAT SHE HAS

"I wish I could have what she has. Her voice, the way she can sing. She's so musically talented and I can't sing at all. If I could just be a little bit like her."

This kind of thinking causes us to become jealous of others. I can remember many times my husband saying, "Boy, I wish I could sing or play guitar." But it ended up that all the wishing we did for ourselves to sing and play an instrument was realized in our girls. God said to me, "I put that gift of singing in your children for your enjoyment, not for you to resent all of these other people who can sing or to wish that you could sing." God didn't put that gift of singing in them for them only, but He put it in them for us, so we could enjoy their beautiful voices as they sing songs to worship the Lord. To envy, covet or to be jealous of another person only causes disappointment in one's self. So know that God has given you the gifts that he wants you to have. He has granted others gifts to be a gift for you also. Don't be jealous or envious of others, but rejoice in their gift, because God gave them their gift for us to unwrap.

I WOULD SELL IT ALL,
EVEN MYSELF

"I can remember a time when I was all that. I had it 'goin on,' as some would say. The clothes, hair, makeup, car and home. But it wasn't enough, once my drugs came into the picture. I needed money, and more of it." I spoke to many women here at Marysville and this seemed to be their stories. I've heard many women quote these same words, over and over again. Never enough, it was just never enough. These women have spoken of selling their children's diapers and even selling their own bodies for money and for drugs. They sunk so low in the drug world that they didn't even care about themselves or others. They neglected their bodies so badly that some have lost all of their hair and teeth before the age of 30. They got to the point where as long as they got their drugs, then nothing else mattered. Leaving their children alone for hours to fend for themselves, sleeping with men that they had never met before, and living a life on the streets that eventually sent them here. But God sold it all, even Himself for us. His price was free. He freely died for our sins. God freely gave his only begotten son for us. He gave His all. It is my prayer that these women can seek Jesus' love, His free unconditional love. Just know that Jesus died for you, and freely forgives all who ask.

I'D DO IT ALL OVER AGAIN

Today, March 5th, 2005, at 8:17 pm my bunkmate at the Ohio Reformatory for Women gave her heart to the Lord. For many days now she has asked me questions about the Bible. Questions about salvation, baptism and the love of Jesus. But today was a different day for her. Today she asked how she could truly feel Jesus in her heart. So, with nine other inmates in the room, we held hands and prayed together, asking Jesus to forgive her of her sins and to save her soul. Today, coming to this prison and with Lindsey getting saved, made all of this worthwhile. Today, I can truly say, I would do it all over again in a heartbeat. Just knowing that Lindsey will be going to heaven with me. I never dreamed I would ever say those words, but today God blessed my heart. God allowed me to pray with another inmate. God allowed me to witness to nine other inmates and to plant a seed that will forever be sown deep within their hearts. Thank you Jesus for the opportunity to be at the Marysville Prison where I can spread the good news of the gospel. Today I can truly say I'd do it all over again for that one lost soul. Lindsey's soul.

IF I COULD TURN BACK TIME

If I could turn back time! I'm sure that all of us have said that at least one time in our life. What would you want to change? What is it that you would do differently? If you could turn back time today and make your past disappear, would you do it? If you could erase all of the trials and tribulations in your life, would you do it? Well, I'm not sure that I would want to do that, because my trials and tribulations have made me into the woman that I am today. I might be sitting in the pen today, but in time I will be kneeling at my Savior's feet and praising Him for all of my many blessings. You cannot have blessings without trials. If I could turn back time, I would still want the past experiences of life that I have had because I want so much to help others who have walked the same path that I have taken. I want so badly to help these other women, so they won't have to face the wickedness this world has to offer to them. But I can't do that. What I can do, is witness and testify of my past mistakes and of the time I have to do because of my many fears. If I could turn back time, I would have given my heart to the Lord at a very young age. But, why dwell on the past when my future holds eternal life for me. Why would you want to turn back time and start all over again when today you can start your life all over with Jesus Christ as your Savior?

IF I DON'T TALK ABOUT IT, I DON'T HAVE TO THINK ABOUT IT!

"If I don't talk about it then I don't have to think about it." These are words that are frequently said by the women here at the Scioto County Jail. They think that if they don't talk about Christmas coming up then they don't have to think about missing their families. I know that the first few days I was here, I thought the same thing. I thought, well I'm not going to call my family or even talk about them, maybe that way I don't have to think about them. I won't have to worry if they're okay or not. That only lasted a few days. I couldn't do it. The more I tried not to think of them, the more I worried. Well, I got to meet a girl this week named Sam. When I first met her I thought boy, she's a hard one. Her face had no expression and the look in her eyes portrayed the hard past that she's had. Jail, prison, the streets, and time are what her past entailed. Time is all she has had for the last few years. But once I got to know her, I could read through the concrete expressions and see a heart of gold. I could see the love for her children and the love for her friend Mandy. She wants to have feelings, but for some reason they seem to be trapped inside her. If she doesn't express them, or think about things, then maybe she won't have to worry. She knows right from wrong, but sometimes I think she feels more content doing wrong. She feels content being trapped in a bubble with no feelings or emotions. But I know that one day God will break her and allow her to love Him with a love that she's never felt or expressed before.

"If I don't have to think about it, Then I won't have to worry."

IF I ONLY KNEW

If I knew it would be the last time that I'd see you fall asleep, I would tuck you in more tightly and pray the Lord your soul to keep.
If I knew it would be the last time I would see you walk out the door, I would give you a hug and kiss, and call you back for one more.
If I knew it would be the last time, I could spare an extra minute or two to stop and say, "I love you," instead of assuming that you know I do.
If I knew it would be the last time I would be there to share your day, well, I'm sure you'll have so many more, so I can let this one slip away. For surely there's always tomorrow to make up for the oversight, and we always get a second

125

chance to make things right. There will always be another day to say "I love you." Certainly there is another chance to say "Anything I can do?"

But just in case I might be wrong, and today is all I get, I'd like to say how much I love you, and hope to never forget. Tomorrow is not promised to anyone, young or old alike, and today may be the last chance you get to hold your loved ones tight.

So if you are waiting for tomorrow, why not do it today? For if tomorrow never comes, you'll surely regret the day that you didn't take the extra time for a smile, a hug, or a kiss. You were too busy to grant someone what turned out to be their one last wish.

Hold your loved ones closely today, whisper in their ear. Tell them how much you love them and that you will always hold them dear.

Please take the time to say, "I'm sorry," "Please forgive me," "Thank you," or "It's okay."

If I had only known, I would have done all of this.

I love you girls. I miss you dearly. It won't be long and I'll be tucking you into bed again. Holding you, hugging you and telling you I love you, every chance I get.

If I only knew.

I'LL NEVER GIVE UP

Well, I've been away from my family now for almost six months, and this last week has probably been the hardest for me. I am so homesick that I can hardly even think sometimes. As I sit in group,I find myself day dreaming out the window, staring through the bars and thinking about playing outside in the yard with my kids. I find myself getting upset every time I call home, because I just can't imagine all that I have missed. I find myself praying to God that they don't forget me or that their love for me doesn't fade away. Sometimes I feel myself growing weaker instead of stronger. But then I realize what they are going through at home. They're not just living life without me, they're existing with the presence of God as He carries them through. Today I make a promise to God and my family that I will never give up, because they refuse to give up on me. As much as they have been through they still remain faithful to me, and to God. They refuse to give in or to give up. Today I will not give up no matter how difficult prison is. I have to believe that God will bring me through.

IMAGINE A PLACE

Imagine a place of violence and pain. Imagine a place where freedom is only a state of mind. A place where thieves are waiting for just the right time to come and take all that you own. A place where your backyard is a razor wired fence. Imagine a war zone on the front line, watching and waiting for the attack to come at any time. Imagine a place where you are told when to wake up, when to go to bed and when and where you will sleep. Imagine your home as a 6X6 foot room with bars on your windows and a door that's locked most of the day. Imagine a place where you have no name, no identity, and you are just a number. Imagine a place where the squirrels and birds fly free, but you are the animal, locked inside a cage. Imagine a place where dreams are just that, dreams. Imagine a place where sin overrules and salvation means that you have lived and beat the streets. You have survived death for the 4th or 5th time; where you have lived through another beating or another overdose. Just imagine a place! This place is prison. This place is the step right before death. This place is real. I know because I eat, sleep and breathe it every day! Just imagine!

IN HIS HANDS

Have you ever seen pictures or portraits of Jesus Christ? Portraits of how others portray Him. His hair, face, skin color, all the way down to His hands. I had never thought of this or noticed the size of Jesus' hands. Figurines and pictures portray Jesus' hands as much larger than normal size hands. I feel that there are many reasons for this. First, His hands must be large to help carry us in our time of need. His hands must be large enough to hold you when you fall. As He holds you up and He places one hand over your heart, He is ready and waiting to give you a new heart and a new life. His hands are larger because sometimes we just grow so tired and we need Jesus to wrap us up in His arms and hold us. Jesus' large wounded hands are placed over our hearts to show us His desire to change all of our hearts by the power of His love. The blood that flowed from His precious hands signifies the washing away of our sins, my sins, and justification before God. Jesus' hands show His strength. His hands remind us that we have to be totally dependent on Him. His hands represent to me how small my hands truly are. We must all place our little hands in His so He can guide our way and remind us that we all must keep our little hand in His big hand.

IN MY PLACE

While in prison I have had the opportunity to talk to many women who have been in and out of prison for years. Some have 4 to 5 numbers from 4 to 5 different crimes and prisons. But when I was told about this one particular prison, tears filled my eyes. That prison is called Humaita Prison in Sao Jose dos Campos in Brazil. It is so different than the one I am in for numerous reasons. It only has two full time staff; the other work is done by the 730 inmates serving time. Every prisoner is assigned another inmate to be a mentor for. They take classes on character and are encouraged to participate in religious programs. This differs so much from where I am. It's hard to even get a smile from a lot of these women at Marysville, let alone having a mentor. But one day a young man in Humaita was assigned a mentor. His mentor was a strong, faithful Christian. He began by showing this young man around the prison. When he got to the cell which is known as "The Hole" or solitary confinement, the young man became afraid. He had never been to prison, let alone been in "The Hole". But the elder man proceeded to take out his keys and unlock the door. The young man asked, "Are you sure we should go in here while there's a prisoner in here?" The older man replied, "Of course, this man won't mind because he's been in here for years." When he opened the door the only thing in the room was a crucifix, beautifully carved, with Jesus hanging on the cross! Otherwise the room was empty. The young man asked, "Where is the prisoner?" The man replied, "Right there, pointing to the cross, he's doing time for the rest of us."

INTERMARRIAGE WITH THE HEATHEN

I was always taught as a child that you are who your friends are. When we spend a lot of time with people, we can easily pick up their attitudes and begin to imitate their actions. When you live under the same prison roof with unbelievers, you must beware of the influence they can have on you. Some here have decided to fall into the trap. They walked into this prison one way and will leave another. They have picked up bad behaviors while sitting here in prison. They have intermarried with the heathen. The day I arrived here I met a woman, a quiet laid-back woman, who was here on a drug charge. It has been almost 3 months now and I can hardly even recognize her. Her attitude is so different. Her mouth is so foul most of the time that most can't stand to be around her. She made a choice, and that choice was to be a follower. It takes courage to stand on your own; to be the one with the positive attitude. To be the one with the positive influence on others and to point them to Jesus. Instead of falling into the trap of Satan and his followers, stand on your own. Let Jesus carry you through your times of trouble. Let Jesus be your guide.

IS A DIAMOND LESS VALUABLE IF FOUND IN A CLOGGED DRAIN?

A few years ago while I was at work, I realized that I had lost the diamond out of my wedding ring. I frantically began searching the office to find the precious stone. It wasn't only precious because of its monetary value, but it was precious to me because it was given to me by my husband as our bond of marriage. After several hours I realized that it was gone, lost forever. Then, a co-worker walked up to me with what looked like a small piece of glass in her hand. She said, "I think this is the diamond that you have been looking for." I couldn't believe it. It had fallen out on the medication table and it was scuffed up and covered with marks, but it didn't matter where they found it or what it looked like, it was found. That's all that mattered to me. It was precious to me. I loved that diamond no matter what it looked like. As I sat and thought of the sentimental value this ring had to me, I thought of what we mean to Jesus. No matter if you are in prison, laying in gutter or sitting on a bar stool, Jesus loves you. You are valuable to him no matter how scuffed up or scarred that you are. It doesn't matter what you have done or where you have been, Jesus loves you and wants you to accept Him as your Savior. You are just as valuable as the Christian that has been saved for 20 years. You are worthy.

IT CAN HAPPEN TO YOU TOO

As I sit here in prison, I wonder how I got here. I realize that I am no different than anyone else in here. Why? Because it can happen to you too. I can remember as a child when my parents would scold me for playing too close to the road, I would say "Aw, Mom nothing's going to happen to me, I'll be careful, I know what I am doing." But, I could have gotten hurt or even killed. You think that it will never happen to you, but it can, it happened to me. I was careful. I was strong, but the pills were stronger than I was. The pills were conniving, deceiving and manipulative. The pills became my best friend and my worst enemy all at the same time. They talked to me. They told me that it was okay. But, just like the devil, they too were liars. I sit here in prison today with doctors, lawyers, Sunday school teachers and even a nun. It can happen to you. Drugs can make you do and say anything. It will make you do things that you never thought you could do. They can and will rob your heart, mind, body, soul, family and your freedom all at the same time. How do I know? Because it happened to me.

IT COULD BE YOU

At this time in my life, as within every woman's life, I had to take a closer look at myself. Not at my circumstances, not at what I did, not at how unfair life is, or not at how or what made me do it. But I had to look at myself in all my glory and imperfections. Have you ever admired a woman who has been through changes in her life? I have. Or have you just made up your mind that she is just MESSED UP! So, before you make this mistake, take a closer look. As a woman who has endured the most unusual life, I am now a woman of courage. I am woman who has been chosen by God to go through things only to make me stronger. Think of all of the great women in the Bible; Mary Magdalene, Ruth, Naomi, the woman with the issue of blood, Esther, to name a few. Mary was a prostitute, a very uneasy woman. But by the time Jesus was done with her, she was one of his closest followers. Esther was unfortunate in marrying an abusive man, but by the time God was done with her, she had married one of the wealthiest men in the land. Society is so quick to beat the next person down instead of trying to hold them up. Before you wonder, "What's up with her?" ask yourself, "What's up with me?" Because that person could be your mother, your sister, aunt, father, brother, mother or friend. That person could be me. Women are the carriers of life, not the channels of death. Let's build and encourage each other, as did Ruth and Naomi. Encourage, love, forgive and forget, because that person could be you!

IT IS WRITTEN

This is the life of my bunkmate Tabitha. The words were left as they were written by Tabitha. She wants to change her lifestyle and live for God but she just doesn't know how. She doesn't have much of an education, but she does know of God's love. Today, she asked me to read her story because she knew that she could trust me and that I would help her. I was honored to read it. I gave her the scripture, Romans 10:13 and I read it to her. I walked her through the Romans road. She climbed back on her top bunk (which she now calls her closet) and asked Jesus into her heart. She had many questions, but I told her that for right now all she needed to know was that she was worthy. Please pray for Tabitha for spiritual strength. She is facing two years at Marysville and she has four children waiting at home for their new mommy.

I Tabitha, birthday Feb.5th 1973, age of 31 years old. This is my life style I'm living every day and every night. When I wake up in the morning, all I do is think about a hit. After I take that hit, it's all over. I'm running all over the west side looking for another hit. First I see who can I get some credit from and tell them a lie. I pay them when my man Bo gets paid, or steal something out of Family Dollar, CVS, or Speedway to support my habit. Crack is the high for me. I can't pay for crack cocaine; I can't spell well because I can't remember anything. Going up and down the street all day and all night looking for someone I can have sex with or oral sex, not even use anything. White man, black man, it doesn't matter what color they are. As long as I got $3.00 dollars, $10.00 dollars, $20.00 dollars, or a hit. I put the crack on the glass pipe, take a lighter in my right hand and put the glass pipe to my mouth, light the lighter and pull on and I pull. Then I look on the floor. Think people in the house with me, watch me, talking about me. I be want to mess around with women. I lost my self respect. I lost life. I've got rape in my own apartment because I choose to smoke that dope up and I thought I was going to pay. I was so scared. The inside and the outside, scared to death. Walk the street, look for help, talk to God, look for crack and tricks at the same time. Sometimes I want to get hurt to see if anybody loved me, because it was hard telling from the lifestyle I lived every day. I know I'm a good person. I love to do what I can on my own, but crack got the best of me. I hate I can't do anything about it. I tried to stop on my own, I could for at least 2 months, but four days later start back again. This is the lifestyle. I'm tired of the right here, I can't do anything about it: because I'm too weak from crack. I love to smoke crack and look crazy. I love to sell me. I've been doing it so long. I can't stop on my own. I want to stop but how can I God? How can I stop? God I'm asking you to change me inside and out. Please, I love my family. I want to stop, I'm weak, and I need you. Don't leave me God , I'm scared you are going to leave me, because I'm been real with you. I'm scared that you are not going to do nothing for me. God, I'm scared I'll mess up because I'm telling you all of this. That I want to live that way.

December 23, 2004

IT'S FRIDAY NOW,
BUT SUNDAY'S COMING

While in jail there's not a whole lot to look forward to other than meals, and they only come 3 times a day. Our breakfast is at 5:00 am, lunch at noon, and dinner at 5:00 pm. Other than that there's not a whole lot more to get excited about. So, since they don't actually have church services and 7 out of 10 girls on my unit are not saved, we decided to have our own church right here in our cells. During the day we have a Bible study reading with questions and answers. Then at bedtime we get into a circle and hold hands and pray. Then we go around the circle and have prayer requests. Most requests have to do with court dates, but over the last few days some have prayed for wisdom and guidance from the Lord. I'm starting to feel more peace around me here and the fights have gotten to a minimal, so now you don't have to watch your back quite as much. So, around here it's never Friday because Sunday's are always here. We don't allow the devil to welcome himself here at all. The other night one of the deputies came back to our unit right after prayer service and she said, "I just wanted to let you all know how proud of you we are." We asked what they were talking about and she said, "Believe me, we see more than you think we do, because we've been watching you all every night before you go to bed." So around here it might be Friday, but Sunday's coming soon.

IT'S ALL RIGHT

These were the words of a Shunamite woman when her son had died. She knew that God wouldn't forsake her. She knew that the promise God had given her was not gone. How can she say, "It's all right", when her only son had died. Her baby boy that God gave to her when she was barren was gone. Her world should have come crashing down on her, but she had faith. There were many times in my life that I thought my world was crashing in on me, but I wasn't quite as faithful. I was afraid. I was doubtful. But the Shunamite woman had faith. She believed that the God that gave her a son could bring life to him again. God sent Elisha to lay his body on top of the boy's cold body. In moments he could feel the life coming back to him. Why? Because, she had faith. When we face uncontrollable circumstances in our lives that we feel are a tragedy, we must have faith. God will work it out. God will never leave us or forsake us. We must have faith like the Shunamite woman. We must believe that no matter what the outcome, "It's going to be all right."

IT'S MY CHOICE, AND TODAY I CHOOSE DEATH

During an encounter today, one of the women here in the program decided death over her life. She chose drugs over her freedom. She chose drugs over her children. She chose drugs over her life. She has been to prison twice already. She has lost her children to the system, and she has lost all of her family support. Still she chooses to use drugs. I've asked myself the question, "Why?" over and over again in my mind. Why wouldn't she want to stop? Why wouldn't she want to live, free of drugs and get her family back? But, no answers came to mind. The only conclusion I have is that she has no hope left. No hope to live free of drugs. No hope to live a happy life. She has no hope, without Jesus. She wants to leave this program so she can get out into population to be closer to the drugs. She says, she just cannot live without them. However, I am here today to tell you that there is hope. Jesus is your hope. Jesus can give you a life free of drugs, a life of happiness and true freedom. It is your choice. What will you do? Do you choose to live or to die?

I'VE FALLEN
AND I CAN'T GET UP

How many times have you heard someone say, I can't do this anymore? Well, these past few months I've heard those words hundreds of times. They've said, I just have gone so deep in sin and God will never take me back. Or, you just don't know what I've done. A lot of these women feel like they've fallen too deep in sin to ever get back up. Well, let me tell you, God has sent me to the worst prison in Ohio, to give these women the best news they've ever heard. Don't give up yet ladies, because God is still in control. You've not fallen too far down because I can see God all over this prison. He's been here ever since I walked through these doors and when I leave he'll still be here. Don't ever let anyone tell you that God will never forgive you because your sin was too great. God loves us all the same. If he could save me, he can definitely save you. I have fallen many times, and this last time, I fell hard. But the one thing I learned through my church family was to never give up, because if they can love me with such unconditional love, then my God surely loves me too.

JAIL BIRD

About two weeks ago we had a bird fly into our dorm here at the farm. The farm is also known as the Ohio Correctional Facility for Women in Marysville, Ohio. I am staying in admissions at the "Hale Cottage" for theft of drugs. I became addicted to pain pills and I took pills from patients when I was going through withdrawals. I have been here for about two weeks now. It is about ten degrees outside and the snow is thick. But two weeks ago, when this little birdie flew into prison, it probably never knew that the doors would be locked behind it. I'm sure it just flew in to get warm. All that it wanted to do was get out of the cold. It just wanted a good meal and a place to make its nest. But this little jail bird didn't know what it was flying into. Many times as women come and go from here, they enter these prison doors not knowing when they'll get out. They entered these doors because all they wanted was a hot meal, or a warm place to stay. They wanted to provide for their little nest eggs at home, but they ended up stealing for their meals, sleeping in garages that belong to someone else, and they ended up here without their little ones to take care of. They didn't want to become jail birds; all that they wanted was for their families to finally be free. Free from the pain and poverty of life.

138

JAIL HOUSE RELIGION

Don't just talk the talk, walk the walk. Bibles are everywhere. Scriptures are quoted, gospel hymns are sung and then the Lord's name is used in vain. Anger is raging, power struggles and most women use the jailhouse religion to get through it. Don't get me wrong, I'm not here to judge, I'm only here to help. I see them as they do horrible things to hurt someone else by hurtful words or angry threats. They read their Bible, then talk about getting out and getting back on the streets. They say, "Don't worry God will protect me from harm. He'll keep me from diseases, because I pray every day to keep me safe." They are so confused. They are so confused by religion and not faith. They can't comprehend God's true love. They can't comprehend true peace in Jesus Christ until they finally accept Him as their one and only Savior. They cannot have true love for Jesus or others until they can find love for themselves first. Jailhouse religion is only a phase, not the truth. God's word is the truth and the light but we cannot be blinded by religion. We must share God's love to all that we meet. Don't share religion to others, share God's love. Walk the walk, don't just talk the talk. Let others see Jesus in you.

JAILS, INSTITUTIONS, AND THEN DEATH

We've all heard the saying, "Jails, Institutions and Death, oh my", but it doesn't seem to hit reality until you actually face it. The quote is so true. I never believed that I would end up in jail, let alone prison. But it happened. The only thing left for me is death.   I realize today that I don't have any more chances in the addiction.   I've heard many women say, "I just want to use one more time."   But, I don't have one more use in me.   I came to realize this after we received an alumni letter from a woman who had left the prison Tapestry Program.   Usually, the letters tell about what they have achieved since they have been out, but this letter was different.   This letter was a desperate cry for help.   She cried out to the only family that she's ever known, her Tapestry sisters.   As another sister began to read the letter tears filled my eyes.   This woman had just left prison and she had gone back to using, "just one more time."   She was living on the streets, cold and hungry and she had no place to turn for help.   Her words were jumbled and they jumped back and forth.   She cried out for help from 94 women who couldn't help her physically, but only through prayer.   Her last use would eventually turn into her last chance in life.   She has not been seen or heard from since the letter.   She thought that she could use just one more time.   But this time her addiction used her.   Her addiction sent her to jail, an institution and now death, oh my.

JESUS HEALED ALL WHO TOUCHED HIM

If they were to only touch the hem of His garment, they would be perfectly whole.   They recognized Jesus as the great healer, but I wonder how many really understood who He truly was.   They came to Jesus for physical healing as so many of us do today.   We fail to realize that physical healing only prolongs our life on earth, but it doesn't secure us or eternal life.   We search for hope to relieve the physical pain, but we fail to realize that what we really need is healing of spiritual pain, healing our souls. For many years I searched for healing of my fibromyalgia. I went from doctor to doctor, just to find relief. But it only led me on a path of disaster. The pills relieved the pain momentarily, but as it wore off, the pain was back even stronger. I recognized Jesus as the great healer but I never truly understood who He was. It took being sent to prison to realize the "Power of His Touch." The day I reached out to touch the hem of His garment was the day I was made spiritually whole. I no longer had to search for healing of physical pain because as He made me spiritually whole, He relieved the physical pain too. I had to realize that without spiritual healing, the pain of my past would be too hard to handle. Each day Jesus soothes the pain, fear, shame and guilt of my past with one gently touch that had made me perfectly whole. Jesus heals all who touch Him, so reach out and touch the hem of His garment and you too can be made perfectly whole. Remember, it's not the robe, but it's your faith that makes you whole.

JESUS I SEEK YOUR LOVE

1-14-05

As I look through the bars of this prison
The guilt arises within me
The pain of my past, the fear within
Blinds me, unable to see.

To see what is waiting there for me
Outside these walls of fear
Jesus please complete me
And open my ears to hear.

141

Undo these chains that bind me
The shackles that hold me still
Free the fears that keep me
Behind these bars, so real.

Jesus I seek your love
A love to meet all my needs
To wrap your arms around me
And comfort my soul that bleeds.

JESUS IS THE REASON FOR THE SEASON

What is the true meaning of Christmas? What does Christmas mean to you? Is it candy, cookies, or presents? Or perhaps Christmas carols, snowflakes, and holly? The true meaning of Christmas is the celebration of Jesus' birth. Jesus is the one and only reason for this season. One of our correctional officers said today "Well, Christmas is just another day to me", and the girl beside me answered back, "It's just another day to us too." I had to let her know that it might just be another day to them, but not for me. Christmas is so different for me this year. I now have the opportunity to do time. Time to think, time to pray, time to read, and time to realize what the true meaning of Christmas really is, Jesus. Where did all my time for Jesus really go when I was on the outside? How could I not realize what the true meaning was? Don't get me wrong, I always knew the story of Jesus' birth and I always knew what Jesus did for all of us. But now, with all this time on my hands, Jesus is now all of my time. Jesus is the reason for me being alive. Jesus is the reason for me being saved and for me being able to spend Eternity with my true Reason for the Season.

JESUS: OUR PAIN RELIEVER

"I am a cutter. It takes away my emotional pains and frustrations. When I'm anxious or upset, I cut myself. For some reason the physical pain eases the mental and emotional pain. I use anything I can find. I cut my arms, my legs and even my stomach. Sometimes I do it multiple times a day. Why? I can't really say, only that I'm in pain and this is the only way to stop it." These are the words of a bunkmate of mine. For many years she's tormented herself by finding ways to ease her emotional pain. She relieves her pain by causing pain. She lies in bed all day long rocking back and forth. She is so tormented by her past that she has withdrawn from the outside world. However she is no different than many of us that have held onto our pasts. We've tormented ourselves with drugs and alcohol, trying to find a way to relieve our pain. The best part is that there is relief. Jesus is our relief. He can ease the mental and emotional pain that we have longed to stop for so many years. But we must ask to receive. So, today let Jesus take away your pain. Let Jesus be your pain reliever.

JOY COMETH IN THE MORNING

I had the pleasure of getting to know another inmate from Portsmouth. Her husband had been murdered in front of her. She thought that she would never be able to make it. The scenes of his death flash in her mind, night and day. How could she ever be happy again? She found what she thought was happiness in drugs. She numbed her mind and her pain with the pills, but her addiction led her to end up in prison. She was still unable to find happiness, but she continued to search for it day and night. Then one day she found it. She found what she'd been searching for since her husband's death. She found something that could take her pain away. She found something that took away her addiction. She found a man called Jesus. He is the only one who does all things. He's the only one who could heal her broken heart and mend it back together. He is the one that granted her happiness. He granted her life back to her. She now has happiness through Jesus Christ. No more drugs, no more running and no more pain. God healed her. God gave her what she's been searching for all of her life, Jesus.

JUST IMAGINE

Imagine a place where time stands still
Where nothing you do is of your free will
Stripped of your freedom, your hopes and dreams
Surrounded by strangers, how frightening it seems

Imagine a place where you're told not to talk
And where you can and cannot walk

Imagine a place surrounded by hate
And made to feel worthless, at any rate

Imagine a place where time crawls like a snail
And all you look forward to is the morning mail
Imagine a place surrounded by wire
And to walk away from here, is your only desire

A place like this, so hard to conceive
Here I sit, I can hardly believe

Written by: A friend of mine in the Tapestry Program

JUST STOP FEEDING IT

I can remember as a child, the love that I had for animals.
So, when I would see a stray cat around our house, I would
run inside and get food to feed it. The more I fed it, the
more it stayed around. But, after so long, my mom told
me that I needed to stop feeding it. We had too many
animals already, and we didn't need any more. So, I had
to stop feeding it, and after about a week, the cat went
away. It went searching for someone else to feed it. This
reminded me so much of my addiction, the temptations and
the cravings, that would feed on my mind. The only way to
rid my mind of it was to stop feeding it. Just as the devil
tries to tempt you into sinning, you must stop feeding him.
We must not give him any reason to hang around. After so
long without food, the devil will go searching for someone
else to feed off of. I learned that the best way to do this
was to feed my soul with God's word; to fill my mind with
scripture, to fight off the devil as he comes to tempt me. I
tell the devil out loud every day, that he's not welcome here

anymore, just as my mom would do with the stray cat, shooing it away, time after time. But, eventually it went away. So stop feeding into the devil's lies and feed your soul with what God really intends for you-a happy life, with Jesus as your Savior.

JUST WEEDS

While walking to chow one day, I noticed an area of grass where a large amount of weeds were growing. They weren't beautiful to look at. They really didn't seem to have any purpose, they were just weeds. I didn't even know if they had a name. The next day I saw those same weeds in a beautiful vase sitting on the Cox's desk. They looked like a beautiful flowing fountain. I found out that they did have a name, they were called "fountain grasses." Somehow knowing their name made it easier for me to see their beauty. The weeds were beautiful once placed in their new setting. Some of us see God's people as just weeds without a purpose, weeds that don't have a name or a beauty within. But once we put these human "weeds" in a different setting they are looked upon differently. Would it help us to see people less as weeds and more like God's children if we only knew their names? Some of us don't come from such a beautiful place but we do have a name, and when we accepted Jesus as our Savior we were no longer just weeds but became a beautiful flower. I might not be so beautiful to everyone, but when Jesus wrote my name down and placed me in a different setting (on the rock) I became as a flowing fountain, ready to shower my love on all that were "just weeds."

KNEELING AND PRAYING
ON PRISON FLOORS

Another lady approached me this morning from Portsmouth, to come and pray with a young girl. I went out front into the recreational area to find a young 22 year old girl crying uncontrollably. She had just received word from one of the correctional officers that her mother's cancer had advanced and they didn't know if she would make it through the weekend. She said that two years ago she had lost her father to health problems and now she would lose her mother, but this time she wouldn't be present. I did the only thing I knew to do. I knelt down on the cement prison floor, took her hand and prayed. I couldn't hear the confusion around me, only the little girl asking Jesus to heal her mommy. I prayed for Jesus to give her strength, and to heal her mother of her cancer. I prayed for her to find peace behind these walls and to have God use her in a mighty way. This was the first time since I've been here that I have knelt to pray on the prison floors. I have prayed many times here behind these walls, but never down on my knees. I felt God's presence in a mighty way and in no time she was taken to see a chaplain. I know that the times I prayed before, in my bed, in the bathroom, or even just sitting in the yard, He heard my prayers. When I knelt down and prayed with this little girl in front of 200 inmates, I knew that God was hearing my prayer. I knew that God was behind these walls with me, and I knew that God would help this child in need.

KNOW THAT HE IS GOD

After Jesus' death and resurrection, an angel appeared to Mary and Mary Magdalene. The angel announced the Good News of the resurrection to the women, but also the angel was sending them a message. The angel was telling them not to be frightened and when you are afraid, to go to the empty tomb; as we all should today. When I'm frightened or afraid, I go to the empty tomb. I look in and see that He has risen. He is in control. The angel was also trying to tell us that He wasn't there. He's alive. Come in and see for yourself, and know that He is God. Then go quickly and tell all that He has risen, He isn't there, so don't be afraid, because He is God. As I sit in this prison and my heart aches for home, I go to the empty tomb, look inside and see that He has risen. I know that my God can do any and all things. Know that my God is in control of the court system. My God is in control of my judicial release. My God knows the time and date of my freedom. I will go and tell all, that my Jesus has resurrected. That my Jesus can save you from the prison you are in, because my Jesus loved you enough to bleed and die for your sins. Know that He is God.

LET BOTH GROW TOGETHER UNTIL THE HARVEST

Tares (weeds) and young blades of wheat look exactly the same and can't be distinguished until they are grown and ready for harvest. A man sowed good seed in his field. But as he slept, the enemy came and sowed weeds among the wheat. They both began to grow and as the servants came to the field, they saw the weeds among the wheat that had brought forth fruit. The servant asked if he should pull the weeds and the man said to wait, so the wheat wouldn't be uprooted also. He said, let them grow together until the harvest and then first gather the weeds and burn them and then gather the wheat into the barn.

Tares represent the unbelievers and wheat represents the believers in this world. Both must live side by side. Just as the farmer allowed the tares to remain in his field until harvest, Jesus also allows the unbelievers to remain. But, at harvest time (God's judgment) the tares (unbelievers) will be uprooted from the field and thrown away. God's harvest (the judgment) is coming soon. So, we must be ready for the Harvest time. Keep your field cleaned out and allow God to bring forth His fruits.

LETTING GO OF SHAME

I can remember a few years ago when my nine-year-old daughter Aleah was playing out in the backyard with a neighbor friend, Dara. Aleah and Dara had their shovels and were digging in the dirt around their playhouse. They had found a special spot to dig their very own garden. They were so proud of their accomplishment. "Look at me, Mom. Look what we did." They wanted to show everyone what they had made. But they showed me. "Just look at you girls," I said. "You're a mess. Look how dirty you are. You oughta be ashamed of yourselves." Aleah dropped her head to the ground. She saw her dirty little hands and began to feel dirty on the inside. She probably felt that she had been bad and that maybe she was so bad that she would never get clean. She went through a physical shame, as today I go through an intellectual shame. Shame produces such powerful feelings. It is easy to underestimate the importance of our thoughts in recording, labeling and increasing our emotions. Shame is a mental process. Self-hatred starts developing one insult at a time. But today we need to let go of our shame, no matter what we've been told. We need to remove the mask of shame and search for the soul that we lost because of it. No matter who you are or what you've done, you are worthy.

LIFE AS A SOAP OPERA

When you read about Joseph and his family in the Bible, his story tends to make a daytime soap opera look mild. Sadly, his family is just like a lot of our typical families today. Joseph's family went through starvation, guilt, depression, resentment and even imprisonment. Does any of this sound familiar? It does to me, especially in the lives of my friends here in prison. Many of these women's homes have been jail cells, homeless shelters and now prison cells. As with Joseph, many of these women have been betrayed and deserted by their own families. But, as with Joseph, I myself have survived and prospered where most would have failed and given up. One of the biggest lessons I have learned in this soap opera called life, is that with God's help, any situation can be used for good, even when others intend it for evil. What matters are not so much the events or circumstances of life, but your response to them. So, "As the World Turns" and you begin to see the beautiful "Guiding Light", know that you are created by God to be "Bold and Beautiful."

LIFE ON THE FARM

What does life mean to you? Is it family, friends, happiness, or love? What does life in prison mean to you? Is it bars, razor-wired fences, guards, or cells? Life in prison means death and dying behind these walls. Buried in a lonely grave in the back corner of the penitentiary, life in prison: never to be released, just buried without family and without friends. The only way for many to escape this prison is through their spirit. Many women have entered this prison to spend their life sentence here, and some died alone on this farm: no viewing, no funeral, just buried in the dirt never to see the outside world again. A few have left this prison through death to die in the arms of Jesus, to live again in Heaven with Jesus. They may have never seen the outside world again, but with Jesus they'll spend eternity walking the streets of gold. God is in this prison. Just allow Him to come into your heart; it may be your only way out. It is the only way!

LIFE'S LESSONS THAT I'VE LEARNED

I cannot hide from God. What I offer to God must be from the heart. God doesn't always protect me from trouble, but cares for me in spite of it. God wants me to do more than drift through life. God's plans make use of my mistakes. God responds to faith even in the midst of failure. Patience often brings rewards. God's plans are larger than people. God is faithful even when I complicate things. I am always responsible for my own actions. All I do is woven into God's ongoing plan. God's plan can not be stopped. With God's help any situation can be used for good. God is in control far beyond my immediate situation. God is ready to use my unique qualities to accomplish His work. God will use me in spite of my limitations and failures. Even those who make great spiritual progress can easily fall back into a sinful lifestyle. My background does not prevent God from working powerfully in my life. God hears and answers all of my prayers. Life is more than simply reacting, it demands action. My willingness to be honest will help me remember my need for God's guidance and help. God has a purpose for the situation that I am in today. Excellence is shown by how hard we work when no one else is even noticing. Real freedom doesn't come until we no longer have to prove our freedom.

LIFE'S ROAD

God isn't one to compromise; there is no other way.
He isn't one to bend the rules; or lead us all astray.
Life's road is straight and narrow, with mountains we must climb,
and the only way to get there, is one step at a time.
We must focus on the Savior or else we'll lose our way.
Life's road is straight and narrow, as we live from Day to Day.

LITTLE GIRL LOST

Little girl lost in a world that's free
Blind to her freedom, of what she could be
Locked in her mind of pain and fear
Crying inside, with only silent tears
Lost in her past of addiction and pain
Locked in this prison with guilt and shame
Only to arise and to conquer her dreams
The Lord she has found, to quiet her screams
Little girl lost, in her prison from within
Washed by His blood, and released of her sin
Clothed with His word, and healed of her pain
Free from her prison, with eternity to gain

LIVING FREE

Galatians 5:1 "Stand fast therefore in the liberty where with Christ hath made us free, and be not entangled again with the yoke of bondage." Christ came to set us free; to live unselfishly; to be free from the bondage of sin. To live free in this prison that holds me captive. The devil wants us back in bondage to be entangled in this sinful world. He wants to steal your joy, the joy that Jesus has so graciously set before you. But you must be willing to be set free. You must be willing to live free. The devil will send all of his followers to the doorstep of your heart. He will try to entice you with the sin of this world. But, stand fast. Stand firm. Stand free. Christ freely gave His life for you. He freely died and graciously rose again three days later. Jesus gives you a choice. We are at liberty to accept or reject that choice to follow Him. So, it's your choice. What will you choose freedom or bondage? I choose to be

free today. I live freely in this prison because I have
freedom in my heart.

LIVING IN THE LAND OF OZ

I'm living in the Land of Oz; women, searching their hearts
for strength, courage and wisdom. They are searching for
that one person who can give them the answers.
Searching through this prison for what they already have,
but they just can't see it. They've walked the yellow brick
road and the witches of addiction, fear and pain travel
closely behind following them wherever they go. They
search for the red slippers to click their heels and go home
but they are nowhere to be found. They search through a
pill or a bottle to find the heart of the tin man, the courage
of the lion and the knowledge and wisdom of the scarecrow.
But, they only get lost deeper and deeper into the forest of
this prison. There is one who has all of the answers. No,
it is not the "Great and powerful Oz" but it is the "Great and
powerful Jesus". The one that can give you a pure heart.
The one that can give you the courage to fight this battle
called sin, and the one that can give you the wisdom
through His word. Jesus can help you find those "red
slippers" to click your heels and find your way home. Seek
out the great and powerful Jesus. He's ready and willing
to guide you on your path. To walk you down the streets of
gold, instead of the yellow brick road that only leads you to
the devil, waiting patiently for you to pull back the curtain
of sin and death.

LIVING IN THE LAND
OF THE HURTING

Many of us were brought up in middle class homes with middle class problems. Problems that were kept behind the doors of your own home. We surrounded ourselves with middle or upper class people, not people with "real problems." Not hurting, abused people or those with an addiction or infirmity. But Jesus did, He searched out the land of the hurting. When he saw a hurting person, he reached out to them. We may reach out, but we still keep a distance from them because they're different than us. Jesus sat with prostitutes, drunks, the poor, the bleeding and the hurting people. Jesus didn't surround himself with the upper class. Just as Jesus surrounded himself with hurting people, so do I as I sit here in prison. I'm living in the land of the hurting. Jesus has called me to the forefront because I was willing and able to share my pain with others. Today I live daily with broken, bleeding women in this prison. Today, all classes of people surround me, and today they are all broken in some way. So reach out to those as Jesus did. When we help others to overcome, we too can overcome with them.

LIVING WITH LIFE
AS YOUR SERVANT

Both life and death are our servants. The nonbelievers of Jesus Christ are victims of this life. They live day to day wondering what the true meaning of life is. They get swept up in a life that tells them that there is no meaning. They go day to day pondering about the true meaning of life.

While on the other hand, believers use life to its fullest. They know the true meaning of life. The biggest fear for a nonbeliever is death. The uncertainty of death overcomes them in a way that makes living impossible. For us believers in Christ, death holds no fear. Christ has conquered all of our fears. He has given us a path to follow in life. He can show us the way if we just obey Him. Don't let life be your servant. Take your life and put it into God's hands, because death is only the beginning to eternal life with Jesus Christ. Don't be a servant to life, because a servant only does what its master asks him to do. Serve Christ, and fear no more, for He is life, life eternal. Serve Jesus and He will make your life complete. He will give you life that you didn't think was possible. He will give you heaven as your home, when all you ever knew was hell on earth.

LOOSE ME AND LET ME GO

When Jesus stood at the tomb where Lazarus lay dead, Jesus called out, "Lazarus come forth." But the Bible tells us that Lazarus was still bound up in his grave clothes. They were wrapped around him tightly. So, Jesus said, "Loose him and let him go." He was not only loosed of his grave clothes but also loosed of the stench of death. Just like Lazarus, we were bound by our sins. Our self-centered habits still have us bound. But we were born again. We were born of God, but our old habits still have us bound. Jesus wants the same for us. He wants to set us free. He wants us loosed from our sins. He wants us to walk in his love. But our grave clothes, those habits of anger, impatience and selfishness, have to be loosed. We must be willing to allow God to raise us up and set us free. Free the grave clothes that held us hostage for so long.

156

Don't be trapped inside of a body of sin. Don't let anything hold you back anymore. Break free. Step out into the supernatural. Don't let sin hold you down anymore. Let Jesus love you. Loose yourself so you can wrap your arms around your loving Savior.

LOVE LETTER TO YOU

Kayla, Tori and Aleah, I Love You! I shed my own blood for you to make you clean. You are clean now so believe that it's true. You are lovely in my eyes and I created you to be just as you are. Do not criticize yourself or get down for not being perfect in your own eyes. This leads to frustration. I want you to trust me -- one step one day at a time. Dwell in my power and in my love and be free. Be yourself! Don't allow other people to control you. I will guide you, if you let me. Be aware of my presence in everything. I give you patience, love, joy, peace and life. Look to me for your answers. I am your Shepherd and I will lead you. Follow ME only. Do not forget this. Listen to me and I will tell you my will. I Love You! -- I Love You! Let my love flow from you and spill over to all you touch. Do not be concerned with yourself-- you are my responsibility. I will change you, and you will hardly know that it's happening. You are to love yourself and love others, and love others simply because I love you! Take your eyes off of yourself. Look at me! I lead -- I change -- I create, but not when you are trying to do it on your own. I won't fight your efforts. You are mine. Let me give you joy, peace, and kindness. No one else can. Do you see, you belong to me? It is really none of your business how I deal with you. Do not struggle, just relax in my love. My will is perfect. My love is sufficient. I will supply all of your needs according to my riches in Glory. Look to me.

I Love You.   Trust Me.

Love,

Your Heavenly Father

LOVE LIFTED ME

Love lifted me out of the miry clay and placed me upon the highest mountain.   Love is what took my past and made my future bright and alive.   Love called me by my name, called me beautiful and unique.   Love granted me freedom in this place called prison.   Love lifted my burdens and love carried them for me.   Love gave me a will and a desire to survive for the first time in my life.   Love gave me the patience and grace to walk with my head held high.   Love gave me the wisdom to share with all the broken-hearted behind these bars.   Love mercifully saved my black heart and washed it white as snow.   Love covered me with the blood and cleansed me of my sins.   Love lifted me up when I couldn't lift myself up.   Love can lift you and place you on the solid rock.   Love is my Jesus, who chose to love old sinners like you and me.

LOVE OR LUST

I met a woman today who has been sentenced to eighteen months here in prison. She proceeded to tell me her story: a story that I don't know if I can ever comprehend. Ridgley met her boyfriend six years ago and they have a five year old daughter. When their daughter was two months old she was afflicted with colic. Ridgley said, "She just wouldn't quit crying so my boyfriend spanked her. He just wasn't sure how to make her stop crying." Children Services got involved and put him on probation. She said that she asked for parenting classes but no one would give her the phone number so they just disciplined the child however they thought was right. For the next five years their daughter went through undeserved spankings. Three months ago their home caught on fire and Ridgley and her boyfriend got out, leaving the baby behind. She said "I'm here for child endangerment because we just couldn't think straight, so we left the house." The firemen entered the home and brought out the little five year old girl, burnt and suffering from smoke inhalation. The child had been chained to her bed with a dog collar and a chain, which she wore like a harness around her waist. Ridgley said "We chain her up every night so she doesn't get into trouble." She and her boyfriend have now lost all custody of their daughter. The sad part is that Ridgley said, "I just can't live without my boyfriend, so I want my daughter to be adopted by someone else." She just doesn't comprehend true love. She has chosen lust over her child. She feels like she needs her boyfriend to make her happy because no one ever loved her like he does. She chose to love a sick man instead of the love for her child. A mother's love for her child should be unconditional. Jesus teaches us to love not lust. I pray that one day she can find Jesus. I pray that one day she can feel true love, the love of Jesus, and choose the right path, the better way. Maybe someday she can see that love is more than just a word.

LOVING SOMEONE
IS LIKE HOLDING SAND

Loving someone is like holding sand. If you close your hand tightly, you lose some. But if you leave your hand open, all of the sand remains. We must be willing and ready to allow our partners to go out and do their work and Christian Services for God. I can remember when my husband was first called to preach and then called to be a Pastor. I began holding my hand closed tightly. At times I felt like the more he had to leave, the more that something was wrong with me. I had put it in my mind that he just wanted to get away for a while. I had to realize that my own insecurities were holding him back from God's work and it was beginning to put a strain on our relationship. It took a long time to realize that I was holding way too tight to my husband, just to ease my own insecurities. I learned that I had to sacrifice my own personal discomfort to tend to my husband's needs and desires of God. These insecurities helped me on my way to prison. I tried ways to fill the void that I had in my heart. But, today as we are apart, God has opened my eyes to His will and not mine. God has filled the void in my heart that held me captive for so many years. So, today my marriage stands firm and will not slip away as tiny grains of sand.

MAKE A FRESH START

Do you have hopes and dreams that you know God gave to you? I do. Do you ever get discouraged and think to yourself, "It's never going to happen" or "God could never use me." Well, believe me, he wants to use you. With each new day He wants to give you a new chance at life. God wants to help you accomplish His purposes for your life, no matter where you are or what you've done. I'm sure people have looked at me and thought that there's nothing out there in life for me. Many times I have felt like giving up. But, it was the enemy that was throwing temptations into my life because he knew what my greatest struggles were. It can be conquered. It's not easy, but I can do it, and so can you. Make a decision to begin your journey, to fulfill His calling. Make a fresh start, and start it with Jesus. It's easy to give up and give in. What is difficult is to change. But believe me, it gets easier and easier with God on my side. Choose to receive God's daily mercy in your life. God is not limited by what we think he can do. God has a plan for your life, but you must exchange your old life for a new one.

MANY PEOPLE YOU DON'T EXPECT TO SEE IN THE KINGDOM OF HEAVEN WILL BE THERE

Forgiveness and grace comes to all that ask. Life is not only about rewards, but salvation. The despised, the outcasts, and the sinners that turn to Jesus for forgiveness will be there. You may despise them now and you can't get yourself to witness to them because they are sinners, but

God loves them. They are locked up behind bars for unthinkable crimes. They are unwanted, the unloved and the forgotten ones but not to Jesus. Jesus accepts their forgiveness. Can you? As I sit here in prison, saved by God's grace, I'm blessed to see the beautiful transformation of women from sinner to saved, from outcast to child of the King. From despised and wicked to loved and accepted by our Heavenly Father. One day they'll all be in heaven with you, if you are saved. The thief sitting will be beside you at the River of Joy. The murderer, will be sitting at Jesus' feet, praising Him for eternity, and I get to sit in Heaven with those who have believed and served God for many years. If God can accept us, why can't you? You might not expect to see us enter into the kingdom of Heaven, but just look around, we'll be there. Just as you were, we were also forgiven, washed by the blood, and saved by Grace. Always expect the unexpected. Go out and witness to those that you don't expect to see in Heaven with you.

MATERIALISTIC MOM

Tonight was a very entertaining evening here at the Scioto County jail. One of the older women (a drug dealer) went off on a few of the girls and pulled the fire alarm. She's in jail waiting to go to the pen for 10 to 15 years. So, in her mind she thought that this might get her there quicker. She has two children, a boy that's 22 years old, and a 17 year old daughter.   These two kids are totally different. The first week I met her she told me about her life and her children. She talked only of having a boy. She said that he was a perfect child. She said that he only smokes marijuana and does pills occasionally. She said that he has stood by her while she has sold dope for years. But, her 17 year old daughter thinks that she is too good for

162

a drug dealing mom. She said that her daughter didn't want anything to do with her dope money. So she told her daughter that she didn't want anything to do with her. She said that if her daughter really loved her then she would want that life to live. Sometimes people see love through materialistic eyes. They can only see what they can give them in vanity and not in love. If she could only see what she's done to her boy over all the years of selling drugs and her addiction. His mother is now gone for the next 10 to 15 years. He doesn't have anyone. He doesn't have anyone to help him get through the hard times. He's now homeless, no money, and no mother. Her daughter lives with her father and has a home with love that she's always grateful for. A love that God gives to parents that should be passed down to their children. A love that's not built on money, but a love built by love.

MAY MY DREAMS COME TRUE

The dreams are happening again. I woke up last night scared to death. I had dreamed that I got out of prison and went to find my daughter. I searched for her and eventually found her at school. I had lost all custody of her when the courts came to get her, due to my drug abuse. I had to kidnap her to get her back. I had to kidnap my own daughter from school. When I arrived at school, she was outside at the playground. So, I ran up to her, grabbed her and ran to the car. She was so happy. She began crying and said, "Mommy, I knew you always loved me. I knew that you never forgot me, Mommy. Please don't ever leave me again. I can't live in a foster home anymore. I love you, Mommy. You do love me, don't you Mommy?" I began to cry. I told her, "Yes, baby mommy loves you. Mommy has always loved you and I need you too." But, that's when I woke up. This was a dream that one of my bunkmates had last night. She awoke crying, because when she opened her eyes, she was sitting in prison and her daughter was still in foster care. She loved her daughter, but her drugs came first. Today she sits behind these prison walls, praying to God that one day she'll see her daughter again, and   that her dreams will become reality. There are so many women in this prison that have lost custody of their kids. It's not that they didn't love them, but they fell into the trap of temptation, that eventually led to addiction. Please pray for these women and their children, that one day soon they will be re-united.

MEN IN BLACK

Here in Marysville we have a place called, ARN 4, the hole. The hole has four brick walls with a mat on the floor to sleep on. The only way you get sent to the hole is if you disobey a direct order. The hole is dark and dreary. When a person is caught disobeying a direct order, they are sent up to the front desk to wait for the men in black to arrive. Once they walk into the "Hale", my cottage, they immediately handcuff the person and shake them down. We always know when we see the men in black that someone is going to the hole. We call them the men in black because they are decked out all in black clothing; black hat, shirt, pants and even a black jacket. We know when they arrive; someone is going to that dark and dreary hole. God has given us a direct order. He has asked us to obey Him. Obey His commandments, and to accept Him as our Savior. If we are unwilling to accept Jesus into out hearts, eventually the men in black will arrive and we will be sent to the hole, otherwise known as hell. The men in black remind me of the devil as he stalks us and eventually comes to get you. He waits in the darkness, waiting for that call, waiting for the lost sinner to be taken to the hole of hell. Accept Jesus' calling. Don't wait for the arrival of the men in black. Wait upon the Lord. Spend your eternity in heaven with Jesus. Don't wait to be taken to the hole of hell when you can be with Jesus in your Heavenly Home.

MIND WHAT YOU SAY
OR YOU MIGHT SAY WHATEVER
COMES TO MIND

The other day while I was reading, I came across an unusual bird, the Tauras Crane. These birds inhabit the Tauras Mountains on Southern Turkey. What makes them so odd is their constant cackling, especially when they fly. The noise tends to get the attention of awaiting eagles that swoop down and take them for their meal. But some of the more experienced cranes have learned to avoid these attacks by filling their mouths with stones, large enough to fill their mouths full. This prevents them from cackling and being eaten by the eagle. I know many people with the same problem. They just can't stop cackling off at the mouth. They just can't control their tongues. During my first few months in prison, keeping my mouth closed was the first thing that I learned. It prevents a lot of heartache and troubles. Sometimes we open our mouths before we think. This usually causes heartache to the one that we are speaking to. Guard your mouth with your life, because it could make the difference in the life of someone else. Mind what you say or you might say whatever comes to your mind.

MIXED UP FEELINGS

From the Scioto County Jail to the Ohio Correctional Facility for Women sure gives you some real mixed up feelings. Really, it is some of the prisoners and inmates that have some real mixed up feelings. I have seen so many things in the last few months that you can only read about in books, magazines, or headline news. I've met murderers, child molesters, thieves, men haters, and many, many lesbians. Being a lesbian seems to be the trend here at the penitentiary. I had the opportunity to sit down and witness to a lady that has been a lesbian for about 25 years. I asked her what she thought made her want to be with another woman. She began her story at about the age of 5 years old. She was molested by her father. When she was around 10 years old, her father murdered four innocent people and now he's doing life in prison. She said she cries every time a man comes close to her. Does it still make homosexuality right? No, but it sure caused a 5 year old child to have some real mixed up feelings. Can God heal her and give her peace with her father and men? Yes, he can. I have been able to see God move in mighty ways these last few months. I know of God's miracles and I know He can mend her broken heart and grant her freedom from her sins and freedom of a past of mixed up feelings.

MOLDY BREAD

I read of a woman today facing seven years in prison for drug charges. She spoke of her little 5 year old, now living with her parents. Not to humiliate the child in front of his peers, the mother told her son that she was away at school. This is very common with women in prison, to tell their children that they are away at school or a job that's had to keep them away. But as the mother called home one night, the young boy asked her once again when she would be coming home. Her response, like always was "Real soon honey; it won't be too much longer." So the son replied by asking the mother if they could go to the pond and feed the ducks when she got home. The mother told her son that she would love to do that. The young child said, "Great Mommy, cause I've been saving up bread to feed the ducks for when you get home." Several days later the woman received her 25-dollar a month state pay. This was her only income there at the prison. That day a woman approached her wanting to sell her a pain pill for 20 dollars. That wouldn't leave her much to spend after she bought the pill. But being the addict that she was, she felt like one pill wouldn't hurt anything and she would have 5 dollars left. After discussing it with a friend, the friend said, "You're an adult and you can make your own decisions, but think of how much bread you could buy with that 25 dollars."

MY HELPER

Ten iron bars lock me in a cell of stone and steel
Forty eight square feet of room
Fear is what I feel

I see the hurt and all of the pain
In this place each day
So why can I smile?
What took my fear away?
Yes, I'm a prisoner in this jail
But not in my heart you see
Because there's someone special
Who's always here with me
So don't feel bad because I'm here
You see there's a good part
I have my Bible and my faith
And Jesus in my heart
He gives me strength to hang on
Hope to face each day
When things get rough, I close my eyes
And see him when I pray.

MY GOD AS A FETUS

Have you ever thought about Jesus being in Mary's womb
as a fetus? The one that was larger than life itself as an
embryo, so gently placed in Mary's womb, the holiest of
holiest, sleeping in a woman's womb. Our creator of life
was being created. Created like any other child on the
outside; hair, eyes, nose, eyebrows, liver and heart. A
heart like no other heart ever created, a pure and perfect
heart, a heart of unconditional love. Can you imagine our
Lord sucking his thumb? Imagine Jesus playing with other
kids, running up and down the streets of Jerusalem.
Crying as He fell down and skinned His knee. Mary, the
woman that first cradled Him, tired and worn from giving
birth. Joseph, the man that gave him piggyback rides and
carried Him to bed, having calloused and dirty hands from
his carpentry work.

But the Hands that placed Him so gently into Mary's womb, hands so pure and clean. Jesus' hands that were pierced at the age of 33, for you and for me. His hands, so precious and perfect. His hands that touched so many lives and performed so many miracles. But His nail scarred hands, are no longer bruised and bleeding, they are now healed and pure. My God, once a fetus rolling around in Mary's womb, now a Savior in Heaven waiting for you there.

MY HEAVENLY FRIEND

Lord, I couldn't live a single day,
without You in my heart.
I couldn't face this troubled world,
or have the will to start.
But You, Oh Lord, have given me,
the courage to endure.
When life gets harder, You are there,
with footsteps strong and sure.
When life seems cold, your breath is warm
upon my troubled brow.
I know your hand is holding mine,
And You are with me now.
Yes, life was harder yesterday,
Before I let you in.
But now You live inside my heart . . .
I'm safe with You, my friend.

MY HEROES AND SHEROES

I am an inmate at the Ohio Correctional Facility for Women in Marysville, and I just wanted to let you know a little about my unsung hero. He is not an inmate, but my mate. My husband Barry has now had to turn his role around from a father into Mr. Mom. He has made tremendous sacrifices for me and our girls during my time here. My family has paid a greater price for the crime I committed than I have. He now makes all the hands-on decisions of 2 teenage girls and one 9 year old girl, while my role here as an inmate is waking, eating, sleeping and working one hour a night. He is my hero, and my daughters are my "sheroes". They make the journey to see me twice a month no matter what the weather holds. I receive mail almost daily from one of them, just to inspire my day. Despite the sacrifices they make, they never fail to make it to my visitations. He was running the girls to basketball games, coaching, preaching, cooking, cleaning and much more. But through God's grace and their faith, they find the strength, courage and ability to meet and accept the challenges laid before them. I thank you for being my hero and my sheroes.

MY SECRET HIDING PLACE

All of us have secrets, but I had a secret hiding place. I would take my fears and hide them in my heart. I took my pain and hid it in a pill. I took my shame and hid it in my mind. I took my rape and hid it in my past. I took my dreams and hid them in a box. I took my friends and hid them from myself. I took my Jesus and hid Him from my faith. I was always good at hide and seek. No one could ever find me. After thirty-five years Jesus found all my hiding places. He always knew where they were, but I would never come out. I stayed hidden because I was afraid; afraid of what people thought of me. I was afraid of never being good enough. I was afraid of being found in my hiding place because I didn't know what coming out would be like. I was afraid that I was the only preacher's wife with an addiction. I have hid many things in my past, but never again will I hide my Jesus. God has granted me the gift of love. He has shown me that even when I'm in my hiding place I'm still not alone. God has shown me true love and true friendship when for all these years I ran and hid from it. The next time I participate in a game of hide and seek I'll be the one seeking, not hiding.

MY SOMETIMES HEAVY LOAD

My load is so heavy, too heavy to carry. I'm weighed down so   far that I can't even stand to my feet. They keep putting more stuff on my back and I don't think I can carry anymore. But I let them. I can't say no. I'm what you call a people pleasure. Yeah, I'm that one with the low self esteem, unable to take charge. Unable to get my life in order because I'm too worried about getting everyone else's in order. I want to be able to say no, but they'll get mad at me. That's what I used to think. This was me, and in some way it still is. I just want to see others happy. I was gradually stripping myself of my happiness day by day, hour by hour, and minute by minute. Until one day it over took my life. Who was I? What had I become? An addict, addicted to every opiate almost imaginable. It eased the pain, and calmed my fears. It made me miserable. I became so over loaded with pain in my heart that the load was too much for me to bear. The load this time took me down on my face, flat on my face. But this time, I had God on my side because when I fell, He caught me right before I hit the ground. So, give your heart to Jesus, so He can keep you in His big hands. He can take your heavy load and place it on His back to carry. He and only He can pick you up and carry your load.

NAIL SCARRED HANDS

Each morning as I wake up in prison, I gaze at the pictures on my wall. Thanking God for my family and the blessings He has given us. But, today as I sat looking at the pictures, I saw something that I had never seen before. It was a picture of the men from New Beginnings Freedom Hall House (a home for recovering addicts). The men were standing side by side, posing for the camera. In the middle was Brian, one of the men that live in the house. His hands were down to his side and the staples from the mailroom had pierced both of his hands directly in his palms. My heart began to pound and my eyes filled with tears. I thought to myself, He died for you and me. He died for Brian and all of the other men in the house. He died for drug addicts, prostitutes, thieves and murderers. As I look at the picture I see ten men who were dead inside, until Jesus gave them life. He took ten drug addicts and picked them up from their life of sin and gave them the most precious gift, salvation. They might slip and fall, as we all do, but they now have someone to pick them up and guide them back on their way. Jesus can do the same for you, as He did for all of them. Jesus can set you free from the world of sin, and give you eternal life.

172

"I was Naked and Ye Clothed Me, I was Sick and Ye Visited Me, I was in prison, and ye came unto me." Matthew 25:36

I was naked and ye clothed me. I gave my all to you. I released every fear, every pain of my past. I laid it out in front of you only for you to clothe me in your love, to clothe me in your armor and your word. I was sick and ye visited me. You took my disease of addiction, and you gave me life. You came to me when I was at my bottom, and you picked me up, brushed me off and placed me in this prison to heal. You healed my heart, mind, soul and cleansed me of my past. I was in prison and ye came unto me. You unlocked the chains that held me captive in my own body. You set me free in this prison. Unlocking each issue one by one, releasing the shame and guilt that held me prisoner in my own heart and mind. You came unto me in my dark and dreary cell and broke through the bars that I clung to for peace and serenity. You allowed me to see for the first time in my life, to see who I am and not who I was. You never left me, nor forsake me. You, my Jesus have clothed me when I was naked, healed me when I was sick, and have set me free in this prison. Thank you Jesus for your promise.

NATIONAL WEATHER ADVISORY-PLEASE BE ADVISED

This is a national weather advisory, brought to you by a cold-hearted sinner. Today will be cold and snowy, which may cause hardened hearts to turn ice cold. Due to high winds there will be a shortage of parishioners at church today. If you need to reach any of them you can find them at the new ski club down the street. Snow drifting may be as high as ten feet, so you might have to walk right over someone today to get to the top of the bank. Be very careful approaching some people due to the fact that they might shatter when you approach them. Their cold hearts have caused ice water to run through their veins. If you need any assistance cleaning off the church parking lot, just wait for someone else to do it, because it's way too cold out for you. If you don't get a call from your pastor or deacons to check on you, just don't speak to them the next time you see them, that will show them. Be advised of possible flooding when the snow begins to dissolve. You better wear your high boots to church next week, just in case the gossip gets too deep.

Don't live as a cold-hearted sinner. Look out for others. Take them under your wing. Share the love of Jesus Christ and spread the Good News (not the bad news) to all that are willing to listen. Make today a nice summer day even if it is cold and rainy outside. Keep yourself a warm heart and share your blessings in life with others.

NEGATIVE SELF-TALK

How many of you have ever suddenly realized you were talking to yourself? I know I have. I can remember many times while growing up, looking in the mirror and saying, "You are so fat and ugly." I held this conversation in my head many times. My negative self-talk came so often and eventually I came to believe it. It's kind of like when I used to work as a nurse in a pediatrician's office. Everyday I heard the screams of children, either a happy or sad scream, and eventually I no longer heard the screams. I became so immune to them that I tuned them out, not purposely, but mentally. This is how negative self-talk would begin. I would degrade myself, tell myself I was bad, then eventually I felt unworthy of love and happiness. But today, my self-talk has become positive, only because I learned how to love myself. Each day I wake up I tell myself, "I am a strong and beautiful woman, worthy to be loved." After telling myself this for so long I finally came to believe it. I finally came to see what God sees in me. A unique woman of courage, made special by the hands of God.

NEVER WILL IT HAPPEN AGAIN

Never will I allow my children to have to walk through these prison gates. Never will I subject them to the angry hateful officers at this prison. Never will I allow myself to hold onto fears and pain. Never will I allow temptation of this world to interfere with my eternal destination. Never will I sit back and watch another hurting soul. Never will I not forgive myself for mistakes, not failures, but mistakes. Never will I rely on others to make me happy when today my happiness comes from within. Never will I not stand up for what's right, even if it means that someone may not like me for it. Never will I not share my past to help other addicts, because of shame and embarrassment. Never will I take for granted the small things in life, like a walk in the park or a kiss goodnight from my girls. Always will I put my Jesus first before any and all things in this life.

NEW BEGINNINGS –
A HOSPITAL OF HEALING SOULS

When my family arrived at New Beginnings Outreach Ministries Church, we arrived at a hospital that was ready to help heal our wounds. New Beginnings had many nurses on duty to provide their services to bandage us up. Our wounds were very deep, but it didn't matter. My past was broken, but they were willing to stand by me to fix it. It's a hospital for broken lives, broken dreams, and broken people. We only have one doctor on duty at all times Jesus. No matter what your past holds, they are prepared to assist you in carrying your load. We have to realize that we all have stuff in our lives, but there are people out there who care. People that are willing to give their love, prayers and time to nurse you back to life. They're prepared to share with you their pasts and their broken dreams, but they are also prepared to expose their scars. They don't hide them because they're not ashamed. They're not ashamed of what God has done for them. He has healed they're fears, pain, and shame. But most of all they are willing to share the word of God to all who enter. All who are willing to show their wounds. When you enter New Beginnings, be prepared, because their arms are open and waiting for your arrival. Awaiting your arrival at the hospital for your soul healing process. But remember, your wounds can never be healed unless you clean it out and expose it to the air. So, we welcome you to New Beginnings Outreach Ministries. The staff here is always willing to assist you anytime.

NEWS BULLETIN:
GOD LOVES EVEN THE
PROSTITUTES ON WALLER STREET

The first week I spent in jail I got to know the girl who became my bunkie. It was so unusual just how the situation all fell into place. Just two weeks before I was arrested, we helped a young girl who prostituted on the streets of Portsmouth to feed her drug addiction. She had just spent eight months, in the Scioto County Jail. It turned out that my new bunkie was her best friend. Jo, the prostitute, came to Piketon where our program was and she gave her heart to the Lord. I was telling my bunkie about the girl that I was helping with her addiction, had gotten saved. When I said her name Jo, my bunkie began to cry. She said, "She's my best friend. I can't believe that she's clean, saved and living for the Lord." I told her that she could have the same, and all that she needed to do was ask the Lord to come into her heart and ask for forgiveness. Tonight as we were speaking about God again, my bunkie, Tiffany, broke down crying. She was thinking back to about a year ago when she had given her heart to the Lord. She told me of the time the Lord spoke to her to get up, go to the altar and give her heart to the Lord. She then told me how afraid she was now, because she would be getting released from jail in a couple of days. If only she could get her faith back, the kind of faith that her friend Jo had. The kind of faith that she had a year ago when she trusted God to save her soul. But, Tiffany could not believe that Jesus would take her back, so she left jail and returned to the streets of Portsmouth. Two girls with the same past, now have two totally different futures with two different eternities.

NO 'DO-OVERS' IN PRISON

I can remember playing ball out in the front yard as a child. Once we had the front yard all set up to start a softball game. The yard was full of kids and I was up to bat. They pitched the ball and I missed it, strike one. They pitched the ball again, strike two. Then the last pitch, strike three, "You're out!" they yelled. I immediately yelled back, "Do-over, she didn't pitch it right. Do-over, it's not fair." "Do-over." Well, it seemed to work as a child, but as an adult "do-over's" just don't work. It would be so nice to just say to the judge, "Do-over." But it just doesn't work that way. There is one thing that we can say, "Go over." We can "go over" things and move on in our lives. We can't redo what we've made a mess of, but we can "go over" them. We can move ahead in our struggle. We can go over the top and move on. We must go on. There's no looking back now. Prison is just a piece of my past. There's no do-over's in prison. There's only the future to look to today, and I will "go over" and be an over comer.

NO PREFERENCE

NFL football players, bikers, biker chicks, fast cars and Jesus. Bill Glass and his team of soul winners came to ORW today for "The Champion of Souls Weekend." They showed up in their gear, ready to win the souls of the women here in prison. They arrived on Harley Davidson bikes, with their black leather jackets that said, "Bikers for Jesus Prison Team." They preached the gospel of Jesus Christ in a way that these women could understand. They gave their personal testimonies. From drug addiction, prostitution, and prison, to now-strong men and women saved by the precious blood of Jesus. As they shared the gospel I saw tears flowing down the cheeks of some of the toughest women in here. I saw women forming a circle, holding hands, and asking Jesus to save their souls. One of the speakers was a woman that was a friend of the well-known Jimi Hendrix. She told us how she used to be a prostitute and drug addict. How she spent her life using drugs with Jimi Hendrix, his wife, and many other rock & roll stars. She told us of how great it was to know such famous people, but she said Jesus had changed her life. Jesus saved her soul. It was Jesus that kept her clean and sober for the last 25 years. They told us that no matter who you are, famous, rich, poor, white, black, male, or female, that sin and the devil have no preference. We must realize that Jesus also has no preference. He loves us all and He is waiting for you to call on His name. Thank you, Bill Glass for a wonderful and uplifting weekend.

NOT AS GLAMOROUS,
BUT JUST AS IMPORTANT

The mother of James and John asked Jesus to give her sons special positions in His Kingdom of Heaven. We, as parents naturally want to see our children promoted and honored, but this desire is dangerous if it causes them to lose sight of God's specific will for our children. God may have different work for them. They failed to understand the suffering that they would face for living in the Kingdom. Their work would not be quite as glamorous, but just as important. Life is not about rewards, but salvation. James was put to death for his faith and John was exiled. The reward came when James and John maintained their commitment to Jesus in spite of their trials. We, as

Christians tend to glamorize positions in the church and even in society. But, it's not about the position, but how we use ourselves in the position for God's Glory, not ours. As I sit in prison and look around, I see nothing glamorous. We all wear the same clothes, shoes and even eat the same exact foods. There is nothing glamorous here at all. But my purpose here is important. My purpose is to heal myself from within and to reach out to other hurting women. It may not be a position that you would ever desire, but its God's will today, not mine. My life may not be glamorous, but it is definitely important.

NOT STRONG, BUT PREPARED

Proverbs 30:25. The ants are a people not strong yet they prepare their meat in the summer. They may be weak physically, but mentally they know how to survive. Preparing in the summer for a hard winter, stocking up, carrying their meals on their backs to survive. To make it yet, another year. To keep their families alive. Marching in a line, inch by inch, mile to mile, for survival. Ants aren't known as the smartest insects alive, but to me they are. They are prepared for the future. Not even knowing what their future holds day to day. Christians are blessed to know what their future holds for them. But, are we prepared spiritually and mentally? Have we prayed up and read His word? Have we spread the gospel to anyone today? Are you prepared for the future? Ask Jesus into your hearts today. Prepare for your eternal future with Jesus. Some of us are not as strong physically as others, but spiritually we can be. We need to be prepared for what our future holds. We can be strong if we work at it. We can be prepared if we work hard enough. Allow yourself to prepare your meat in the summer and to be prepared for the long winter storms.

OH LORD, MY ROCK

Fear is one of the darkest shadows that envelopes us and ultimately imprisons us within ourselves. We all have become prisoners to our own fears at some point in our lives. Our biggest fear is to face our fears head on. We let ourselves fall right back into all of the fears, when all that we needed to do was stand on the rock. David's greatest desire was to live in God's presence each day of his life. He was ready and prepared to handle any test. He awoke on the rock and went to sleep on the rock. You never saw him leaning on the rock, because he was always standing. Standing for Jesus. Many of us have had sad experiences in our lives that have left us feeling forsaken by others. Drugs, alcohol, broken homes, and even the loss of a child---the pain of these experiences linger up into adulthood causing us to fall out of His presence. God can take the place of the voids in our past. The voids that we took with us for many years. He can heal the hurt. He can direct our way and direct us to others that can fill the void of a parent. They can take over the role as a father and a mother. God's love is sufficient for all of us. God is our rock. We just have to take that one step upon the rock. We must be willing to make that move, to take one step up and not one step back. Let God be your Rock. He will never leave you nor forsake you.

ONE TREE IN THE MIDST
OF THE FOREST

As you're walking through the forest searching for that one special tree, it's hard to find it because they all seem to look alike. Even though they have different purposes, a lot of them bear fruit to feed the world while others give you wood to keep you warm when it's cold. Some are used by children to climb on a warm sunny day, while others are used to carve love notes to that one special person in your life. But that one tree that you're searching for seems so hard to find. You search for days, checking each tree to see if it's the one. You pull apples from one tree and peaches from another. It tastes good but it's not the tree that you are looking for. You climb to the top of another to check out the view, and you cut down the next one to keep you warm on that cold winter day. But, none of them are the one that you are looking for. Then finally you see it, The Tree of Life, blooming from top to bottom. The vine is growing out so long that it wraps around every branch. It's got everything you need and everything that you want. It bears fruit, it keeps you warm, and it keeps the rain off of you and it even gives you shelter. But most of all it supplies every breath that you take. It gives you the air that you breathe. It's the one and lonely tree, the tree of life. He is the vine and we are the branches.

ONLY EXISTING IN THIS
PLACE CALLED PRISON

For twenty years she has only existed in this placed called prison. Fourteen of those she spent in "The Hole." No one to talk to, no one to listen to, for she has never called on the name of Jesus. She only exists here as a prisoner, an inmate, a number. Never facing her fears, her pain or even her past. No remorse for her crime, only anger toward the one she victimized. What does it mean to only exist here? It means a life of crime behind these prison walls. To walk alone, with no family or friends to support or guide her. It means to live a life without true hope in this prison, without Jesus. But today a seed was planted. A seed that may never grow, but will always remain planted deep within her heart. She was shown Christian love for the first time in twenty years. I asked a friend of mine, Jamie Bakenhaster, to visit Tracey here at prison. This was her first and only visit in twenty years. Jamie may never know what that visit meant, not only to her, but to the prison guards who witnessed Tracey's first visitor. Tracey did not get saved, but a seed was planted in her heart and in the hearts of those who watched Tracey walk into the visiting hall for the very first time. Thank you Jamie for your unending love of the Lord and the hurting souls around you.

ORANGE, GREEN, PINK, OR BLUE, THERE'S ONLY ONE DIFFERENCE AND THAT'S THE COLOR THAT YOU WEAR

She walks down the sidewalk, handcuffed and escorted by two armed guards. She is to remain ten feet away from all other inmates. She walks in her orange shirt and beige pants, and the only difference between her and me is the color of her shirt. She is an inmate just as I am. She is a woman with a past, just as I have. She is a woman with fears and pain, just as I have. She has the same red blood flowing through her veins, just as I do. She may have committed an awful crime, but she too is worthy to be loved. She too is worthy of God's forgiveness. She may never be forgiven by those she harmed, but if she asks, God will forgive her. She may never have the opportunity to be free in the outside world or to walk out of those gates without shekels or handcuffs, but God can free her of her sins. She does have a chance to be free in her heart, mind, body and soul. God can free her of her past, her sins and her fears. I don't know if this woman in the orange shirt (a death row inmate) is a Christian or not, but I do know that God loves her the same as He loves you and me.

OUT OF THE HOG PEN AND INTO THE PALACE

How could anyone think of jail as a palace? I could! Jail has been my palace for the last 15 days. God has brought me from pain pill addiction, heartache, lies, and much more to a life of blessings that are so undeserved. While in jail, God brought my family together to be so strong. We have all learned the real and true meaning of family. I not only have my husband and 3 girls, I now have an extended family. My family now consists of drug addicts, prostitutes, thieves and many more. God allowed me to be put in the Scioto County Jail and within 15 days I've been blessed to pray through for salvation with five women. I have been able to share the good news of the Gospel with women who might not be alive long enough to hear it. Can you be in a place that looks like a hog pen, but still be in a palace? Yes, you can! Your palace can be anywhere as long as you have God in your heart and you are willing to accept Him and share His good news.

December 8th, 2004

OVER THE EDGE

What makes a fifteen year old girl slip over the edge, enter a dark moment of the soul, or think that violence will take care of all of her problems?   To take the life of both of her parents, and now, never to see freedom again.   As a child, she spent her days away from home as much as possible, growing up outside like some wild weed.   Creating a world of her own, happily away from the noise and chaos that she found inside.   She didn't know that when she woke up every morning if she would meet a smiling, loving mother or the manipulative, overwhelmed, alcoholic mother consumed with life's pressures.   She could hear her father yelling at her mom, then threatening to kill her and the children.   She suffered privately, alone in her room. Crying in her pillows, late at night, alone and afraid.   As she got older she found the only thing that could take the pain away, drugs.   Now, at age 15 her life has become consumed with drugs and alcohol like her mother.   She didn't realize how living in a home filled with alcoholism and abuse would sow the deep seeds of guilt, disgrace, loneliness and insecurity that helped shape her into a murderer.   Today this child sits in prison serving a 25 year to life sentence.   The pain still remains and the shame and the guilt are still overwhelming.   So, what makes a 15 year old girl slip over the edge, into a dark moment of the soul, or think that violence will take care of her problems?   Sin! Sin can change a beautiful child into a convicted murderer, and sin can take your life too.

OVERCOME WITH JOY

What does it mean to overcome? Even better, to be overcome with joy? How can you be overcome with joy sitting behind prison walls? Well, let me tell you how. To overcome is to triumph over the obstacle or obstacles that have held you down. To overcome is to move on, to grow, to achieve whatever it is in life that you've desired. Today I am an 'overcomer.' Prison has opened my eyes to many things about myself. Prison has shown me a love for others that I never had before. It has given me a peace within myself that I've never had before. Today I am overcome with joy that I was blessed to be behind these walls. Don't get me wrong, it is the most difficult thing I've ever had to do in my life, but I will overcome. I have been able to overcome so much from my past that held me hostage for so long. I have been able to feel free for the first time in my life because of this trial. I know that today I can and will overcome any and all obstacles that are placed before me because today I have the joy of the Lord in my heart. Today I see with my heart and no longer with my eyes. Today I am overcome with the joy of the Lord.

PENNIES FOR A PRICE

She was just a five year old little girl. She had two sisters and one brother. For many years she was sexually abused. Come in here, he would say. "I'll give you pennies, so you can go to the store and buy a candy bar". "Candy" she thought, I love candy. So one day she went, but only for a price. The price she paid cost much more than pennies. The price was her self-esteem, self-worth and dignity. She didn't realize this until she was much older. Pennies for candy was a big price to pay. Her brother sexually abused her and her sisters for many years. But she loved him, and at the same time she hated him for what he had done. It was easy to forget about it with all the drugs. She was numb then. She didn't have to face her fears anymore with the drugs. But the price was too high for her. The thought of pennies made her sick. It wasn't actually the pennies, but the price she paid to get them. Just before she was sentenced to the Ohio Reformatory for Women, her brother committed suicide. No funeral, no viewing and no memorial service. Today she lives as a prisoner at the Ohio Reformatory for Women and as a prisoner for pennies. She is still unable to get rid of the pain of the past. A pain that has cost her a high price in her life today.

PLEASE ACCEPT ME

I am I.
Do not change me,
Condemn me,
Nor put me down.
Accept me for what I am.
No, you need not agree with me.
But accept me.
For I am total in being.
I have my faults.
I have my guilt.
But this is who I am.
Perfect I will never be.
Allow me to be uninhibited.
Do not pressure me into feeling,
What I do not feel.
Accept me, when I am flying high,

As I have accepted you when
You were flying high.
Do not put me down . . . nor make
me feel unhappy about me.
I am I,
and I like being what I am.
ME!

PLEASE GOD,
I WANNA GO HOME

On December 9th, 2004, an 18 year old girl had awakened
after 3 days in a crack coma. A crack coma is a deep sleep
that occurs after being up for weeks to months at a time
high on crack. On the third day she awoke and began to
cry. She had just realized where she was in jail. For those
three days we would wake her up for her 3 meals a day and
back to sleep she would go. But, this day was different.
Right after she woke up she began to tell us a little bit about
herself. She started out by telling us about how she got her
tricks. First she said, I would strut myself down Waller
street. After a few minutes a car would pull up beside me
and the man would say, "Hey baby how are you doing?"
She answered, "I'm doing just fine, how about you?" Then
he would ask her, "Would you like a ride?" She thought
to herself well not really, but she murmured her reply, "Yes
that would be great." She got into the car and they took off.
As he began to drive he asked, " So, what do you want?"
There was silence. As she began to finish her story tears ran
down her face. She said to me, "I'll tell you what I want. I
want to go home. I want to be a little girl again and I want
my mom to hold me just like when I was a little girl." I
picked her up in my arms and held her while rocking back

and forth. I kissed her on the forehead and caressed her hair like a mother would do with her own child. A few moments later she called and spoke to her daddy for the first time since she left home. Her daddy told her that he wanted her to come home. She looked at me and said, "Angie, my daddy misses me and he wants me to come home. They really do love me."

The Prodigal Son,

Amy 18 yrs old

PRAY BLESSINGS
ON YOUR ENEMIES

I can remember clearly the day that I was sentenced to prison. As I walked into the courtroom, the daughter of my victim was glaring at me and my family. At first, I didn't even know who she was, until they were called up by the prosecutor to give their testimony of their feelings on my crime. The first daughter stepped up and shoved a picture of her mother into my face. She looked at me and called me a parasite and then read the definition of it. Then she said that what I did to her mother was so horrible that she hoped one day that one of my children would get kidnapped off the school grounds, so I could feel the same pain. She proceeded to look at my children and say, "I hope that your children suffer like my mother had to while you spend your two years in prison." My children began to cry hysterically. After the hearing my oldest daughter Kayla walked up to her and said, "I'm sorry for all that has happened, but my mother is a drug addict." She looked at my daughter and said, "Shut-up little girl and keep playing your violin because your not getting any sympathy from me." My girls were crushed, Barry was crushed and I was crushed. I couldn't even speak. I stood to my feet and told them how truly sorry I was and I asked for their forgiveness. After the hearing many things fogged my mind. Anger, fear, and even hatred for what they had said to my children. But today, I've learned that I have to forgive them and I have to pray blessings down upon them. I pray that one day they will find peace in their hearts. I pray that one day they will find Jesus as their Savior. Today, I no longer sit here in anger and hatred, but I sit in this prison with peace and love, and I will continue to pray blessings upon these women.

PRECIOUS FATHER

O Precious Father, give me time-time to meditate on you
Grant me Godly wisdom, when deciding what to do.
Bless me with serenity, when I seek your perfect way.
And diligence to walk the path, that I should never stray.
Keep my heart and eyes affixed, to the life you proclaim;
Help me accept your chastisement when I'm the one to blame.
Lord, through your Holy Spirit, keep me in your fold,
And when I need to face the world, the strength that I'll behold.
Help me sow the seeds of faith-as others weed and hoe,
And anoint my steps with righteousness wherever I may go.
Remember me when things go wrong-that I'm a stranger in this land;
Please keep the fire lit for me, and don't let go of my hand.

190

PRISON LIFE

Waiting on letters when you're doing time and your family won't send a dime.
It's waiting on visits that never take place, from friends or loved ones who forget your face.
It's hearing them lie and say they are trying, making you promises, but you know they are lying.
It's making plans with someone you thought you knew, but their plans suddenly change and they don't include you.
It's hearing them say how much they care, but in your time of need, they are never there.
It's hearing their promise and it goes straight to your head, but when push comes to shove they leave you for dead.
Its feeling love, honor and pride; pain, emotions and hurting inside.
It's expressing yourself to your loved ones and friends, but they can't feel your pain because you're in the pen.
It's all messed up, just doing time, but that's prison life, out of sight, out of mind.

PRISON TEARS

Behind these walls there is a different world. Prison is a cold and uncaring place. Only those of us that have been in prison know what it's like to try to survive. We have to hide our pain by wearing a mask; a mask that tells everyone else that we're okay. We don't show tears behind these walls for fear of someone taking advantage of us. Tears that flow behind these walls are a sign of weakness. We must try to live as we did when prison wasn't a part of our lives. We talk about 'what ifs' and 'what about that's.' We have to focus on the good times before prison, otherwise the tears will begin to flow and prison tears are hard to stop once they get started. We must show strength to survive in prison, and tears in prison show our weakness. We must look to the future. Life outside these prison walls. Life with our family and times when we can let our tears flow without getting ridiculed! Tears of joy when they open that gate and set us free. Free to let the tears flow, for we'll never have to hold them back again. Never have to fear tears of joy, sadness or happiness. Some of us have prison tears on the outside of these walls. We are unable to share tears when we want to for fear of showing our weakness. But one of the best days I have had was when I saw my husband cry tears of joy for the first time. It wasn't weakness to me; it was strength. He showed me that he wasn't afraid to cry. He was strong. He didn't have prison tears, he had powerful tears.

PRISON WILL DESTROY YOU IF YOU ALLOW IT

Prison has been the most degrading experience that I have ever faced. At times it seems that degradation is the main purpose of this prison. Strip searches, dress codes, serial numbers, keys, buzzers, horns, bells, no privacy and rules that are so many and too long for anyone to remember. Rules that are used to humiliate and tear you down so low, mentally, physically, emotionally, and even spiritually.

Prison is a negative environment. Prison has some of the most negative people with negative thoughts in this world. Prison has defeated women who are broken in mind and spirit. They have failed in life because they feel that there is no turning back. But, we are not the losers that you think we are. We must believe in ourselves when no one else believes in us. We must see ourselves as God sees us. We must see ourselves as worthy, because our thoughts are powerful. They can create and give us life or they can destroy and cause death. So, believe in yourself as God believes in you and you can overcome this place called prison.

PULLING APART THE COBWEBS

As I lay in bed at night and l look up through the bars, I try to see out the windows at the top of the bars. As I stare up into the ceiling, I have to move my head back and forth just to see around all of the cob webs. I know that the cob webs had to have been there a long time because they're all broken apart and just hanging there. I'm sure that the spiders that made the webs have moved on by now, seeing that they've left behind their broken homes. I think many of us can relate to having cob webs in our lives. When looking back at the cobwebs of our past, we try pulling them apart one by one. We try to pull them off but they are sticky and too hard to get off. Just like some of our pasts, their hard to get rid of. They're hard to forget and hard to pull apart. But to move on with our futures we must be able to see the future clearly. We can't look through cob webs the rest of our lives. The way to make a clear future is to forgive our past. I am so grateful that six women in this jail cell have asked for forgiveness of their past sins and are now able to see through the bars clearly. There are no more cob webs blocking their view.

QUIETING THE DEMONS

Why did I use drugs? To quiet the demons that held me captive. The demons that hid in my past to try and destroy my future. The demons that talked to me each and every day telling me that I was unworthy. Telling me that I deserved what I got. Telling me that I was a failure. These demons haunted me day in and day out. I had to shut them down. I had to quiet them. The drugs took care of that. The drugs quieted them in my mind, but not in my heart. They were temporarily quiet, temporarily numb. These demons haunt you like a bad nightmare. You try to pinpoint one, and another comes at you. They speak to your thoughts, your mind, your heart and your soul. But, as the drugs began to kick in, the demons began to quiet down. I allowed these demons to take control of me. I allowed my addiction to control my every thought. The demons have quieted today, only through the Lord. He has given me counselors and sisters here in prison to talk about my fears, my pain and my past. The demons try to come back, but Jesus has put His words in my mouth to quiet them. He has put a new presence in my heart, and a new love in my soul. You too can quiet the demons, but you must try Jesus first.

RECOVERY IS LIKE WALKING UP AN ESCALATOR GOING DOWN

Recovery from addiction is like walking up an escalator going down. There is no time to stand still, because if you do, it takes you right back down to where you started from, the bottom. Recovery is constantly moving, moving through a process that eventually leads you to freedom, the top. We must remind ourselves daily that we are suffering from an addiction. If you fail to take the appropriate recovery steps, then it could lead you to a place you never intended to relapse. Recovery is just like salvation. It's a process. Yes, the moment you ask Jesus into your heart, you are saved. But, being a Christian isn't easy. Like recovery, it's impossible to stand still because the devil is always at the bottom, ready and waiting for the escalator to stop. Relapse is like backsliding. It comes on like a thief in the night. You never meant for it to happen. It was a process, a process that can take you up the escalator of life, or back to the bottom sin. But to stay clean and sober you must have an active recovery program. The same goes for being a Christian. You must stay active; reading your Bible, praying, going to church and witnessing. The moment you stop, the escalator takes you right back down and you're in relapse mode once again.

RELAPSING WITHOUT EVER TAKING A DRUG

Forty-seven years old, married with two teenage daughters and seven years clean. She had a firm conviction the she would never use again, even if it killed her. She was a hard worker, working at her job for 15 years. She received a shift change that caused her to give up the extra jobs that she had. The financial problems were causing her to lose sleep and she began to notice that the little things in life were really beginning to bother her. But, she remained clean. She was going to be okay. She would say, "I'll just adjust to the changes and everything will be all right." Before long, she began skipping her NA/AA meetings because they were too hard for her to get to because of her job. She felt like her husband was picking fights with her on purpose, just to irritate her. She began to withdraw from everyone. She didn't know how much longer she could take it. She seldom ate with the family and began snacking rather than having meals. She began calling in sick, making bad financial decisions, and her husband was to the point of threatening divorce; but she stayed clean, she didn't use, even if it killed her. Staying committed to not using, she began to plan her suicide. "If I make it look like the car ran off of the road, then maybe everyone will believe it." She sought treatment for her relapse even though she had never picked up a drug. Always remember, you don't have to pick up to relapse.

REMEMBER THE WALK

I can remember many places that I have walked. I've walked through the park on a bright, sunny day with my daughters. I've walked the beach hand in hand with my husband. I've walked the mall on a Christmas Eve shopping for special things on my list. I've walked through a dream that soon became a nightmare. I've walked through fears that I've never been able to recover from. But this walk is different. This walk that I'm walking now is behind a razor wired fence. A walk behind bars; a walk that I will never forget. This walk I began almost a year ago. This walk began with addiction and ended with prison. This walk began in fear, anger and pain and will end as a blessing in disguise. This walk saved my life. This is a walk that Jesus has carried me through. I will always remember this walk, just like the others, because this walk has changed my life. Many of my walks before, I was going too fast to see the blessings around me. Too fast to ever notice the beauty of God's work. I even walked too fast sometimes to listen to my children's wants. I could hear them when I walked, but I was too busy to listen. But now, this walk has opened my eyes. This walk is a slow walk. A walk on a path that Jesus sent me on, in a prison full of hurting women. This walk has healed my fears and has opened the doors to bigger and better things. This walk has given me blessings. This walk has shown me that I am worthy, I am loved and I am someone. This is a walk that I'll always remember.

RESENTMENTS

I've met many women here in prison, and I'd say 99% of them have resentments toward someone else: their co-defendant, their mother, father, siblings, even their spouses. But I realized one thing as they began to speak, they have become a slave to this person. The moment you start to resent a person you become their slave. They control your dreams, they absorb your digestion, rob you of your peace of mind and good will, and they take away the pleasure in your life. When you resent a person it ruins your spirituality and nullifies your prayers. You take them along to the park, out to dinner and even on vacation with you. They destroy your mental freedom and hound you wherever you go. There is no way to escape the person you resent. They go with you to the doctor and require you to take medication for stomach problems, fatigue and headaches. That person even steals your dreams while you sleep. So give in and let it go. If you don't, you'll remain a slave to your own resentments. Be free today and let it go.

ROBBED OF A PRICELESS GIFT

We had a topic group today on "budgeting your money." I couldn't understand why we needed to budget in prison, because most women here don't have anything anyway. Once the lecturer began to speak I realized what her reasoning was. She asked us the question, "How much money do you think you spent buying your drugs during your addiction?" I first thought, well, not very much because I only got it from a doctor, I didn't buy off the streets. Then I remembered all of the emergency room visits, the doctor visits and the possibly unneeded surgeries. When I totaled it up it ranged over $100,000.00. I couldn't believe it. Then she asked us what we would do with that money today? Then it hit me. I would buy my girls an ice cream cone and go to the park. I would take them to a ball game and watch the smiles on their faces, because all of that is priceless to me today. I did spend an overwhelming amount of money that I know I'll never get back. But today I realize that I robbed my children of not only monetary things but I robbed them of the most priceless gift they could ever want, their mommy.

SADDENED BY MY SURROUNDINGS

Like Habakkuk, I am saddened by the corruption that is all around me. Many times I have wondered, "Why is there so much evil in this world?" "Why do they seem to be winning?" Sometimes the other prisoners here look at you differently the more you get into trouble; but I just can't do it. I just can't live for this evil world anymore. I feel like I am on my own many times, in a wicked world right here in this prison. Then I remember that I must rejoice in my salvation. The Lord is my strength. I cannot find strength in people any longer, I must seek the Lord for my strength. I must learn how to play this game called life and have Jesus as my only coach. I am searching daily for teammates. Teammates who have won their game and prisoners who haven't found the right team. I must have confidence that my Jesus will protect me. I am in a room with 200 women; at least one quarter are lifers. They are here for twenty-five years or more for brutal crimes. Some have changed and asked for forgiveness, but others are still playing the game. Thieving, cheating and conniving to get anything and everything they can from this prison and from me. They think their only hope is vanity, not salvation. Their only dreams are to get out and continue living the same wicked life just as before. Some have become cynical and hardened. They reject the only thing in life that can help and change them, Jesus. I see a dying world around me and it breaks my heart. Many times I feel that they can never change, but deep down I know that Jesus is still in control. Now, I must listen closely for God's answers to my many questions. I must now rejoice in the mighty work that He is doing in my life, and I must wait patiently for Jesus to guide me with His wisdom to help free these women of their sin and corruption. I shall not cry for myself any longer, but cry for those who refuse life, eternal life.

SAFE HAVEN FOR RECKONING SINNERS

I know that we are all sinners who have come short of the Glory of God, but some of us have led lives that caused us guilt, pain and shame from our sinful pasts. It caused our lives to be different from other people's lives. We have to go to rehab, jail and even prison just to recover from our deepest sins. My recovery started in jail. I knew that over the last six months or so that this addiction had to end, but it had became so overpowering that I didn't even know how to start the process to end it. Around 5 months ago we started a program for men called "Safe Haven." It is a recovery program for drug addicts and alcoholics. These men were some of the hardest men I've ever met. The stories of their pasts were stories you would read in a book or see in the Columbus paper. But these were still men and God loved them and so do I. God showed me just enough to get through my first 5 days in jail. God had it all planned out. He showed me what can happen when you're in deep sin. But then he showed what could happen when God sends you to the "Safe Haven for Reckoning Sinners" and He can make you clean just by His loving care.

SAMSON, THE PHILISTINES ARE UPON YOU

Have any of you had the opportunity to meet a real life Delilah? I have. I've met hundreds here at the pen. "How can you say you love me if you won't confide in me?" These were the words of Delilah as she planned to betray her Samson for money. She could weaken him by passion.

But Samson would overcome before his death. These women have done so many things in their lives for money. They have taken food from their own children's mouths to get what they wanted. But in the end, their walls came tumbling down. They ended it all just for a few dollars or an 8 ball to smoke. They had the Philistines on them quick. It all backfired. They lost it all for a long trip to the pen. Don't allow vanity to overcome your life. Don't allow the Delilah in you to take over. You must live for Jesus. Let Him take control, not you. You can overcome just like Samson. Even the Delilah's here at the pen can be forgiven, but they must want it more than they want for the desires of this world.

SEEING WITH HIS HEART

Matthew 9:36   "But when He saw the multitudes, He was moved with compassion on them, because they fainted, and were scattered abroad, as sheep, having no shepherd."

A friend of mine in prison recently lost her 6 month old daughter to SIDS. My friend, a convicted felon, was deeply grieving. I could not look at her as just another number. I saw her only with my heart. A heart of compassion. I had to see her as Jesus sees you and me as shepherdless sheep lying prostrate from exhaustion. Jesus sees with His heart into ours. We have to change the way we look at people. Man sees only the appearance, but God sees into our hearts. Jesus can help us see with His heart by first showing us the spiritual condition of those we see. This will, in turn, change the way that we look at them. As with my friend that was grieving over the loss of her child, I could see her with a more compassionate heart. Likewise, when we see the lost, enslaved in bondage, and blind spiritually, we will see them differently and our hearts will be moved with pity as Jesus was. When we finally begin to witness to all people, we no longer see them as faceless numbers, or anonymous, but as broken hearts that need to be mended by the love of God. So open your heart, so you can see more clearly.

SENT TO BE A
WORLD CHANGER

Who is a world changer? Are you a world changer or are you changed by the world? Today, I am and will be a world changer. World changers use the strategy of overcoming evil with good. They have the humility to admit when they are wrong, and change it. They act out of faith tempered by the test of this life. They see potential in every human being. They speak out for those who do not have a voice. They may get knocked down, but they refuse to stay down. They are persistent in their pursuit to those things they know are of God's desire. They have humble hearts and they use whatever means available to help others in need. They often turn their personal suffering into a search for those things that bring benefit to other sufferers. They help others who cannot help themselves. They are motivated from within and refuse to be discouraged by criticism or external factors they seek to serve more than to be served. They seek to save lives, even if their efforts mean putting their own life at risk. They look to God for the help they need. They change things wherever they may be, whether in church, home or in prison. For today, I am a world changer sent by God to help change your life. You too can change the world. You too can use what God has given you; a unique gift to be an inspiration and a disciple for Jesus Christ. Together we can change the world. Together we can make a difference.

SHARED PAIN IS HALF THE PAIN

Many of us go through life hanging on to the past, and I am one of them. When I was 16 years old I went to a party with a friend and got drunk. Within a few hours I was so sick from drinking too much that I decided to lay down. I went up to her bedroom to lay down to see if I would feel better. Within minutes I was passed out. What I awoke to was horrifying. A teenage boy in the room with me, the door locked, and I was being raped. I couldn't move. I couldn't lift my arms to defend myself. I couldn't open my mouth to scream. How could I have been so stupid? How could I let this happen? For 20 years I kept this secret pain hidden deep within my heart. Overwhelming feelings of guilt of the rape brought me into a deep depression. I just couldn't tell anyone. Over the years I became so fearful of men, even my own husband. I was afraid of the dark, afraid to be alone, and even afraid to go to sleep sometimes because of the dreams that would awaken me. But six months ago, I shared my pain. I emptied my heart to another woman here at prison. The overwhelming feelings of guilt started to finally subside. The anger of the past finally turned into freedom from my past. I finally shared my pain with someone else and now, today I live with only half the pain because my sister here at prison carries the other half for me.

SHUNNED BY THE OUTSIDE

I met a woman in the Tapestry Program today who was sentenced to 25 years to life in prison for murdering her husband. When she first got here to Marysville she received cards and letters and was able to talk to her children and other family members on the phone. She has been in prison now for 12 years and in the Tapestry Program for a year now. As we began to talk she told us about what life in prison was like 10 years ago. She had so much love and support. But today, 10 years later she sits in this prison alone. No mail in the last 8 years. The phone numbers of family members have either changed or been blocked and most of all, no visits from home. She has been disassociated completely from the outside. She says that she feels like she's been forgotten. She's alone and afraid, but 2 years ago, she gave her heart to the Lord. She now puts all of her fears and pain in the arms of Jesus. He now carries her burdens of home. I asked her how she makes it here in prison without any communication from home: no letters, no visits, no love from her family. She turned to me and said, "Jesus. Jesus is the only reason that I am still alive here in this prison. Today I may not have the love and support from family and friends, but today I have Jesus. Jesus is my daughter that I no longer get to see, Jesus is my mother that I no longer hear from, Jesus is my father who no longer wants me in his life. Jesus is my everything, and most of all, my reason for living."

SIGN OF LOVE

I met a young twenty-two year old girl the other day who is doing a two and a half year sentence for burglary. She had proceeded to tell me about the night she was arrested and how when she arrived in jail, the women wouldn't even speak to her (because of her crime). She has been an addict now for 5 years and she came from a family where her father promoted her addiction. He also is an alcoholic and drug addict. He taught his daughter that the only way to have fun was to be high. So, that's what she did. But, as the years went by she fell so deep into her addiction that lead to her crime. She and her co-defendant began robbing churches. They stole stereo systems, sound equipment, and literally anything else that they could find to pawn to support their habit. But the last church they went to was the church that her son had just performed in the Easter program. She went inside the church and walked up on the stage. She immediately felt sick. All she could see was her son up on stage saying his little piece for the program. She began to cry hysterically. So her co-defendant decided they should leave. As she left the church and they began to pull away, she saw a sign that was hanging under the church sign. It said, "Today is Sunday, but Monday brings a new day." Even though she was so high off of all the drugs, she knew that she had to change and that Monday would be a new day for her. Monday would be the beginning of the rest of her life. On Monday she was arrested and sent to prison, to start preparing for her new future. Yesterday she opened her Bible for the very first time in her life and she started reading Mark 1:14-15. "Now after that John was put in prison. Jesus came into Galilee, preaching the gospel of the Kingdom of God. And saying, the time is fulfilled and the Kingdom of God is at hand; repent ye, and believe the gospel." God has blessed her with a second chance at life, and I know that one day very soon, she'll give her heart and soul to the Lord.

SILENCE OF THE LAMBS

I sit here in silence, but am able to speak. I sit here in wonder, but am able to think. I choose to be silent, only to hear Him speak. I choose to be silent, to hear Him think. God has silenced my past, not my mouth. He has silenced my fears and my painful heart. God has silenced his little lamb, but only to help me grow. He has silenced this prison to begin my work. Jesus' plan that He's trying to fulfill. But I had to be silenced, to hear His words. I had to be silenced to hear His plan and fill my heart with scripture and song; to share with women about His word and to give them "life" behind these bars. I had to be silenced to spiritually grow. I had to be quiet to learn what was right. I speak for my Jesus now, to women in pain: to share with them that there is hope for them to attain. I live for my Jesus behind these bars, to reign in His kingdom above the stars. I am silenced today, but only by choice. To give what He gave, that lives in my heart. Sometimes we must be silenced to hear His voice. So listen carefully; it is your choice.

SLIPPING THROUGH THE CRACK

Slipping and falling, then slipping and falling again and again. That's all that I've seen since I've been here. These

206

girls come in because of messing up on probation. They had to be on probation for some reason, and that reason seems to be crack. That's crack cocaine. They were prostituting for it, stealing, lying, cheating, and more, much more. Then once they're in jail and they do their time, they're sent right back out on the streets. They're sent right back out to slip and fall and slip and fall again. Then eventually because of crack, they slip through the cracks and do it all over again. They're forgotten because they're prostitutes, crack users, and drug dealers. But before that they were moms, aunts, grandmas, our children, and your children and God's children. They're just people that made bad choices. Now they are paying for it. They're labeled now. People say, "Don't talk to them and don't associate with them." But, why? Do you think they're contagious? Do you think you will catch what they have? Do you think they'll let you fall through the cracks just because you made a bad choice? Think about it, sin is sin, isn't it?

SNOW ON A BRIGHT SUNNY DAY

I've been on "The Farm" now for over 5 months, and many times I've seen it snow on a bright sunny day. I sit inside my dorm and watch the "snow" fly all around the farm. But this "snow" is a little different. This snow is white, puffy clouds of cotton that flow through the air as they blow off the trees. I can remember many times during my life that the snow fell on me on a bright sunny day. My day would be going so well, and then "boom" the snow would fall and my day would turn from happiness to gloom. The clouds came and covered up the beautiful rays of sun that shone so brightly on my day. But today when the snow begins to fall on my day, I remember the puffs of cotton on the trees and how beautiful they were when they fell like clouds flowing through the air. I can now see through the dark clouds and look directly at the "Son," for today every day is a beautiful day in Marysville, because no matter where I am the "Son" shines brightly over me. Even though the snow may fall, and the dark clouds may cover my day, I just put my hand out and catch the beauty of the cotton puffs as they fly through the air, so beautiful and so free.

SO HELP ME GOD,
I REALLY WANT TO CHANGE

I was given the opportunity to be a registered nurse for 10 years. God allowed me to work for a Christian Pediatrician for 8 of those 10 years. While working there I took care of a little girl named Natasha. At 8 months of age she was struck with a fatal disease that caused destruction to the grey matter in her brain. Ta Ta, which is her nickname, became seriously ill over the next few years. She is now restricted to a wheelchair, unable to walk. Over the years her mother worked so hard with her to get her to speak. Natasha is now 7 years old and she is able to say four or five words. Her favorite word is Mum, Mum. It's also her mother's favorite as well. After knowing this strong Christian family for all those years, I was placed in the Scioto County Jail and the first person I saw was Natasha's mother. As my heart began to ache for my family, I ached for her family too. Patty, Natasha's mother, became so overwhelmed with Natasha's disease and care over the years that her faith dwindled down to nothing. Patty turned to drugs and alcohol for her pain instead of Jesus. Now, faith is all Patty has left and she's still unable to grasp it. Anger and fear has overtaken her life and her way of coping is, not to cope. Patty had expressed many times that she couldn't feel God anymore behind these bars, but she knows He's there. I prayed hard for Patty just to feel His presence again, one more time to let the tears flow and the anger to be released. During our last jail church service, God opened doors and words were spoken to Patty from God and the tears began to flow once again. Patty said "Oh God, please help me, I really want to change." Patty felt Jesus once more through her tears that day, but still she struggles with her pain and fear. So pray for Patty and her baby, because I know that she really wants to change...

Patty – written 12-12-04

"SO THAT WE MAY BOLDLY SAY, THE LORD IS MY HELPER, AND I WILL NOT FEAR WHAT MAN SHALL DO UNTO ME."

Hebrews 13:6

Do not be afraid. Do not run from fear, run to God in prayer. Fear is normal, but don't let fear paralyze you as for many years it did to me. Fear can keep you from many opportunities. Fear can keep you from utilizing God's power. Fear can immobilize you. But fear evaporates when we trust God. We can overcome fear and turn it into joy. For many years I feared man. I did all that I could to get approval from man. But today I can boldly say, "The Lord is my helper, and I will not fear what man shall do unto me." Why? Because no matter the outcome of what my earthly judge decides, I know today that my Heavenly Judge is in control. By my faith, I have overcome my fears. I have been strengthened by His love, His word and His promise. I will not be in this prison one day longer than necessary. Today, I no longer run from man or from the fear of man. I run to God in prayer. God is my helper today. I have hope. Today I am not afraid to face man's judgment, because today I am not overcome by fear but am overcome by the love of God. I stand firmly on His promise!

SOME ARE PRODUCTS OF THEIR PASTS BUT THEY DON'T HAVE TO BE PRISONERS TO IT

They are manipulated by the memories of their pasts. Guilt-driven, they allow their past to control their future. Just as Cain, we too become disconnected from the feeling of God's presence because of overwhelming guilt. You then just exist on this earth as a restless wanderer. We are not limited by our past. We are not committed to our past, because of the loving forgiveness of our precious Father. Moses, a murderer, was turned into a compassionate leader. Gideon, a coward, was changed into a courageous hero. Paul, a persecutor of Christians, changed into a preacher for Christ. They were not products of their pasts, because Jesus set them free from the bondage of their sins. Your past is your past. Let it go! You can't change it and you're only hurting yourself by hanging on to it. God's well-formed love banished their fear of their pasts. Fear causes us to live a crippled life. We miss opportunities because we're too afraid of change. But God wants change. God has a purpose for our life. He can, and will, give you a hope and future with Him. But we must ask to receive. So, remember we are not products of our pasts, and we don't have to be prisoners to it. So set yourself free; allow God to love you. Reach for the future: eternal life with Him.

SOMEBODY'S WATCHING ME

The young girl looked up at her mother and said, "Mama, how do you live for Jesus"? The mother looked happily into her precious daughter's eyes and said, "Just watch." Years went by and the young girl grew up into a beautiful woman, having two children of her own. The mother grew older in her years, but stayed true to God's word, and lived as an example to her daughter of how to follow Jesus. Yet, the daughter often lived her life in a way that was not pleasing to God. One day the daughter came to visit her mother for what would be the last time. The mother lay there dying, and the daughter leaned over the bed and heard her mother whisper these simple words, "Did you watch"? The daughter thought for a moment, and then realized what her mother was saying, "Just watch." "Follow me, imitate me as if I also imitate Jesus." Is somebody watching you? I have three daughters watching me each and every day. Today I can tell them, Kayla, Tori and Aleah, "Just watch." Do you have somebody watching you?

SOMETIMES MOMMIES
GO AWAY

When I first held you in my arms, I swore I'd hold you every
day,
But there was something I forgot to tell you, sometimes
mommies go away.

I never meant to hurt you and I hope, someday you'll
understand . . .
That any tears I've caused you, was not a part of my plan.

Sometimes bad things happen and it's hard to tell you why.
It always breaks a mother's heart to see her children cry.

Now, I hope you are listening, it's important that you do,
For I want to tell you all about the love I have for you.

A mother's love is special; it's a bond we'll always share.
Look inside your heart, you'll always find me there.

There has not been a single day that I have not thought of
you,
And said a special prayer, for God to see you through.

No I can't change the past, God knows that I wish I could.
For I don't always do the things I know I should.

I guess I'm asking for forgiveness for all the pain I've
caused.
For leaving your little heart and mind feeling so lost.

Now it's almost time to make a brand new start.
I promise never again to break your little hearts.
Time to start a life that's right for me and you.
A life full of love, to show you that it's true.

But with your hand in mine, up the mountains we will

climb,
Saying "I love you" more with each passing day,
And never again will your mommy go away.

SPRITUAL PRIDE

As water flows from a waterfall the stream runs downward.
When water runs from a faucet it flows downward. When
it rains on a hillside the water flows down hill. Such is our
personal influence on others, it flows to surrounding
families, friends and church members. Some of us think
that we must witness to the "important people." Athletes,
movie stars, top businessmen and the influential people in
society. But Christ came to seek and save the lost, not to
seek and save only the wealthy influential people in society.
Christ came to seek and save even the "down-and-out."
Just like Jerusalem, we must be careful to avoid spiritual
pride. I have been to quite a few churches since I've been
saved and some were filled with the spiritual pride. Not
many stand and testify of the times they spent in prison, or
the time they were without food or clothing but they speak
of illnesses or pregnancies, healings when they were sick.
They seem too proud to speak of their twenties when they
were an alcoholic, or when they were raped or abused as a
child. They carry pride with them as a burden, unable to
release it to others because they fear what people might
think. But I am now at a church, "Chapel Hill", that
carries not only their burdens but yours and mine also.
They testify of their shameful pasts only to help others.
They testify of their prison sentence, rape or drug addiction
to let others know that they have made it through their
trials, called life. Sin is a part of life, no matter how big or
how small. So don't be ashamed and carry spiritual pride
around. The only way to help someone just like you is to

let them know that you've been there. God wants to use your past, not to shame you, but to gain you. To gain strength to share with others so they can get rid of their shame, and release their burdens of sin, shame and doubt.

SPRITUAL WARFARE

These past few weeks have been very difficult for me on a spiritual basis. I have been questioned by many women about my faith. "If I was really a good Christian, then why don't I go to church"? Only real women of God go to church. I've been called judgmental, a hypocrite and more. I had to sit back and process what was being said, instead of lashing out like the devil wanted me to do. I had to look at where it was coming from and to realize that faith and peace comes from within. I read a book on a preacher that was sentenced to prison. He went to church there for the first time and decided that it wasn't what God wanted him to do. At first, I couldn't understand how a preacher couldn't attend church when the doors were open. Until I came to prison and did the same exact thing. It just wasn't what God wanted for me. I couldn't sit in a service and hear the word of God from a lesbian. I couldn't even fake it. I was so disturbed when I left the service that I couldn't even think straight. So, I decided to continue worshipping my Jesus from my cell. As the questioning continued, I prayed to God for help. He told me, "Angie, you must do what is right for you." So I did. Before I came to prison I was such a people pleaser. I would have sat back and listened to what they had to say, and then I would do it just because I was so worried about what other people thought of me. What I really needed to worry about was what Jesus wanted for me. So, today as I sit in my cell praying and studying the word of God, I know I did what was right.

I know I've pleased God for obeying Him instead of trying to please others. Don't let others persuade you out of God's will. Stand up, stand fast and stand firm.

STONE COLD

About five months ago we had our very 1st meeting at the Safe Haven Home. The home is a place for men who are recovering from drugs and alcohol addiction. Most of these men have lived hard lives in the short time of being an addict. Most have spent time in the homeless shelters, jail, and even prison. For all of their lives they have only looked at the bad things they've done and not the good. They've been labeled and judged for the bad choices they have made from their addiction. They've had to fight for their lives and fight till death, knowing that they would end up in hell if they were to die.

Since I'm an addict, I know personally how it feels to be judged. I know how it feels to be hit by a stone thrown from a cold heart; to be hit square in the forehead by another Christian. So, for the first meeting I felt it fair to give everyone their own stone, this way they could throw their own stone at us addicts only if they were completely free of sin. If they have no sin in their lives, then I felt it was right for them to cast their stones, and cast them hard. Well to everyone's dismay, I wasn't hit that night. The only thing I saw that night was cold hearts beginning to thaw, and tears beginning to fall down their checks melting the ice frozen from time. After the meeting everyone was told to carry their stone with them at all times, and when they felt judgment rising in their heart, they could reach in their pocket and remember they too are just a sinner saved by grace.

215

STOP REMEMBERING WHAT GOD HAS FORGOTTEN

God created us, but today He's willing and able to recreate you. To be recreated in Christ means that first we were created, then we messed up, and now we're in need of repair. But we must be willing to let go of the past. We made a mess, but with God's help, we'll be able to clean ourselves up, dust ourselves off, and move on to the future. Satan wants us to remain prisoners of our past. But Jesus wants us to be "prisoners of hope." We have to "let go and let God." We all have pasts, but some of us have ones that are more unpleasant. So we live our lives trying to gain the approval from others, when all we really need is God's approval. People don't forget our pasts like Jesus does. So, often times we are misjudged. Know that the day you asked God for forgiveness it was forgotten, as far as the east is from the west. So quit hanging onto something that is no longer there. Let Go, and let God.

STOP! YOU'VE JUST ENTERED MY COMFORT ZONE

How many of you have a comfort zone? Some of our comfort zones have a hundred mile radius, and some of them are inches away. I realized this the day I was shoved by another inmate because I was in her "comfort zone." This is a physical comfort zone, not an emotional one. Don't get me wrong; when I was shoved she definitely entered my physical and emotional comfort zone. Yes, I did think for a second that I wanted to enter into her comfort zone, but I knew that it wouldn't be the right thing to do. Why? Because being in here you have to pray real hard for self control. Some of us have very small emotional comfort zones. I am one of them. Due to a date rape as teenager, my comfort zone is much smaller than most other people. It caused a fear in me that I had never felt before. A fear of men that I held onto for 20 years. I was unable to get my comfort zone opened, until I gave it to Jesus. I had a fear of my husband, not that he would physically or emotionally hurt me, like when I was a teenager, but a fear that was so misunderstood in my mind. Many women have faced rape as a child, teen or even an adult. Because of this they have closed themselves off, unable to even have a comfort zone. But there is one man, a perfect man that I have allowed myself to open my heart up and give it to, Jesus, because he was the only one I thought I could trust. Give all of your fears and pain to Jesus, so he can allow your comfort zone to be opened once again.

"STRETCH FORTH THINE HAND, AND HE STRETCHED IT FORTH AND IT WAS RESTORED WHOLE."
Matthew 12:13

The devil has been fighting me these last few weeks by putting things in my head that just aren't true. So, I got out my Bible and opened it to Matthew 12:13 and I prayed. I prayed with my hand outstretched in front of me. I prayed for Jesus to take hold of this withered, beaten down body, and to restore me whole. As I prayed, I felt Jesus take hold of my hand. I felt his overwhelming love all around me. I felt the warmth of His touch. He restored me today, in many ways. I was ready to give up. I was ready to stop fighting, but He touched me. He said, "Angie, you've come too far to go back now." You're a winner, either way, if I leave this prison or if I stay. After I closed my Bible, the devil began fighting again. I went downstairs to pick up my mail and I had received a letter from a friend of mine. When I opened it up it was a card with a beautiful picture. It was Jesus with His hands outstretched. The words on the front were, "Christ meets us where we are." He met me today in prison. He touched me and made me whole again. He restored my joy, my peace, and my hope. But I had to have faith. I had to put my withered hand that once was used for taking pills and putting them into my beaten down body, into His hand. I had to allow Jesus to restore me. Today, I stretched out my hand and Jesus held it. He restored me whole.

SUFFERING FROM
SPIRITUAL ARROGANCE

I have to say that I envy those Christians that have found and experienced salvation as a child. Living a life of Christianity and knowing the love of God as a child. I relate it to being sheltered from a storm that passes through your town. You can see and smell the rain, but you're covered from it. Living victoriously, and knowing that you are never alone. But most of us in this prison did not have that advantage. But there are those who have lived that life who suffer from spiritual arrogance. They define holiness as what people look like, what they wear and even what they eat. Monitoring and living their life on an outward appearance. Tattoos, earrings, and long hair, they must not be Christians, because of the way they look. I know that when I was saved that I was not given a badge of righteousness to wear. I was given a new heart. We all have sinned and come short of the glory of God, but sometimes we forget. Being here in prison has opened my eyes to many women of different races, ethnicities and earthly backgrounds. But, today I see the inside, their hearts and no longer see the tattoos, hair or outward features. I no longer suffer from "Spiritual Arrogance" because God has humbled me in a way that I never dreamed that He would. I truly have to say that if I had not ended up in this prison, that I might still be out in the world suffering from "Spiritual Arrogance". I pray that if you suffer from "Spiritual Arrogance" that one day soon you can see what really matters to Jesus and that is our hearts. If we continue to focus on the outside of our brothers and sisters then we might as well exclude the majority of these women here in prison from ever walking through the doors of our churches.

SWEEPING THE SUNSHINE

One of our rules here at the Tapestry Program is to not stare at the clock and keep our minds focused on group. We have group meetings, case loads and counseling sessions, and sometimes our minds go adrift. You start looking out the windows, looking at your watch, and daydreaming, and pretty soon you are thinking about home. But if you get caught staring at the clock, they assume that you just want to hurry the group up. They assume that you're trying to wish the time away, so you can go and do something else. So the punishment for this is to "Sweep the Sunshine." You receive a broom and a dustpan and you're sent off to find the sunshine. You have to find one spot where the sun shines through the window and continually sweep it for 15 minutes. I tried to think about the reasoning behind this and I concluded that sweeping the sunshine is a way to see the goodness in that spot. To see the beauty of what's going on around you. Even though you stay in that one spot, the sun continues to shine. The spot may get cleaner, but it never goes away until the sun goes down. We must spend our time searching for the goodness in everything. Searching for the sun to shine on us, to brighten our day. Just this same way we should continually search for the "Son" to shine on our day. So today, take some time out to "Sweep the Sunshine," and let the "Son" shine down on you.

TABITHA'S PRAYER

"Precious Heavenly Father" your daughter Tabitha is coming back to you asking forgiveness for her sins. I need for you Precious Heavenly Father to give me a salvation heart. Precious Heavenly Father I need for you to move this mountain out of my life quick. There are addictions, stealing out of stores and sale your precious body. Lord, help me to find another way to support my family and for myself, to empower me on the inside too. Precious Heavenly Father make me beautiful on the inside and on the outside as well. Precious Holy Spirit help me to stay focused on Jesus instead of myself and what I don't have like, money, support on the inside of jail, coffee, sugar, creamer, food, lotion, hair grease. Precious Heavenly Father help me to say no when I need to and stick to no, and yes when I need to say yes. Precious Heavenly Father you said ask and you shall be saved and confess with your mouth. I'm confessing with my heart and mouth to be saved as well as my mind. I need a new heart. Father you said have faith as small as a mustard seed, that you would move mountains out of my way. Help me through this day so I can do your will. Give me someone that I can tell Jesus about and what you have done for me. Precious Heavenly Father I really need this bad. Help me to hate, hate, hate, hate, and hate crack, crack, crack, crack cocaine more than anything in this world. Precious Heavenly Father I need for you to make a way for me and Gregory to be together when I get out of jail. You know my heart's desire is to marry him. Also change his heart to live right. Pray for his addiction. Gregory take time out for me Tabitha to write me and get block off the phone. Let me know he is alright. Father make it possible for me to get all the things I need and want. Put it on someone's heart to help me. Precious Holy Spirit show me who I can trust, like who I can talk to. I'm dependent on you Precious Holy Spirit to help to pray in the Spirit for what I need.

Amen

(This was written by Tabitha on December 23rd, 2004 after she was saved at Marysville Penitentiary. I believe she was saved by God's Grace. I am so blessed to have been able to help lead her to the Lord. Thank you Jesus for allowing me to see eight souls saved since my incarceration. This is all for your Glory.)

TEARS OF PAIN

I could see their tears of pain as they watched and observed us for the week. In the beginning they had a rough and tough exterior. They've worked as counselors for only about two months now, in different institutions all over Ohio. For one week in Tapestry, we had what's called Immersion Training. Counselors from all over come in to observe how the Tapestry Program works, so they can take what they have learned back with them to their prisons. One man made a comment that he knew all there was to being a counselor. While, another said that she just didn't know if our program was strict enough. But by the end of the week, they all got what they were meant to get, tears of pain. By Friday, they all wept for our pain. They saw something in us women that they never saw before in their prisons, and that was worth fighting for; you see, they never really saw their clients as people. They saw them as prisoners. Because our counselors allowed us to give personal testimonies, it allowed them to see that we were worthy. By the time they left, they shared with us a joy that they never had before, only because they shared with us our pain, through their tears.

THE ABILITY TO FORGIVE

The ability to forgive is one of the greatest expressions of love that you can give to yourself and others. To forgive means to pardon. To overlook an offense and treat your offender as not guilty. People offend us everyday, but the way you act or react to the offense will determine the outcome of your day, and eventually, determine the outcome of your eternity. We are powerless to forgive others without the power of God living within us. When you refuse to forgive, you are allowing Satan to steal the love, peace and joy you have in your heart. Many women sit in this prison alone, no family or friends to love them, due to one word, "un-forgiveness." But you must know that if we choose not to forgive others for their offenses, then God will not and cannot forgive us. Don't let the enemy deceive you into thinking that you are not worthy of being forgiven. The devil can and will torment your life by holding onto your past. Do you have the ability to forgive? The love of God can override anger, hatred, and un-forgiveness. You just have to allow Him to do it.

THE ANOINTED STEP

Several years ago, God called my husband Barry to Pastor a church in Waverly, Ohio. When God called us to that church, we didn't realize that he was going to allow us to meet the most anointed, kind, and loving people in the world. Just a few weeks after pasturing the church, one of the men in the church was called by God to come to our home with several men of the church to anoint the front steps of our home. They prayed that every person that walked over that step would be touched by God in a mighty way. I have never had the privilege to be around such anointed men. They had no problem kneeling down in our front yard in front of our neighbors and our dog Grace, to obey God's will. As we knelt down and prayed, I never dreamed that the next day God would send us a man who had been addicted to drugs for over 30 years. But God had a plan. This man was a good friend of ours that had spent over 10 years in prison due to his drug addiction. He had seen more in his 44 years of life then anyone should have to see in their lifetime. As Mike pulled up to our home and walked across that front step, the tears began to flow like a waterfall. He was sick and tired of being sick and tired. He was ready to do God's will instead of Mike's will. That day Mike was gloriously saved in our home and to this day he is clean, sober, saved and eternally grateful for men who were willing to obey God's word.

Mike was saved July 5th, 2004.

THE BAG OF BURDENS

A friend of mine told me a story that goes something like this. An old man was carrying a bag over his shoulder, when a younger man passed by. He too was carrying a bag, but his bag seemed much larger. So the young man asked the older man if he would like to trade, since the older man's bag was smaller. But the older man, answered by saying, "No son, I think I'll keep my bag, because I'm not sure what's in yours." Well, my bag is full of life's burdens. It has a test I took in Algebra with an "F" on it. It has my baseball glove that broke from my last game, and it has all the pieces to my bicycle from where I wrecked it the other day. The older man smiled at the younger man saying, "My bag may be smaller, but the burdens in it are much heavier." My bag is full of broken dreams and broken promises, deaths, prison and addiction. We never know what's inside the bag of burdens that another person carries. It may look light, or even empty to you, but until you see inside, inside their heart, you'll never know what they are carrying. Some are just heavier than others. Thank you for sharing with me such a beautiful story, and your strong words of wisdom.

THE BATTLE IS MINE,
VICTORY IS HIS

Then David said to the Philistine, "Thou comest to me with a sword, and with a spear and with a shield; but I come to thee in the name of the lord of hosts, the God of the armies of Israel, whom thou hast defied." I came to this prison in the name of the Lord with Bible in hand and the word of God in my heart to fight these philistines with the love of God. Today I had to fight another prisoner, not with my hands but with my heart. I do have to say that if I did not have the love of God on my side then the battle may not have turned out the way that it did. I was hit by horrible words. Words that cut deep like a sword. Words were slung about my Jesus that fell deep into my heart. But I fought back with the word of God. I fought back with the love of God and the word of God, spoken as a sword cutting through the flesh and soul, exposing the very intentions of my heart. Not to destroy or condemn another likened as to the woman at the well, but to expose the word of the Lord, to display His splendor. Today the philistine was defeated by the love of God and victory was His.

THE BIBLE

Within this ample volume lies
The mystery of mysteries.
Happiest they of human race
To whom their God has given grace
To read, to fear, to hope, to pray,
To lift the latch, to force the way;
But better had they ne'er been born
That read to doubt or read to scorn.

Sitting still and wishing
Makes no person great.
The good Lord sends the fishing,
But you must dig the bait.

With every rising of the sun,
Think of your life as just begun.
The past has shrived and buried deep
All yesterdays; there let them sleep.
Concern yourself with but today,
Woo it, and teach it to obey
Your will and wish.   Since time began
Today has been the friend of man;
But in his blindness and his sorrow,
He looks to yesterday and tomorrow.
You, and today! A soul sublime.
And yet the great pregnant hour of time,
With God himself to bind the twain!
Go forth, I say -- attain, attain!
With God himself to bind the twain!

If I have faltered more or less
In my great task of happiness;
If I have moved among my race
And shown no shining morning face;
If beams from happy human eyes
Have moved me not; if morning skies,
Books, and food, and summer rain

Knocked my sullen heart in vain; -
Lord, thy most pointed pleasure take
And stab my spirit broad awake.

THE CAUGHT VERSUS
THE UNCAUGHT

Have you ever cheated on a test at school and never got
caught? Have you ever gossiped about a friend and she
never found out? Have you ever taken something from
someone else and never got caught? Well, I guess this is
your unlucky day because you've been caught. By whom
you ask? Jesus Christ, he sees all and knows all. There
were many times in my life that I've done things wrong and
thought to myself, boy! I hope no one knows I did that.
But this time I was caught. Just when you thought you got
away with it, wrong, you're caught. I wanted to be caught
so this addiction could end. The power of this addiction
had overtaken my life. It's by the grace of God that you're
not sitting right here with me in the Marysville
Penitentiary. You just were never caught. So, think
about your blessings from God. Remember where you
came from. Did you live a perfect life? Haven't you ever
made a mistake? You were just blessed not to get caught.
It's only by God's grace that this pen isn't full of more
women just like you, the uncaught. The ones that haven't
had to pay for their mistakes will one day, the Day of
Judgment. There will be a day when we all stand before
him, caught and the uncaught. Give it all to him today.

THE COMMITTEE IN MY HEAD

How many of you have ever been on a committee? You have people talking all the time, giving their opinions, whether good or bad. Some like to tell you how they think it should be done, while others just sit back and make smart remarks about everyone else. Well, I happen to have my own committee right in my head. I have the ones that tell me to keep taking those pills because no one will ever know. I have the ones that say, "Angie, what have you gotten yourself into?" Then, I have the one, you know, The One, Jesus Christ telling me, "Angie, my daughter, you are my child and just do my will not yours." Sometimes the committee just talks way too loud and I just can't figure out who it is that's speaking. But you have to listen close, really close so you can hear His voice. Follow His voice only. Sometimes you follow those voices that seem to overwhelm you. But nothing good ever seems to come out of it. You must heed God's calling. Don't mistake the voices in your committee. Fire all the others in your committee and only have one voice, God's voice. Make Him the one and only in your committee. Make Him the chairman.

THE CON ARTIST

I sat and ate chow today with a friend of mine from my home town, Kim Little. She was with another woman that she takes to chow daily, in a wheelchair. This woman is in her upper fifties, with a very hard demeanor. I got to talking with her and she told me of her first time ever in prison. It was at the age of 16 at Rikert Island Prison in

New York. She was there for attempted murder. She spent one year at this prison, where she was taught to be a con-artist. When I asked her what brought her back to prison she said, "Well, I've been a con for most of my life, I can't stay in one place very long, so I've pretty much traveled the world." She began telling me that her whole life was filled with lies -- cheating and conning anyone that she could. Moving from place to place to keep from being caught. But now, she's grown tired. She's in a wheelchair, unable to travel alone, and is ready for this life of conning to end. She said she just doesn't know any other way. So I began telling her of a place she's never been. A place where there's happiness; a place of no more pain, no heartache, and no more conning. I told her of Heaven and eternal life with Jesus. At this time in her life she wasn't ready to accept Jesus as her Savior, but the seed was planted. I know that one day she'll desire this place called "Heaven". One day she'll know that the only true happiness is in Jesus.

THE DAY I FINALLY STOOD UP

When I entered these prison walls, I was like a scared little child. I had low self-esteem, no self-worth and I was unable to stand up for myself. So, I prayed and I prayed to God to help me become an assertive woman of courage. I prayed that I could learn to stand up for myself. To be the woman that Jesus wanted me to be. Well, Jesus began answering my prayers by sending me on a test. A test that I never dreamed I would make it through. I finally had to stand up for myself, but I had to stand up to a white-shirt (a sergeant) and a correctional officer. When you're in prison these are two people that you never want to have to stand up to. They have total control over the prisoners, except when Jesus is in control, and today He gave me strength. A correctional officer sent me to another cottage for an appointment. When I arrived there, I went to the sergeant and handed her my pass and asked her who I needed to see. She responded by asking me why the officer who sent me didn't call her before he sent me over. I answered by showing her my pass, and explaining to her that I didn't know. She stood up from her seat and told me that I was just another manipulative inmate who thinks that I know everything. My first reaction was to cry, but not this time. God gave me the courage to first thank her for her time, and second to walk away and go back to my correctional officer and ask him why he didn't call first. His response was that he didn't have to call. I explained to him how I was treated because he didn't want to call over to the other cottage before I went over. I finally did it. I am an inmate but I am also a person. I give respect and I deserve respect. I thank God today for the trial I went through, because of this trial I realized that I am growing as a Christian and as a woman of courage.

THE DOORWAY OF PAIN

The door was open, so I took a step in
Into my past, to relive it again
To face my fears, my anger and pain
To heal my soul, to live life once again
Just one step in and his face I did see
That horrible night, what he did to me
I struggled to fight, but my body lay still
Lifeless and drunk, just a little girl
He took from me, my hopes and dreams
And left behind, a heart that screams
So I turned to run, back through the door

230

I just can't take it, I can't hide anymore
The weight of my past, too heavy to carry
Dreams and nightmares, as a child so scary
I wanted to run, but my feet wouldn't go
But I saw the light, like a bright white snow
The door stayed open, but fear held me back
To the nightmare of rape, the horrible attack
Unable to leave it, behind the closed door
So, today I will face it, I will end the war.

THE EMOTIONALLY HANDICAPPED

When I think of someone that's emotionally handicapped, I think of the 2,000 plus women on this farm. These women have truly been hurt by their problems of life. Wounded to the point that they are unable to really deal with life on life's terms. They have scars so deep that they feel that they can never be healed. Paralyzed by fear and shame, unable to even lift their voices to fight. When I came to this farm I never considered myself as one of the many women who were emotionally handicapped, until I started to deal with my own fears and pain of the past. I never knew that my emotions and feelings had paralyzed me for so long. I was unable to walk into a room without feeling shame. Without wondering what someone thought of me, because of my past? But coming to prison was the best thing that ever happened to me. I realized how much I had in common with these women. I realized that I was not alone on this journey called life. And most of all, I realized that I could be healed of my fears and pain that held me captive for so many years. So, use this "time" to heal your emotions, so you don't have to stay in your wheelchair for life, remaining emotionally handicapped.

231

THE ENCOUNTER

Here at the Tapestry Program we have a group that's called "Encounters." We all sit in a large circle and the counselor hands out concern slips. The concern slips were written by other sisters in the house to bring you up on your negative behaviors. Once they're handed out to the sisters, the encounter begins. The first sister begins by reading her concern slip, then they all look at you and say, "Ms. Pelphrey, you need to get receptive." When I heard those words yesterday, my heart sank. They started reading the concerns, one by one, and my tears began to flow. Each concern hit me straight between the eyes. My words began to flow about my fears, my pain, and my past. I began to open up to 80 women and tell them why I was in prison. For the 1st time in my life the shame and guilt of my past began to leave me. I began to realize that I was worthy of being forgiven. That the past is the past, but the future is just the beginning of a new and improved life. Thank you Tapestry, for loving me enough to help save my life.

THE EXAMPLE

January 5th, 2005, I sat waiting at the Pike County Courthouse for my pre-trial to begin. My lawyer approached me and escorted me to a back room. I knew by her facial expression that what she was about to tell me wasn't going to be good news. She said, "Angie, remember how I told you a while back that the prosecutor might want to use you as an example? Well, he is. He is asking for 2 years in the Marysville Penitentiary for Women." I could hardly breathe. First, anger then the pain hit. I felt pain for my children, my husband and my parents. I knew I could do the 2 years, but could my husband, children and parents. My lawyer spoke to me saying, "With you being a nurse, a preacher's wife, and a Christian, the prosecution wants to show the victims, their families and Pike County that no matter who you are or what you've done, that you still have to pay a price for your crime." I could feel anger building inside of me. They want me to pay by taking me away from my children who need me, and place me in a prison instead of a rehab center for my actual problem, addiction. Why do I have to be the example? But, then I thought of Jesus, and the example He was for all of us as He died on the cross for a crime He didn't commit. I did the crime. I took the pills to feed my disgusting addiction. So, I will be the example. I will be an example for all of those Christians who are struggling with addiction. I will do my time serving Jesus. I will praise Him each and every day that I wake up behind those prison bars. I will make my family proud. I will make my church proud. I will make my Jesus proud. I will be a light to those lost in the darkness of sin. I will tell others of the good news for Jesus Christ. I will be an example, but I will be the example that God wants me to be, not what man wants me to be. I am a Christian. I am a Child of the King. I am Forgiven. I am a soul winner for Him. I am the EXAMPLE!

THE FEAR DANCE

The dance of fear is not one that I choose to do today, but it comes with any and all relationships. We all have fears, but I tend to react when my fear button gets pushed. I react because of my feelings of inadequacy. I fear that I just don't measure up to the expectations that my husband has for me, and that I have for myself. When I would get into an argument with my husband, Barry, we would use our emotions to cause each other to feel anger, sadness and even disconnection. He would feel like a failure because he was not in control. He was losing power and as a man, this was a large fear. My fears caused me to separate from my one true love, my husband. I disconnected from friends and family and lived my life in a closet of fear. We danced this dance for a long time. We stepped on each other's toes, we bumped heads and even forgot the steps. But today our dance is a different dance. It's the dance of love, peace and joy. Today we use the dance steps set before us by Jesus. Today we no longer fear our dance, but we live to dance.

THE FEAR OF BEING ALONE

I've never met so many women afraid to be alone. Their lonesome paths have led them into this penitentiary. From the death of a parent, to the death of a spouse, searching and seeking out any type of love they can find. Abusive relationships that have led to murder, or a life of drugs that has kept them from feeling what true love is. No love from their mother, only anger and neglect. They are searching for love out of fear of being alone. These

234

women search behind these walls for a love that is only going to lead to destruction: the love of another woman, which they consider to be companionship.   A love that they consider to be just for while they serve time.   Just to get them through their sentence without being alone.   But they can't see through the fear.   They can't see the destructive path that they're walking, while hand in hand with another woman.   But I can see their broken hearts as they speak about their pasts.   I feel their pain as they speak about their father that raped them.   Never wanting to even look at another man.   So they walk in fear, hand in hand.   They walk in fear with their "mate," but only for a time.   They can't see the end results.   They can't see the fear that they'll be facing in judgment.   They can only see what they think is love.   Love of another woman.   The companionship of their "mate."   But never understanding that with Jesus on their side and in their hearts, they would never walk in fear alone again.

THE FLAMES OF HELL CAN'T BE ANY WORSE THAN MY LIFE NOW

I asked my friend Barbi, "If you could have changed anything in your past, what would it be?"   She replied, "I wouldn't have wanted to be born."   The comment stuck with me all day.   I couldn't imagine that a person's life could make them feel that way.   But when I heard her past, I began to understand.   She began saying, "I was raped by my own daddy."   My stepmom took me out of the bath when I was six years old and put me on top of the coal stove until I was severely blistered.   My first husband raped and beat me.   After the beating she found out that she had lost the baby that she had been carrying. So her husband tied her to the bed for four days, only feeding her bread and water. She remarried again to a drug dealer. When she got out of the mental hospital after the loss of her baby, her second husband shot up everything in the house. He was angry that the police got involved, when she called 911 when he was beating her. She remarried two more times, and both were alcoholics. She had two children after the loss of her baby and before they were two years old she had lost custody of both of them. I asked her why she gave them up on her own and she said because one day her 14 month old wouldn't stop crying and she found herself in the baby's room, holding a pillow over his face, ready to suffocate him. She said, "I was never meant to be a parent, only a crack addict. I don't deserve them; they need a mommy that loves them more than crack." She has been in and out of jail for twenty years and she has been to prison four times. When I asked her why she felt that she couldn't change, she said, "I don't want to change, because when I'm in prison I feel comfortable here, I feel at home here." She said, "You know what the hardest thing for me is when I'm locked up? It's having to leave. It's much harder to adapt to the outside that it is to adapt to prison. The flames of hell couldn't be any worse than the past I've had."

THE FLOWERS ARE BLOOMING AND SO AM I

It's almost summer here on the farm. I get up every morning and go outside just to see the flowers. The colors are so bright and beautiful. Today, I picked a dandelion and sat and looked upon its beauty. Before prison, I saw a dandelion as an aggravating weed that grew in our yard every year. But today that weed has become a beautiful flower that was placed before me in this prison, just for me. For me to see the beauty of life, that I've never seen before. Just as the flowers that are so beautifully blooming, so am I. I have bloomed into a beautiful creature, made so delicately, by the Makers Hands. Formed from a broken vessel, into a beautiful and brightly colored vase. Changed into a masterpiece for all to see. For the brokenhearted to see in me the beauty of life. It wasn't easy turning from a weed to a beautiful blooming flower, but by the grace of God, today I have been fully bloomed into the beautiful flower that God wants me to be.

THE GENERATIONAL CURSE

Twin sisters, half-sisters, cousins, mothers and daughters locked up together in prison, otherwise known as a generational curse. Evil and sin that flows through generation after generation, unable to break the bondage that holds them in sin. It seemed unbelievable for me to see two sets of mothers and daughters here at prison. Both couples arrested on different days and times, but both for drug-related charges. Addiction, a stronghold on their lives, went from mother to daughter before early teenage life. The mothers work the streets for money, dealing, cheating and lying to get what they need to buy their drugs; not realizing that the whole time their young daughters, walking in their footsteps, were only a few feet behind them. Like looking in a mirror these women now see their daughters on a daily basis, but locked up behind these prison walls. They see the monsters they created. They watch as other women shame and harass them, unable to do anything about it. Generational curses flow throughout these prison walls, tearing families apart. Mothers and daughters here have to be separated from each other due to prison rules. They can only watch and wave to each other in passing. Watching and waiting to hold each other once again. To hold and love like they should have. To love them now with a true love, God's love, that at least one mother has found behind these walls. Stop the generational curse before it stops you.

THE GOLDEN NUGGET

Recalling a dream I had, I saw a beautiful clear image of a bronze colored wicker basket. I was placing beautiful gold nuggets into the bottom of this basket. When it was half way full I began placing rocks on top of the nuggets. When I stood on a ladder to look into this large basket, all I could see were the dirty, dingy rocks. But I knew the nuggets were there somewhere and I would just have to keep digging out the rocks until I found the nuggets. If I kept placing rocks on top of the nuggets, all I would truly see were the rocks. But as my life goes on while sitting in this prison, one day all of the rocks will be replaced with gold nuggets. Sometimes our lives are dirty and dingy. It's the way that we have made it. But if we keep our eyes focused on the beauty in the basket, the beauty of our life, then one day we'll reach into that basket called life and a gold nugget will be the only thing we will find. Don't fill your basket full of rocks. Reach into your basket and search for that golden nugget.

THE GREAT ESCAPE

I have escaped from prison many times. The first time I escaped I found myself back at home playing ball in the yard with my children. The second time I escaped I found myself in Israel walking through the wilderness. I have escaped from this prison many more times, but every time was in my mind, in my heart and in my soul. I can escape almost daily, through a letter or card from home, a picture or reading God's Holy word. I can escape, but only for a few hours, then reality sets back in. But for those few hours the escape was a great one. I call it "The Great Escape." I have escaped with Jesus on many occasions as I bow my head in prayer on my bunk. As He walks me through my fears and pain on a path that leads me to healing. My escapes from this prison have always been successful. As I sit in this cold, unfamiliar place called prison, I escape to many places where I long to be. But I know that one day I'll never have to escape again-- I'll be free. I'll be free to go to those places that I've had to escape to in my mind. I'll be free to no longer have to worry about "The Great Escape."

THE HEART OF A SHEPHERD

If you are saved, then the heart of a shepherd is in you. We Christians are followers of Jesus, the "true Shepherd." The heart of a shepherd is not just given to preachers, deacons or Sunday school teachers. But it is granted to all who are saved and are willing to be a follower of Jesus. The true shepherds seek the sheep with needs. To heal the brokenhearted, to bind up their wounds, to proclaim liberty to the captives, to give beauty for ashes and to give the garment of praise in exchange for the spirit of heaviness, shepherds love their sheep. They seek out the one that has gone astray and are sensitive to its needs. Herds and flocks always have their young with them, so shepherds must be patient because the flock can only be led as far as the youngest can endure. The terrain is rough and there may be many scrapes and scratches, so one must be gentle lest the flock die if you push them too hard. The shepherd must constantly observe his whereabouts, their thoughts and their dreams. The shepherd must always remember that sheep are very sensitive animals, and they are to be led ever so gently, as the "Good Shepherd" leads us.

THE HOURS THAT COME BETWEEN

Hour upon hour, minute by minute and second to second. I was sitting and thinking about the time that comes between. What do I do? Where do I go? There is no place because I'm locked up and cant get out. I'm a prisoner. Not just a prisoner in my mind, but a prisoner in the pen. An inmate, a real prisoner that only has the hours that come between. To think and pray, and then think and pray again. To pray for myself, my family, and my extended family, the others locked up with me. How many times in your life have you been able or been given the opportunity to spend most all your time with Jesus? On the outside I spent most of my time running from my past. I would run from the hours that came between by filling it with pills. Pills that could take my mind and put it in another place. I fogged the hours of my day with trying to clean the house, take care of my children, others' children, and being a pastor's wife while also trying to manage a home for recovering drug addicts. I spent my hours with too much on my hands, when I should have placed the hours in between in God's hands. I am blessed to have God in control of my life now. I now spend my time with the Lord and thoughts of my family. I now wish that I had spent those hours that came between with the Lord and quality time with my family. Spend your time with the Lord so you don't have to spend it in a prison, just so you can learn what to do with the hours that come between.

THE JERRY SPRINGER SHOW
LIVE AT MARYSVILLE

"He's my baby's father!"
"I don't care cause he's my man."
"She's my girl."
"Well she's my girl too."
"But she loves me."
"I don't care cause she loved me first."
Fights over men from their home town that they won't see again for the next four years. Words of anger thrown back and forth like a basketball. Friends turning on friends. Fists flying daily over who knows what. It's like live T.V. right here in my front room. At first I thought maybe they just didn't know any better or they were just raised that way. But then I realized that this was a sin problem. Sinning daily, knowing right from wrong, but choosing to do wrong. They know of God, many have even experienced salvation at one time, but they still choose to sin. Do they feel unworthy, unloved and uncared for? Yes, but they can't let anyone know. They have to show strength, and strength to them is to be tough. They call

them thugs around here.   But one day judgment will come.
They will no longer be able to choose because they made
their choice -- sin.   It will be too late.   Too late to take
back all that they've said or done.   Don't wait any longer.
Turn off the Jerry Springer act and give your heart and life
to the Lord.   Show how tough you really are and answer
His call.   Accept Jesus as your Lord and Savior.

THE LOVE OF GOD

Shulam was so concerned for Solomon's whereabouts after
awakening from a dream that she arose in the middle of the
night to search for him.   When you truly love someone,
you will do all you can to ensure their safety.   Even if it
causes you to lose sleep and causes you discomfort.   You'll
do whatever it takes to know that they are okay.   Once
Shulam found Solomon, her mind was eased.   She held
him in her arms, just to feel his presence once again.   Just
as Shulam, there are many parents and husbands and wives
that are searching for their loved ones, just to assure their
safety.   You awake during the night wondering if they're
even alive.   You arise out of bed and search the streets,
wondering if you'll find them beaten by their pimp, drugged
up or lying dead in a back alley.   But once they were sent to
prison, their minds were eased.   One mother said to her
daughter here that she can now sleep at night, knowing that
her daughter was ok.   Jesus loves us so much more than a
parent could ever dream about loving their child.   He waits
up all day and night waiting for us to come home.   He
waits for us to call His name.   He's waiting for you to come
home.

THE ONLY WAY TO HAVE A PERFECT STABLE IS TO KEEP ALL OF THE ANIMALS OUT

The only way to keep your life free of people problems is to keep it free of other people. This is what causes so many of us to abandon relationships. We think that if we just don't have relationships then we won't have problems with people. But this statement is so untrue. How do you keep a stable clean with animals in it? You must work to clean it up. You must help the animals to clean themselves up. If you keep letting it go, and letting it go, the filth just piles up higher and higher until it's almost too far gone to do anything about it. This holds true for people also. The longer you leave a strain on a relationship the messier it gets. Before long you feel like there's no way to clean it up. So what do we do, we just keep everyone out of our stables, so we don't have to work on cleaning it up. The only way to heal past relationships and even current ones is to work together. To clean up the filth that has caused the relationship to sour. We can't live our lives in the prefect stable, because reality is that relationships are what helps restore us. So open up you barn door, and kick out the hay and make room for your relationships to grow.

THE OUTCASTS, THE CRIPPLED, THE LIMPING ONES

Jesus gathered the outcasts of Israel. He healed the broken-hearted and bound up their wounds. Mephibosheth ate at the King's table, even though he was crippled. Jacob was a schemer, a trickster and a swindler;

but he wrestled with God and God would not let him go. God changed and renamed him Israel (Contender with God) and he went away limping. As I read about these outcasts, crippled and limping, I began to see a part of them in these women here at prison. They are outcasts, crippled and limping, that have wrestled with addictions, abuse and anger; for many years they have wrestled with God and gone away limping. They can see nothing in themselves but a liability, a handicap. They have been labeled for years. Once I was shown the love of God and saw that I was accepted even with my handicap, I was able to overcome. I've seen many women at this prison shunned for the crime they've committed, but once they found the love of God and the love and acceptance of other Christian women here, they were able to walk away healed of their disabilities. We must seek to heal the brokenhearted, and not shun them away.

THE PERFECT SNOWLAKE

Have you ever seen a snowflake dropped from Heaven that looked so perfect? It drops down from the clouds as a shining star glowing on the ground. As I walked back from chow at the penitentiary today, it had begun to snow. My first thought was, "Oh, not today, it's too cold." We have to walk about 5 blocks in the snow to get to our meals and I just wanted to get back to our dorm to get warm. But as the snow began to flow more, a girl beside me said, "Have you ever seen such a perfect snowflake?" I looked onto my jacket as another one fell and the sight of it made me glow. It was the most perfect snowflake I had ever seen. It was the shape of the bright and morning star that shown that wonderful night in Bethlehem, that guided the wise men to Jesus. It looked like the kind of snowflake that was cut out

244

so perfectly by a child at school. Once it fell onto my jacket and it began to melt it started to sparkle like a diamond. I had never seen anything so beautiful. I began to thank God for allowing me to see something so beautiful. I began to think of all that I had taken for granted. I had never once stopped what I was doing while on the outside to look at a snowflake that had dropped on my jacket. One thing I noticed about the snowflake was that there were no two flakes that looked alike. But every one that fell just looked so perfect. Every one of them that fell melted within a few moments. But before they melted, all of them gave me a blessing; a blessing that I never expected on this cold winter day. A blessing I never deserved to see while locked up behind a razor wired fence. I thank Jesus, that wherever you may be that He can always send you a little blessing from Heaven no matter how big or how small. All blessings come from Heaven, but today this was a blessing that came straight from the hands of Jesus.

THE PERFECT TEAM

Priscilla and Aquilla: the perfect team. Ministers of the gospel and well educated in their faith, these two were perfect for each other. They complimented each other and built on each other's strengths. They formed the perfect team. They took Apollos into their home and told him about Jesus' life, death and resurrection. He could now go on to preach the full story, and preach it with power. Aquilla and Priscilla are an example of what can happen through a strong, faithful, husband and wife team. Today God is creating another perfect team, my husband and I. He is strengthening our love and faith everyday. We are fulfilling our purpose in this life, to share, as a team, the gospel of Jesus Christ with the broken-hearted and to love the unlovable, God has truly blessed our marriage through this trial. He has given us the opportunity to be the perfect team. One day soon God will free me from this prison to minister the gospel with my husband and to complete his triumphant mission.

THE PLAYGROUND

I had the opportunity to advance from a ten man room down to a two man. But, as I moved my belongings into my new room, I glanced out the window. What I saw was so sad to me. My new view is the yard for juveniles. I watched them for a few moments, playing like little children. Tossing a ball, drawing and singing as children do. They range in age from 15 to 21. To some of them that playground is their backyard for the next 10 to 39 years, and two have life here, never to leave outside those gates again. I watch as they run and play, day after day. I see my own daughters in some of them, and I see the fear in their eyes. I see the pain and anger from their pasts. They could be my children. They could be your children, playing on that playground behind a razor wire fence. I see hope in that playground. I see life in their eyes. They just need our love and the love of our Father. They need to know that someone cares. Do not forget about our children. Take every opportunity to take them to the playground and play with them. You never know if the next playground they might play on will be behind a razor wire fence. God help them!

THE PREACHER'S WIFE TURNED PREACHER

It's Black History Month here at prison, celebrating heroes of yesterday and today; men, women, presidents, sports figures and more. So, our caseload decided to make our presentation into a skit, representing Black History Month. They allowed me to choose whoever I wanted to speak on, so I chose the Rev. Bishop T.D. Jakes. The scene started out on a bus with Rosa Parks walking up to get a seat in the front. We moved on to a church scene, showing the old fashion preacher of the all black churches. Then that's when I came in. I began speaking as T.D. Jakes, preaching to the congregation. Speaking of all of his accomplishments, past and present. Then I told the crowd why I chose Bishop Jakes as my hero. I was able to speak of my salvation, and of my Jesus. I let them know that while they are here in this cold dark prison, that they would never be alone. As I looked out into the crowd I saw tears flowing from row to row. I saw women weep that I had never seen cry before. I saw hard hearts melt. After my presentation the woman that was crying came to me and said, "Ms. Pelphrey, thank you for bringing a little hope to this prison." She said, "As I sat and listened to you speak of T.D. Jakes and your husband being a preacher, I thought to myself, 'Doesn't she realize that today she was the preacher?' Ms. Pelphrey, you must realize that God has sent you here as a messenger for Him, because today you gave something so special to all of us, and that is Hope."

THE PRESENT

I can remember, as a child, sitting and waiting anxiously on Christmas Eve night for the arrival of "Santa Claus" and his great big bag of presents. But these really aren't the type of presents I'm talking about here. I'm talking about 'the present' -- today. Not the past or future, the present. They call it the present, because each day is a precious gift of God. So many of us focus on our pasts and what we've done when we should be focusing on the present so we can make a way for our future. We wake up each morning thinking about what we should or could have done differently. Why and how did we end up behind these prison walls? Let go and let God. Listen for Him to speak to you today. Look for what special gift he is trying to give you. It's the present, His present that will lead you to an eternal future with Him. Make each day a blessing, obey His will and know that He is with you, no matter where you may be.

THE PURPOSE OF PRISON IS...

Some say that the purpose of prison is to make you grow old, run you down, and to cause you to suffer from health problems. Prison is a place of filth; old cottages, dirty floors, rats, bats, and bugs. Lead paint and asbestos absorbing into our skin, without us even knowing. The food is just filler; it has no substance or consistency. It's only used to fill us up and keep us quiet. It's canned and dehydrated and boiled beyond taste. The pork is known to be full of parasites and they fill you with enough potatoes and breads to make you into a walking starch zombie. But for me, I can truly say that Tapestry has changed my life. I don't know if I would have felt the same way living with the angry, hostile and vengeful women out in population. Yes, I do believe that some officers feel that prison is here just to degrade us, but to my counselors here in Tapestry, they build us up and help to create us into that person that we've always dreamed of being. So, to me the purpose of prison was to give me my life back and to make me into the strong and beautiful woman that I've always dreamed of being.

THE RIB THAT HOLDS US TOGETHER

"And the rib, taken from man, made woman." The rib taken from the side of the man -- not taken from the head or the feet, for if taken from the head she would be above him. If taken from the feet she would be below him. But woman was taken from the side so that man could walk side by side with woman. Taken from the rib; the rib that protects the most precious organ, the heart. The rib willing to be crushed before any damage is done to the heart. The rib that wraps around the body much like the arms of Jesus. Why did God choose the rib, such a fragile and delicate bone? Because it can take many blows before it is broken. If broken it can be healed, but never replaced. The rib taken from man causes a nuptial (mystical) union between man and woman that connects the couple's hearts and lives as one. God created man and woman perfect for each other. Marriage is a gift, a gift given to us by God. When your child leaves your home he can't take a piece of your rib, but a piece of your heart gently slips through the rib cage and into their soul. Marriage is good and honorable. Only death should part us as one. You can be away from your spouse in distance, but you can never be separated at the heart. Our hearts are now entwined into one to become complete. My husband, Barry, is my heart.

He is what makes my life complete here on this earth. We are one, we are complete, joined together by God until death do us part.

THE SAD SNOWMAN

As your children bundle up and get ready to play in the snow, thoughts of building a snowman fills their minds. Before they go out they ask for the supplies to build a perfect snowman. They want their snowman to be bigger and better than those of their friends. As you send them on their way, one of them says, "Mommy, I'm going to build a snow mommy just like you." Your face glows with joy as you kiss them on the cheek. As they start rolling their first snowballs you remember back to when you where a child, but building a snowman was something your were never able to do. You smile big as you wave to them through the large glass window, but your mind focuses right back to your abusive childhood. Where was your happiness? Where was your perfect snowman? Your daughters roll and roll until their snowman is ready to be dressed. They place the hat and scarf around its neck, then put on the arms and the shiny red buttons. You smile as you see the glow in your daughters' faces. Then one of them places the coal black eyes, the carrot nose, and the black buttons for the mouth. She steps back to say, "Look how perfect, Mommy." Tears well up in your eyes as you gaze at the snow mommy staring back at you with a sad face. The smile is upside down. Your daughter saw the sadness in your eyes. You never knew that your daughter had seen your pain. You didn't know that your past would become her future. You didn't realize the pain that she carried. Don't carry your sadness to your children. You can get peace and have your own perfect snowman.

THE SHAME BASED WOMAN

I am a wife, a mother, a preacher's wife, a registered nurse and a drug addict. How can you hold your head up after getting addicted to pain pills, then taking pills from your patients and ending up in the penitentiary? For years I lived my life with my head hung down in shame. Many around me saw the smiles that I portrayed to hide the shame underneath. But it took me ending up in the penitentiary to realize that I am no different than anyone else that had made mistakes in their past. All of us have sinned. But do we have to walk around forever in shame with our heads hanging low or do we have the right to look up high towards Jesus? I know that I have the right to keep my head up. To smile without the shame and guilt of my past. I live only for Jesus now, not those who want to judge my past. I am a strong woman now. I am a good woman, good mother, and a good wife. I am forgiven because I am a child of the King. I no longer have to live my life in shame. Today I hold my head up high.

THE SHINING STAR

I have been in prison now about two and a half months, and each and every day I pray to be a light to others, even if it's just a smile or a "good morning" to someone. I pray that I can speak words of wisdom and His word to a hurting person.   Well last night a lady named Robin came to talk to me.   I have spoken to her many times before but this time was different.   As she sat down she began to cry.   She said "Angie, God answered my prayer today."   I told her that was great.   She said, "I have prayed for days for God to send a 'Paul' into this prison, and he did.   It's you.   I have talked with you on and off for a few days and you never had a bad thing to say about anyone or anything."   She said, "You are a star that shines down on this prison.   You were sent here to give me hope.   You are a true mentor of God to me."   I was amazed.   I could hardly speak, but I thanked her and told her that I pray every day for God's wisdom.   I pray that I can be a light to others who still live in a world of darkness.   She said, "Well you are more than just a light, you are a shining star that glows day and night."   She wanted to know how I could be so strong when I'm sitting behind bars.   I told her that at one time in my life, I was very weak.   My addiction, fear and pain of the past weakened me.   But I had to make myself become strong again.   I had to pray and read God's word everyday.   I told her that to get strong physically you have to work out, and that's what I am doing now spiritually.   I spend my time "working out" for the Lord.   Please pray for the still hurting women that are living in darkness of the past.   Be a shining star for Jesus wherever you may be.

THE SPIRITUAL SEED

A single seed planted on a bright sunny day, waiting for a drink of that heavenly water.   If planted in good soil, with good fertilizer, it will grow.   It will grow to be a prosperous seed.   One single seed can produce multiple fruits.   The wind may blow hard enough to take away some of the crop, but some will stand, and stand tall.   Nature may cause the crop to stand still, but in a moment, the sun can come out to provide for the crop. In a moment the fresh water from Heaven above may pour down to provide for the thirsting crop. Today I am a spiritual seed. I am just one of the many fruits off of a crop planted long ago. I am just a small piece of the crop of Jesus Christ. "The Son," shines on me daily to help me grow here in this prison. The wind blows hard and roars on many days, but I remain tall, standing for my Jesus. I am but a seed, planted, plucked and pure in this garden called prison. I share with others of the crop Jesus has planted for them. This seed keeps growing by His spiritual word. This seed of God will grow to be strong. It will stand among others that fall to the wind. I will bear much fruit from my one and only seed, Jesus.

THE STONE WHICH
THE BUILDERS REJECTED

One stone can affect people in many different ways. It all depends on how they relate to it. As the builders place all of their supplies out around the site, the stones are placed to the side, ready and waiting to be set in their perfect position. But as the builders begin their work, one worker hurriedly walks around the stones and trips as he passes by. He knew the stone was there, but he was in a hurry and just didn't pay any attention to it. Another builder goes by and looks at the stones carefully. He tells another worker, "I just don't like the shape and color of the stones, so go get me different ones." The third builder goes by and gently places the stones into their position without the cement to hold them in place. As he begins to walk away, the stones fall from their positions, crushing the man to death. The last builder picks up the stones, places them together with cement, and stands back to gaze upon the beauty of his work. One year later, he returns with more stones, building onto the work he had already done. The stones in this story represent Jesus Christ. Many people hurriedly walk past Jesus, tripping and falling as they pass by. They know He is there, but they don't have time for Him. The other builder doesn't like what he sees, so he jumps from church to church, idol to idol, not realizing that the stones placed before him were a beautiful site after completion. The third man represents the enemy that will be crushed to death on Judgment Day. The last man represents Jesus, Himself, our building block. With Jesus as your Savior you can build your life into a beautiful masterpiece, and in years to come your descendants will come to build off of the life that you lead with Jesus. What will you choose? Life or death?

THE SUBSTANCE FOR A SUBSTITUTION

I have had the pleasure of speaking to hundreds of women on this farm about their addiction. Almost all of them said the same thing; "I used as a substitute for something in my life." They substituted the pills or crack for pain, fear, low self-esteem and more. They substituted the drugs to be someone that they were not. As for myself, I substituted drugs for a fear of rejection, low self-esteem and other hidden pains from my past. But today, my mind is clear, the fog has lifted and reality has set in of who I really am. I have nothing I can substitute, so I must find a solution. The solution for me was to finally face this pain and fear by talking about it. Telling other sisters of my past, of my failures and realizing that they accepted me for me, no matter what I had hidden. I had to agree to change. To change my thinking and to realize that I am the only person who can make "me" happy. I can no longer rely on my husband to make me happy with flowers, compliments or affection. I've come to realize that I substituted drugs in order to increase my self-esteem. I can't rely on my happiness to come from a comment or a flower. I have to realize that the solution is to learn to love me first and then my happiness will come.

THE UNDESIRABLES

They call her "undesirable." She's six feet tall, broad shouldered and built like a football player, but her heart is as soft as a child's heart. At the age of 18 she began using drugs. Within one year she had become an I.V. user. Her addiction took her rapidly down a road of destruction. She shot up with one needle, one time, with one person, one too many times. She had known him for years, and thought that nothing would ever happen to her. In that one needle was the AIDS virus and Hepatitis C virus. Now, 10 years later, she has full blown AIDS. As she walked into prison, she quickly became labeled. She was known as one of the "undesirables." But to her it didn't matter what people thought of her because as long as she had her heart right with the Lord, it didn't matter to her what the rest of her body had wrong with it. One year ago, she gave her heart to the Lord. She no longer felt like a leper. She no longer felt unwanted or unloved. She was healed of her dreaded disease called sin. So, today she may still be labeled one of the "undesirables", but to Jesus she is one of His children. She is loved by the best. She may die of the dreaded disease of AIDS, but she won't die a poor lost sinner and she'll no longer be labeled an "undesirable", because to Jesus she's known only as a desirable.

THE UNLOVABLE

I was 5'4 and 125 pounds and I was so fat. I thought this for many years and sometimes I still do. I would take 20 to 30 diet pills at a time to keep me from eating so much. But the more weight I lost, the fatter I saw myself. I'll never be perfect like a want to be. I had 2 children and because of them I got fat. When I got pregnant with my third child I decided that I would rather be thin than to be pregnant and fat again, so I killed my baby. I had an abortion, just so I could be thin. I killed my child, just so I could look good, but I'll never look the way that I want to, I'll never be thin enough. I would leave my children for days at a time, searching for someone to love me. I was searching for that certain man that would finally see that I was not fat. Eventually, I fell into the trap of crack cocaine. It helped me to see myself as I always wanted to, thin. I could love myself through the mirage of crack. It masked all of my negative feelings. It made me be someone that I wasn't. This is not a story, but the life of a young 20 year old girl in prison. Today she sits behind these prison walls, still fighting her fears and the pain of her past. Weighing herself each week as they bring out the scales, but never happy with the results. She no longer has the crack to hide her true feelings or to numb the pain. Today she weeps for the child that she gave up for abortion. Today, she still searches for that one person to love her. She prays everyday that Jesus will forgive her. Please pray for this young woman, that one day she will accept Jesus, because Jesus is the only one that will love her unconditionally and the only one that will take away her pain and fears of the past.

THE UNSTABLE CISTERNS

Jeremiah 2:13, "For my people have committed two evils; they have forsaken me the fountain of living waters, and hewed them out cisterns." A cistern, a pit that collected rainwater, broken and empty, was set aside and chosen over a fresh, sparkling spring of water by the Israelites. When they could have had the living water of Jesus Christ, they chose instead an unstable cistern, unable to hold water. Unable to provide fresh drinking water. Leaking out the fresh rain as it falls, causing it to become contaminated, and turning it into water that is undrinkable to any man. Many times we choose the old cistern over the fresh living water. We choose second best when we could have it all. Jesus wants us to have His living water. But it's our choice today. What will you have? A pit, broken and empty or will you choose the living water, fresh and available at all times. Choose Jesus! I did.

THE WISH LIST

Today is February 26th, 2005, and I've been in prison now almost three months. I have been moved into the Tapestry Program, a program for recovering addicts. On Tuesday, two days from today, one of our sisters in the program will be leaving to go home after 2 years here on the farm. She came into the program with low self-esteem, anger and suicidal thoughts.   Before her incarceration, she had jumped from an overpass to the concrete below, shattering her arm.   She had wanted to die, and it was just another attempt that had failed.   Well, yesterday she was presented with her wish list.   She was asked to come to the front of the group while the other sisters gathered around her. One by one each sister took her by the hands and presented her with their wishes for her.   For the first time, I saw women in this prison share a love for another inmate that was true.   They took her hands and wished her a life of happiness, a life of freedom from addiction, a life with her girls that she never had before.   They wished her to never have to return to this cold, dark prison.   They wished her to open the beauty shop that she's always dreamed of. Lastly, they wished her to follow God on the path that He had made for her.   I was overwhelmed with a love and peace that I had never felt in this prison.   God was not only answering her prayer for freedom, but He answered my prayer for freedom of love to spread behind these walls.   I am so thankful for being present during her wish list, but most of all I am so thankful for answered prayers.

THE WOMAN BEHIND THE MASK

A couple of days ago I was able to talk to a friend of mine about her new job. She is a porter for ARN 4, "The Hole." The Hole is a place where you never want to be. It is four cement walls, a bunk and a toilet.   There's no communication with anyone, and a porter delivers all meals. My friend began telling me this week of how she was just ready to give up. She said that she was just so tired of this place and her faith was really being tested. "Overall," she said, "I'm just feeling sorry for myself. I have no one to write me, no money on my books, and I've been waiting to hear about my release date and I've never heard a word." So she prayed hard that day for God to help her with her pain.

Well, she went to work today just like usual, but today God let her see something that would change her life forever. She met the 'woman behind the mask.' My friend went to deliver trays to all the women in The Hole. She came upon a woman with a black mask on. The only thing you could see was her eyes. When my friend got ready to hand the woman a tray she saw her eyes fill with tears. My friend smiled at her, and they both began to cry. A moment later the correctional officers came to the door and told the woman that it was time for her shower. The woman refused. The correctional officer said to her, "Either get your shower or I will mace you." The woman replied, with tears in her eyes, "You do to me what you want because I don't have anything to live for anyway." She said, "I've been living in this hole now for 14 years; no cards, no phone calls and no family to say they love me. Death would be better than this!" She took a step back into her cell and wrapped the shower curtain around her neck, then tied it off. She was trying to hang herself. The CO's got her down quickly with mace and force but my friend was weeping uncontrollably. She later told me, "Angie, I have never seen someone that had no hope like that before. But God allowed me to see her today. God allowed me to see what I have to live for. I need to be here at this job just to give her a little hope. I may not be able to speak to her, but I can show her love, God's love, through a simple smile."

THE WORLD OF THE UNKNOWN

Twelve years on the farm and her biggest fear is freedom. The day that the judge slammed his gavel down, she entered into the world of the unknown. Her first week on the farm she was sent to see a psychiatrist (this is normal procedure for all women sentenced to a "life term"). The psychiatrist looked at her and said, "Well, I'm not sure what you expect me to do since you're a lifer, but if you have any trouble sleeping then just let me know." The world of the unknown. For five years she lived in the same cottage, then one day they told her to pack her stuff up, because she and another women were going to be moved. The world of the unknown. She was headed to an NA meeting and went in the cottage to get her friend, and a C.O. told her to go on back in her room and wake her up. As she walked into the world of the unknown, she leaned down and shook her friend to wake her up. There was no movement, no breathing and no heart beat. She turned her over, only to see that she was cold and blue. She had died of a diabetic coma. Nine months later she got word from a lifer friend of hers that another lifer bled to death laying on a cement floor, the night before. The world of the unknown. Within a year another lifer friend hung herself, to escape the torment of her crime that played in her mind each and every day. Half of her family had already passed away while she was in prison. She wakes up every morning not knowing what each day holds for her. Shakedowns, lock downs, shut-up, sit up, stand here, do this and do that. The world of the unknown. What does this world hold for you? Live each day to the fullest. Live each day for Jesus. This is the world of the unknown, but with Jesus, you can one day enter the world of the known, eternity. Be grateful for what God has blessed you with, because each day to a lifer is a gift from God, because to them, freedom is a state of mind.

THE YARD

I'm sitting out in the yard.   It is so beautiful out here.   The birds are chirping.   The dogs are barking and the squirrels are running the trees.   The sun is shining so bright, melting the beautiful white snow.   There isn't a cloud in the sky, just bright blue everywhere I look.   But as I look around past all of this beauty, I see prisoners.   Prisoners walking the walk joy.   Prisoners sitting and talking.   Prisoners everywhere.   I'm sitting in "The Yard" at the Marysville Penitentiary.   I hear women cursing God for being here.   I hear women cursing this beautiful yard.   But I have to look past these walls.   I have to look beyond the anger and pain and see the beauty, the beauty that lies inside these walls.   The beauty of God's nature and His people.   God has blessed me to see beyond these bars.   He's allowed me to see the true blessings in my life.   The yard is a blessing to me.   I can feel peace while I sit on this park bench.   I can feel His presence in the sunrays that beat down on my face.   I can feel His love as I sit and talk to my Jesus.   The yard is a place of peace to me.   The yard is a place of rest.   It's a place where I can look beyond...beyond this prison.   Beyond my past to focus on the future.   As I sit here now, at 1:30 in the afternoon, I can hear the shouts of praise from women in the Elizabeth House.   I can hear them clapping for another woman who just gave her testimony.   I can hear the joy in their voices. This yard is not just a yard.   To me it is beauty.   A beauty that God has allowed me to see.   A beauty that God has allowed me to hear.   A beauty that I'll always have with me wherever I may be.

THINKING OF YOU

I dream of the day when I hold you close, take your hand and walk with you by the River of Joy. When I walk the streets of gold holding onto your nail-scarred hand, talk of my past and say, "Remember when?" When I feast at your table and meet your disciples one by one. When I share my love for you, for all you have done. When I kiss your nail-scarred hands and wash your blessed feet. When I sit with my loved ones, so many to meet. I think of you often, I think of that day. I think of your love and the price you had to pay. To die for me, just a sinner saved by grace. So that I could know that I've won this eternal race. I think of you Jesus when I open my eyes, and I thank you Jesus, that you were willing to die.

THIS CHRISTMAS DAY

Lord,
You tell us in your word that you shall supply all of our needs according to your riches in Glory. I praise you Lord for meeting my needs, because today, I need a miracle. I need a break through. I need my soul to be mended, revived, refreshed and restored. I know that we need to be washed and thoroughly cleansed of all unrighteousness. I praise you Lord, for whenever I have a need you are my supplier. I praise you for the peace that I feel in the midst of my troubles. I praise you for the peace that surpasses "my" understanding. Why doesn't the world understand your peace? By their standards, we should be crying and depressed on this Christmas Day. I praise you because when I thought I would fail, you made me the conqueror. I

praise you on this day, your day, your birthday. Thank you Jesus for your joy that gives me strength. Today is December 25th, 2004 and I am spending it in Marysville Penitentiary. I praise God for all of my blessing's today. I thank you Jesus for your birth, death and resurrection from the dead. Because of you I have eternal life to look forward to. So make this Christmas a merry one, no matter where you have to spend it.

THIS DAY IS MINE
TO MAR OR MAKE

This day is mine, to mar or make. God keep me strong and true;
Let me no erring by-path take, no doubtful action do.
Grant me, when the setting sun this fleeting day shall end,
that I rejoice o'er something done, and be richer by a friend.
Let all I meet along the way speak well of me tonight.
I would not have the humblest say I'd hurt him by a slight.
Let there be something true and fine when night slips down to tell
that I have lived this day of mine, not selfishly, but well.

This is a beautiful song, written by one of our 20 yr. old juveniles who was in prison for aggravated assault to her sister's boyfriend, she stabbed him in the neck.

How did I get here?
Why did this happen to me?
How did it go down this way,
When I got kids at home?
They were my life, my heart.

263

Now they're living on their own
Because I'm sitting in this cell,
Behind these prison walls.

It happened on an October Day,
The sky was clean and the weather was great.
I was still happy from turning "20" the other day
Just pickin' up my kids from my mama's house that day
Never did I think that I would drive up to a fight
And to see that it was my sister, with her man on top
Tears fall from my cheeks and drop.

I just went out of control
Got out of the car without thinking
I just couldn't bear to see what he was doing to her
I can't even remember that day,
It all went so wrong, the cops came and put the cuffs on me
And now I'm sitting here praying on my knees

Never did I think that I would leave my kids this way
God, I don't know what I was thinking
I sit here and wonder each day -- Where would I be;
if   I'd just walked away
Would I be at home with my kids today?
Or would I be here on another case?

God forgive me and let me go home
Lord I beg you to redeem me, since
I didn't know, but now I see;
I played the piper, and all I can do
Now is sit here and weep.   I get down
On my knees and ask you to forgive me
'Cause, Lord, I just need you to tell me,
How did I get here?   Why did this happen to me?
How did it go down this way?
Yes, now I'm sitting here in this prison,
In my cell, behind these prison walls.

Ms. Churchill
'05'

THIS LAND IS YOUR LAND,
THIS LAND IS MY LAND

Your land is filled with milk and honey.   It is flowing from the spout, the spout that is filled by your job, your church and your education.   My land is filled with bread and water from the spout of hunger-a hunger from within.   It is a hunger that can free our souls from our pasts.   It is a hunger that can change our lives from an inmate to a person.   Your land sees the world with eyes as a carnival mirror, distorting reality.   My land sees you for who you are, not where you have been.   My land sees hurting women, abused and broken down so far that the only place to look is up.   Your land sees addiction as a choice.   My land sees drug use as a choice, but addiction as a disease that robs and steals your family, job and your freedom. Your land is my land and my land is your land.   We must all come together as one to see this land called prison; to see our land of addiction and to realize that we're all here for one purpose.   We're all here to serve and worship my Jesus.   We're all sisters and brothers.   We're all one family of different races and ethnicities.   We're all ONE. We may live in different lands, but in Heaven, we are ONE.

THREE HONKS

It's count time. We're stuck in our beds until the guard yells, "Count clear!" The days are long, the weather is hot and I'm homesick. I just want to go home. I'm so tired. So tired of being tired. But then I heard it--the three honks. I get a little touch of home every time the horn blows three times. The three honks come from my dad. My dad drives by the prison Monday through Friday, three times a day. Every time he goes by he blows his horn three times. Every time I hear it a smile comes to my face, because I know that it's his message just for me. The three honks mean I love you, I miss you, I'm praying for you. My dad will never know what those honks mean to me. The days when I start to get down and even depressed, I just sit back and wait for my dad to go by. If I can just hear him go by, I'll be all right. When I hear it my dorm hears it, the whole farm hears it, but it's just for me. My special message from my dad to me. Thank you dad for those three honks. There are many times that I think I can't go on, then I hear them. I hear the honks and I know that there's someone out there with me, my dad.

TILL DEATH DO US PART

I've always taken my wedding vows very seriously. When I married my husband I knew that he was the one for me. I know some people don't believe in love at first sight, but when I saw Barry for the first time, I knew that he was mine. We met for the first time at my sister's and his brother's wedding rehearsal. We went out that same night. He has always said to people "And she hasn't left since". For some reason the words I love you were hard for him to say. But five months after we met, we were married and he hasn't left yet. Through my addiction, I've learned what true love is really all about. The famous quote at all weddings, "Till death do us part" has a lot more meaning now. I've learned about unconditional love through my husband, children, and my family. But while in jail I've learned a lot more about till death do us part with Jesus. I've learned that Jesus has never left me and that I want to spend eternity in Heaven with my family. I want to have that special love, God's love in my heart until death do I part. I want to win as many people to the Lord as I can before I leave this world. I've been in jail three days and I now have six more family members: Three prostitutes, and three addicts, that will spend eternity with me in heaven some day.

TIME WILL TELL

Time seems to tell all. Time is always moving. Time brings change. Time allows today to become yesterday, and tomorrow to become today. I commit to a change of heart, mind, and soul. I commit to allow change to come. I commit to change. Change brings fear, fear brings guilt, and guilt brings shame. Time will tell. Time tells your future. Time tells your past. Time tells your dreams. You can allow time to help you grow, or to let you wither away like a flower in winter. Time is like the wind: fast moving, invisible, and you can't hang on to it. You may try to catch the wind, but like time it is 'uncatchable.' Time will tell of who you truly are, who you truly desire to be, and what you are willing to become. Time is endless, because it will never cease to exist. Time, to me, is an eternity because with Jesus time is forever. However, time does tell all, so use your time wisely.   Use your time doing God's will, because time will surely tell on you.

TO BE A LEADER

Leadership begins with a vision, a revelation by God. Leaders are made, not born.   Leaders encourage change. Not just accept it and tolerate it, but actually encourage it. The problem is that we don't like change.   But life is always changing.   So we must learn how to adapt to the changes in life.   Being a leader involves gaining trust from others; planting a seed for people to follow as you guide them toward their full potential in life.   Today I strive to be that leader, because I have a vision.   A man reaps what he sows. So today I will sow friendship to gain friendship.   I will sow mercy to gain mercy.   I will sow respect, to gain respect.   To be a leader you must focus on the gold and not the dirt.   Today I strive to be a leader for Christ and not a follower.   To be a follower in prison is very difficult, but being a leader is much harder.   So today, with my vision clear, I will strive to lead the followers to a life of freedom--freedom in Jesus Christ.

TO LIVE LIKE YOU WERE DYING

What would you do if you had a death sentence and you were only given 6 months to live?   What would you do? Would you live it up?   Would you go out and party till you

268

dropped? Or would you go and spend all of your money on drugs? I guess that's up to you. Because today's the day, you've been sentenced to death. How long do you have? I don't know, only God knows. He's the judge and he's slammed the gavel down and said, "Death". All of us are going to die. Every one of us has a death sentence, but some of us have a heaven to go to, and some of us have hell as their sentence. But all of us will die. None of us are indispensable. So live, live like it's your day to die. Go and spread the news, the news of God's saving grace. Live like it's your child's death sentence. Tell your children about Jesus, tell your friends about Jesus. Today's the day! Spend your Eternity in heaven with Him. Love Jesus like it's your time to die.

TO LOVE A PRISONER

Loving a prisoner is not easy to do
No one will know this better than you.
It only gets harder day by day
So giving me your heart is a higher price to   pay.
Promising to me and saying you'll wait
Knowing some day they'll open the gate.
Hoping and waiting for a letter each day
For the smile I get when one comes my way.
Loving a prisoner is really not fun
But it's worth the wait, when the time is done.
My life is written in volumes of three
The past, the present, the yet to be.
The past is over and miles away
The present we are living day by day.
But the yet to be is the best of the three
Because we'll spend it together, Just you and me.

Were all prisoners if you're without Jesus Christ? You live a life like a hostage. You look through the bars each day waiting for the judge to release you. So obey God's calling, accept him today as your King and Savior. There's no reason to be a prisoner anymore.

TODAY I SET MY MIND ON ABOVE

Today I set my mind on what is above, not on the things of this earth. The Bible tells us to set our minds and keep them set on things above. For many years I lived my life worrying about what other people thought of me. I wondered if people were pleased with me. Anger and rejection filled my mind every waking moment. I would sit and worry, my mind was spinning out of control. Did I say or do the right thing? I wonder what they think of me. Are they pleased with what I said? But today I spend my time working on pleasing someone other than me and that person is Jesus. I set my mind on above, and not on earthly things. I am no longer a runner in the race for approval, but a runner in the race for freedom. I am free from the bondage of fear and rejection. I am free from the fear of approval. But most of all freedom from my past that's held me captive for so many years. You don't have to live in fear any longer. Where is your mind set today? Set your mind on above and let Jesus set you free.

TRAGEDY OUTSIDE
THESE WALLS

We awoke today to sirens and lockdown. We were unsure of the reason behind the lockdown, until the officer said he had an announcement. He said, "Before you go to your rooms to be locked in, I think we owe you an explanation. One of our officers took his life this morning right outside the gates, while on duty." Why? We thought. Why would a man, that has a family, a good job and his freedom, take his life? One of the girls here commented and said, "You know, I came to this prison with nothing. I lost my family, my job and my freedom and I was at the lowest point in my life. But, no matter how far down I got, I always knew that I had hope. I knew that there was a God out there and I knew that He loved me." So why? Why would he take his gun, point it to his head and pull the trigger? I'm sure we'll never know why this man took his life. But I do know that God loved him and God loves you. No matter how far down this chaotic society takes us, always know that God loves you. There is always Hope. So never give up. Never give in to your addiction. Please pray for this family and for the women that were affected by this tragedy.

UNEXPECTED AND
UNEXPLAINABLE TRAGEDIES

In 2003 there were 380 recorded natural and man-made catastrophes worldwide that claimed the lives of 60,000 people. The Titanic remains one of the largest disasters at sea ever. Tragedy has a way of bringing out the worst and the best in us. When we think of tragedy, we don't think of a grandfather who died of natural causes at the age of 90. It's definitely painful, but I wouldn't describe it as tragic. Tragedies are unexpected, uncontrollable, unimaginable, unprecedented, and they leave our life uncertain. Many feelings go through our minds when tragedy strikes. Your body starts to go through a state of shock. Then the pain sets in and you start dealing with fear. How can you make it? Then the anger comes and you begin to wonder why they left you. Why did you let them leave me? The tragedy on 9/11 affected everyone around the whole world. This tragedy affected families from every state. It was unexplainable and unexpected, but it happened for a reason. I'm not sure what others think about the reason, but I feel that it changed the world. People that hadn't spoken to Jesus in years finally fell to their knees begging for help. People began praying. Men who haven't cried in years, cried out in sorrow. Our nation was taught the importance of family and the importance of living for today, not yesterday. If you have had a tragedy in your life, you begin to learn what truly matters in this life, family, friends and Jesus. Love one another, live for Jesus and He will hold your hand through your time of need.

UNLIKELY PLACES

A few years ago my husband Barry and I had the opportunity to go to Israel. One of the most fascinating places that was there was the "Dead Sea". There was nothing alive in it because of the increased amount of salt in it. There were no fish, no crabs, and not even seaweed. But, around the shoreline, there were olive trees for miles and miles growing prosperously. Some were even inches from the shore line, and they grew even larger than the other ones. They were seeds that grew in a place that seemed unlikely to grow. Every living seed carries a miraculous power and potential of its own. The seed of God's word has a power and potential of its own. It has the ability to spring up, prosper and bear fruit even in places that seem unlikely. Just as the olive trees grew by the Dead Sea, we too, in prison have the potential to prosper and bear fruit, but the seed must be planted. A harvest always comes from sowing the seed, even in what may appear to be an unlikely field. The unlikely field is this prison and in this prison there are thousands of women desperately needing the love and grace of Jesus Christ. The miracle of the harvest becomes reality, only after the faithful laborers have sown the seed. "We shall reap, if we faint not". (Galatians 6:9)

VICTORY OVER DARKNESS

What does the word victory mean to you? Is it a win at the basketball game where you beat them at the buzzer with a three pointer? Is it a victory when you win a prizefight with a knockout punch in the third round. What does victory mean to you, when you live in a world of darkness? Is it victory when you wake up in the morning and you see the sun coming up? Is it victory when you and your husband have tried for years and years to get pregnant and finally hear, "It's a girl!" Victory is God's love and it flows throughout the day when you feel like there's never going to be another day; victory over darkness in a world with no light to glow from the inside. Victory to me is beating this addiction through the faith and love granted by Jesus Christ; victory over darkness such as a child in a world of abuse, anger, and abandonment. Victory to me is peace and forgiveness toward the man who raped me as a teenage girl. Victory appears in many forms. It is light in a world of darkness. Victory is taking back your life through faith and prayer. Why do you need victory in your life? When you feel like you have no hope just look up, because the sun will come up in the morning. Look up and let the "Son" shine on you where darkness is overpowering your life. Don't let yourself get defeated in this dark world, because Jesus is our shining star. Follow him, follow his light and the darkness will fade away and let the light shine on you.

WASTED TIME

The time that I've wasted is my biggest regret
  Spent in this place, I'll never forget
  Just sitting and thinking about the things we've
    done
    The crying, the laughing, the hurt, the fun.

Now it's just me and my hard driven guilt
Behind a wall of emptiness, I allowed to be built
  I'm trapped in my body, just waiting to run
  Back to my youth where there's laughter and fun.

  But the chase is over, there's no place to hide
  Everything is gone including my pride
  With reality suddenly right in my face
  I'm scared and alone, stuck in this place.

Now memories of the past flash through my head
And the pain is obvious by the tears I shed
  I ask myself why and where I went wrong
  I guess I was weak, when I should have been strong.

  Living for the drugs and wings I had grown

My feelings were lost, afraid to be shown
As I look at my past, its so easy to see
The fear that I had, afraid to be me.

I'd pretend to be rugged, so fast and so cool
When actually I was lost like a blinded old fool
I'm getting too old for this tiresome game
Of acting real hard with no sense of shame.

It's time that I change and get on with my life
Fulfilling my dreams for a family and life without strife
What my future will hold, I really don't know

But the years that I've wasted are starting to show.

I just live for the day when I'll get a new start
And the dreams I still hold deep in my heart
I hope I can make it, I at least have to try
Because if I don't, I'm going to die!

L.W.

12-25-04

(This was written by a friend of mine here at Elizabeth.
She's lived a rugged, hard core life, but one month ago she
gave her heart to the Lord.   She no longer lives for the
drugs and the fast life, but today she lives for Jesus.)
       (Angie)

WE ALL FALL SHORT

I once heard this comment; "The Grand Canyon is 9 miles wide." I can jump 6-8 feet. My husband, being taller, can jump 12-13 feet, but a trained broad jumper jumps 24-26 feet. My point is that we are all still very short of the nine miles it would take to jump the Grand Canyon and dead unless someone were to save us. Many times I've told my children, "Just because you can't run as fast as the other girls in school doesn't mean that you're not fast." There's always going to be someone who is faster than even them. Yes, my daughters aren't quite as fast as some others and to some that means they fall short, behind the other kids. It never stopped them from trying harder. All of us fall short of the glory of God. All of us sin. But we must pick ourselves up and try again. We must remember that there is someone out there who will catch us when we fall. There's someone there to pick us up and dust us off. Jesus will be there at the bottom of that canyon as we jump to the other side. Jesus will be there to catch you, to save you from an eternal destiny in hell. We all fall short, but allow God to save you from what could be your destiny.

WE CAN'T RESIST
TEMPTATION ALONE

In the garden of Gethsemane Jesus went to pray. He told Peter to watch and pray. Three times Jesus caught Peter sleeping. He failed to obey Jesus' simple request, to watch and pray. Jesus used Peter's drowsiness to warn him about the lands of temptation he was about to face. Temptation strikes when we are most vulnerable and we can't resist it alone. The only way to overcome temptation is to be alert and pray. We must be aware of what hides in the darkness waiting for us. We must be alert to the subtleness of sin. But we also must be spiritually equipped to fight. We are at war and we must be alert and ready to fight. We can't do this alone. We need Jesus and together we can win this battle. We must pray and join in prayer to overthrow the enemy. It is essential because God's strength can shore up our defenses and defeat Satan's power. So, join in the forces against temptation. Watch and pray. Alert yourself to what lurks in the night, waiting to catch you while you are sleeping. We can't do it alone. We must join together and win this battle, because we can't do it alone.

WE DON'T EVEN KNOW HER NAME

The only name she has is "Potipher's wife." She lived her life with one foot on rich soil and the other in the sand. She was unfaithful and vindictive, ready to lie at any time to get what she wanted. She knew that Joseph was a prosperous man so she accused him of rape. Potipher's wife was a hollow woman whose soul was decaying due to her quest for power. She would do anything to become prosperous, even if it meant sending an innocent man to prison. In this prison I have met many women who would do anything to prosper themselves, no matter who was hurt in the process. Many of these women are prostitutes who sleep with married men, otherwise known as their "sugar daddies." The men provide them with money, cars, and even diamonds just for sleeping with them. The women take men to hotels where they rob them, and eventually help break-up their homes. They will do anything for vanity. Most of the time they don't even know the men's names. Their lives are headed down the path to hell. Their souls are decaying more and more each day. They have lost all respect for themselves and their "sugar daddies". Not caring what happens to their babies at home, or even what happens to themselves, they just want to prosper in their vanity. God wants to know their names and He's waiting for them to call on Him. He's waiting for them to stop in their path and turn their vindictive lives into faithful ones.

WE UNDERSTAND GOD WITH OUR HEARTS, NOT WITH OUR HEADS

How many of us have asked the question why or how? How did Moses part the Red Sea? Why does God love me when I don't love myself? Why did God let my daughter or son die? So many times in our lives we question God with our minds and not our hearts. We tend to question God during the times in our lives when everything seems to be going wrong. So, why don't we question God when things are going right in our lives? Why don't we ask, "why God", when things are going right in our lives? Why didn't you just let me stay in my addiction, instead, you saved my life by sending me to prison? We need to understand that we're not going to be able to comprehend or understand all that God does. We must think with our hearts and not our heads, because God is our heart that gave us life.

WELCOME TO THE FAMILY

As a baby is born, the new mother and father say, "Welcome to the family, baby." When I married into my husband's family, his grandmother said, "Welcome to the family, Angie." They didn't say this because I was now the new housekeeper or the new maid. They said this because I was now "adopted" into their family. I wasn't literally adopted, but I now held a new name. I was Angie Shier for 21 years and once I got married my name changed to Angie Pelphrey. My heart and mind wasn't reborn or changed, only my name. I was still the same person; I just had a different name. But when I was adopted into the family of God, not only did my heart change but so did my name. My name was now written in the Lamb's Book of Life. I was now "Angie Pelphrey, Child of the King". In January of 1995, God gave me a new heart and I new life. I was reborn the day I got saved. Yes, I struggled and failed Him many times, but He never stopped loving me with His unconditional love. Over the past month or so I have been granted the opportunity to help lead eight souls to the Lord. These women are convicts. They were prostitutes, drug dealers, and murderers. But, today they all have new hearts and new names. They are no longer only known as convicts, they are now known as children of the King. They have new lives ahead of them. They all have been adopted into a new family, the family of God. I was so blessed to say to them, "Welcome to the Family of God."

WHAT I ASKED FOR

I asked God to take away my guilt.   God said "No, it is not for me to take it away, but for you to give it up to me."
I asked God to give me patience.   God said, "No, patience is a product of trials and tribulations.   It isn't granted, it's earned."
I asked God to grant my life with happiness, God said "No, I give you blessings from Heaven, happiness is up to you."
I asked God to guide my path. God said "No, you walked the path you chose, and in your time of need I will carry you."
I asked God to spare me of pain. God said " No pain and suffering removes you apart from worldly cares and draws you closer to me."
I asked God to take my sins away.   God said "Yes my child, you are forgiven."

Angie Pelphrey

Many times in our lives we ask for things that we think we need.   But God knows all of our needs and when and how they should be granted.   But there is one thing that God grants upon request, if your heart is truly sincere and that is forgiveness of sins and an Eternity with him.   Ask God today for a new life, a new path, his path, and the way to Eternal life with Him.

WHAT IS HOPE?

Hope is when your day is dark and the sun breaks through the grey stormy sky. Hope is a dove that flies overhead when you've prayed to God to show you a sign of hope. Hope is the words given to my bunk mate that her husband made it through the car wreck. Hope was when Sharon's death penalty sentence was turned into life in prison. Hope is when you walk through the prison yard and the perfect snowflake falls on your coat. Hope is a rainbow that shines in the sky after a thunderstorm. Hope is when your children send you their pictures and a note with an "I love you." Hope is when you've hurt someone and they say the words "I forgive you." Hope is when you've run a long hard race and the finish line is in sight. Hope is when someone gives you a loving smile that says "It's okay." Hope is when the dreams stop and the nightmares go away. Hope is when you get a visit from your family and your children weep when they see you. Hope is when you call your husband and he says, " I'll be there no matter what." Hope is when the judge says that your sentence may be shortened. Hope is the sweet breathe of a new born baby born behind these walls. Hope is a letter, the first letter you've received in ten years. Hope is the day when the judge sets you free. Hope is knowing that one day I'll be free. Hope is knowing that Jesus is with me. Hope is my Bible, my prayers and my faith. Hope is all I have in this prison of fear. Hope is all I can share with these hurting women. Hope is not a dream but a reality with Jesus. Hope is knowing one day that my Jesus will return for me.

WHAT IS IT TO BE FREE?

What is it to be free? To be free for the 1st time in 20 years. To be free to sit on your front porch to watch the rain fall as tear drops from heaven. To watch the lightening flash across the sky and the thunder sound as the storm passes over. To be free to walk hand in hand with your child through the park on a bright sunny day, or is freedom being able to bow your head at your table in the chow hall behind prison walls? Is freedom the ability to kneel down with a sister in your dorm room to pray with her as she weeps from the death of a parent, never to be able to see them again, here on this earth. What does being free, mean to you? To be free is a state of mind. To be free to a sister behind these prison bars, is a choice. You can be free in this prison, but it's a choice. Today a sister in our cottage spoke on what it means to be free behind these prison walls for 12 years. To be free from the pain that she caused by taking the life of her own husband. To me, being free is my choice. To me, freedom only comes through Jesus Christ. Freedom is a state of mind in many ways, but true freedom comes from forgiveness of our sins. One day, I will be free from this prison, but today I know that I am free in my heart. Free to live my life for Jesus behind these walls.

WHAT IS MATURITY?

When I think about the word maturity, I think about a tree and its growth process. First, a seed is planted, and then it is watered. After a few weeks it sprouts up out of the ground. A few years later it blossoms into a full grown tree. When springtime comes, the tree begins to bear fruits. Some of the fruit may fall to the ground and get bruised and tattered, but most turn out to be beautiful bushels. In the fall the tree sheds all of its leaves, turning brown and falling to the ground. But once springtime hits, the tree is covered with beautiful brightly colored leaves and tasty fruit. Why is maturity like a tree to me? Because, growing up as a child, my parents planted a seed in me. I was watered by friends, family, and my peers to make me who I am today. As a teenager I began to sprout into the woman I eventually would become. Many years later I blossomed, bearing fruit. The fruit represents many different things in my life. The fruit represents my qualities in life whether good or bad. Because to be a mature woman you must first be able to fall to the ground and pick yourself up and learn from that mistake. You may be bruised and tattered but you must blossom. It may take you a whole season, but when you finally get up you're brighter and better than you ever were before. A mature woman sees with her heart instead of her eyes. As she sees that bruised fruit lying on the ground, she picks it up, cuts the outer shell off and opens it up to see what's inside. A mature woman doesn't have to be a certain age, because my 14 year old daughter, Kayla, is a mature woman to me. She sees with her heart, never judging, only loving others for who they are, not where they have been. She sees the inner beauty of the fruit I bear, whether I'm bruised or beaten down, she picks me up and kisses the bruises and loves me no matter what. What does maturity mean to me? Maturity is a process. It is a growth from within, a growth that may be stunted at any time, but with a little sunshine and water on it, it can grow to be a beautiful thing.

Kayla, this was an assignment I had to do, and when I did it, I could only think of you. I am so proud of you. You have grown and matured into a beautiful young woman. I am so proud!!!
I love you,
Mommy
(7-16-05)

WHAT IS OUR HOPE? LOVE.

What is my hope? Knowing that God loves me no matter what. Knowing I'm different, unique, and that He has a purpose and plan for my life. Knowing that He meets my every need no matter how great or how small. Knowing that His love goes beyond my natural needs and that He gave me an instruction manual, my Bible, to guide me successfully through this life, no matter what happens. Knowing that I am a part of the family of God and that I will live forever in eternity with Him. Knowing I am able to experience His love and presence in my life and that He gives me peace even in the midst of the storms that arise. Knowing that He loved me enough to lay down His life for me, and that His love sees the best in us, not the worst. Knowing that there is no greater love than the love of Jesus, and that He loves me, Angie Pelphrey, with a love and compassion like no other.

WHAT I'VE LEARNED

What I have learned while here in the pen is that when you say you're "salty" that means you're really mad. When you say you're praying for someone that's considered "good looking out." I am a number not a name. God is used in almost every cuss word. I don't know if they're praying sometimes or cussing someone out. I've learned that breakfast at 4:00 a.m. isn't really so bad, and envelopes are hard to come by because that's the only type of cash that everyone has. But what I've really learned is to be thankful. Thankful that I have a loving husband who supports me. I have a family that's never been taken from me. I've learned that all of us are hurting in some way, even if we're the toughest broad on the bay. I've learned that temptation is a daily piece of life. I've learned that I can witness to even the roughest and toughest woman in this prison if I just ask God to allow me to. I've learned that all of us have tears, and there are some times that we just control it. I've learned that I am worthy, even if you don't think so. I've learned that all of us have fears, and those who are most fearful are the ones who say they're not afraid of anyone or anything. I've learned that Jesus is with you everywhere, even in "Hale." I've learned that even a murderer or child abuser can be saved. I've learned to love some people that have never known love. I've learned that we all have a purpose in life, and mine is to be a mother, wife, friend in need, and a witness to others in need. I've learned that I am loved, I have friends and I am a child of the King.

WHAT WOULD JESUS DO?

When I was first brought into the jail I was locked up in the bull pen for about three hours. The bullpen is a holding cell that's about 5x5 feet. The only thing in the pen is a bench to sit on along the wall. Well, for two hours I sat there waiting for my paperwork to be processed. Unsure at this time what in the world would happen to me and no clue where they were going to take me next. After two hours, they brought in another woman. She was cuffed behind her back and her hair was hanging in her face. She was dirty from head to toe and she ranked of paint fumes. Her teeth were rotted out and she was crying and crying. She would stop crying and look at me and say, "This isn't fair, I shouldn't be here." Well, I was getting pretty anxious at this time, thinking they've put some nut in here with me and she's going to freak out on me any time. I thought to myself, Angie, what would Jesus do at this time. So, I leaned over and told her everything will be okay. I'll be sitting here and praying for you, and whatever happens, it'll be okay. She kept crying and sobbing and saying she was scared. She had been sniffing paint all night and her mind wasn't working well. So, again, I thought what would he do? So, I again moved toward her and put my arms around her and hugged her. She looked up at me and said, "Nobody's ever done that for me." She asked, "What's your name?" I told her, Angie. She said, "Angie, thank you." She sat back and stopped weeping, and said, "Please pray for me."

WHAT'S LOVE GOT TO DO WITH IT? EVERYTHING!

As I was brought into custody, my heart broke. Not for myself, but for my husband and children. For all that they had to go through with my addiction, and now the consequences of the bad choices that I made while Jones' for pills. (Jones' is when you feel like you have to have that pill or you're going to die) While going through my addiction, the only thing on my mind was making sure I had that next pill. Addiction is a selfish disease that overcomes your feelings and emotions, and makes you become as concrete. You're happy when you have it and angry when you don't. But God allowed me to go to jail.

I've been in jail now for 3 weeks and I have been given the opportunity to see what love is all about, everything. God has showed me unconditional love from family and friends. My daughters told me they were proud of me and proud that I am their mother. My husband told me that he would be there to the end. That he will stand behind me no matter what.

At my first trial, 30 members of my church family showed up to support me. The officers thought it was a jury trial. When they found out it was for love and support, they said never in the history of Scioto County has anyone had 30 people show up for a pre-trial. God's love is the greatest love you can ever share with someone, and I am so thankful for his Great Love.

What's love got to do with it? EVERYTHING

Written 12-13-04

WHEN ALL HOPE IS LOST

Addiction had overtaken her life, her hopes and her dreams. She hit her bottom this time. She cried out, but no one was there to hear her. Her daughter died suddenly of an aneurism in the brain and she died inside right along with her. She lost all hope. Was life worth living? She felt like she had nothing left. Death was her only option. She hired a hit man to take her own life. She didn't know the time or the place only that it would happen soon. He was waiting for her in her home. As she walked through the door, he grabbed his knife and stabbed her, once in the back and once in the stomach. Quickly, he grabbed his can of gasoline and doused her with it. He set her on fire and left her for dead. She lay there crying out in pain, begging

God for forgiveness, begging God to let her live and to give her a second chance. Today, she sits in prison with me, determined to live her life free of her addiction and free to serve Jesus. One day she prays that she will see her granddaughter once again. In a time where she thought that all hope was lost, she found Jesus. The scars still remain from that tragic day, but today she is free. Today she has hope. Today she is alive, and alive in Christ.

WHEN GOD'S ON YOUR SIDE

When God is on your side you have nothing to fear. God will protect you. I found this out the second week in Marysville. I was walking by one of the girl's bunks and I stopped to talk to someone, before I knew what happened the girl hopped up off of her bunk and shoved me up against the wall. She started yelling, "If you don't get out of my space, I will go to the hole for killing you today." The hole or ARN 4 is where you are put when you get into any kind of trouble. It is like a jail inside of prison. It has four brick walls with a mat on the floor. You are sentenced there anywhere from a week to a year, or longer. I have never had my life threatened before, so I was very afraid. I couldn't let her see my fear, so I just glared right back at her. She was a black girl about 5'11" and 250 pounds. You can see why I was a little fearful. Well, I got on the phone with my husband and asked him to start praying. He called some of our friends from church to pray for protection over me. Throughout the day as I would pass her bunk, she would make comments aloud about "getting me." I knew the only way that this could be handled was through prayer. I knew that I had someone and something much bigger and stronger than she was, and that was God. After praying, I felt at peace about the situation. I decided to smile at her and try to make small chit chat to ease the situation. Well, it worked. The next day we were both in the bathroom at the same time holding a civil conversation. God was truly on my side. God can turn any bad situation around and turn it into something good. Allow Jesus into your heart so He can be on your side too.

WHEN YOU FLY INTO A RAGE, YOUR LANDING WILL ALWAYS BE ROUGH

"Be ye angry, and sin not" (Ephesians 4:26). Anger is an emotion, and it is important to have these feelings, but it's how we use our anger and how we process it that makes the difference. I have always been one to get easily offended and touchy in certain situations. I had to be treated good to actually feel good about myself. But, in some ways I expected to be treated badly, because I thought I was bad. It was my own insecurities that caused anger toward me and others. The word anger derives from the word DANGER. When you are easily angered, it should send up "danger signs" in your mind. Staying angry allows the devil to gain a foothold on our lives. In Christian lives, Satan gains his ground mostly through resentments, bitterness and unforgiveness. Anger causes you to speak without thinking. Then as your anger begins to fly off the handle, you end up making a landing that has taken out friends and family members. We must realize that sustained anger is sin. God commands us to forgive as freely as he has forgiven us. So, be generous today. Give the healing to others that has been well overdue. Give them forgiveness.

WHEN YOU'RE DOWN TO NOTHIN', GOD'S UP TO SOMETHING

For the last couple days here in Marysville, I've laid in bed sick. Nothing seems worse than having to be sick in prison, because when you become physically ill here you also become mentally and spiritually down. Your heart just seems to ache for home. But this morning, God was up to something. It's two days before Valentine's Day and holidays can sometimes be depressing here. I had prayed that this Valentine's Day would bring some happiness into this prison for me. When my husband told me he was sending me my Valentine's present in the mail, I knew that it had to be special, because we can't receive anything but mail here. When I got to thinking about it, I prayed, "Lord, please just let him send me a picture of the roses that I would have received, like always, on Valentine's Day." Well, as I awoke this morning I rushed to get my mail. I saw a big white envelope from my husband. As I opened the envelope, two pictures fell out. It was my roses -- just like I always received, but they were so much more beautiful this time, because in the picture they will never die. In the card he got me he renewed his wedding vows with me. That was more precious than anything he's ever said or done for me. So when you think that you're so down that you can't look up, just remember, God is always up to something.

WHEN OUR LIFE TURNS INWARD, WE LOSE OUR INTENDED PURPOSE

If we try to protect ourselves from pain, we begin to die

290

spiritually and emotionally. But being a real disciple for the Lord implies real, true commitment. When we give out lives in service to Christ, we discover the real purpose of living. For many years I was just the bystander, watching others carrying the cross through the streets. The Roman method of execution for condemned criminals was to carry their cross through the streets to their site. So after Jesus' death, carrying the cross meant a true commitment, the risk of death, and no turning back. So, today I carry the cross in service for Jesus. There is no turning back. I am a true disciple for the Lord, pledging my whole existence to His service. I can no longer try to save myself from pain or discomfort, because I would risk losing my true eternal life. My life had turned inward, losing the intended purpose for my life. I made choices as though this life were all I had. When in reality this life is just the introduction to eternity. I have turned my will and my life over to God and my life shines outwardly toward my eternal destiny. I no longer see with my eyes but with my heart.

WHO, ME? I'M NOT ANGRY!

There are many types of anger and I can say that I've seen most, if not all, types here in prison. I've learned in prison that I feel two types of anger. The first is due to an anger avoidance behavior, and the second is shame-based anger. For many years I hid from being angry. I hated confrontation. I wanted to always have a feeling of safety. I was a people pleaser. But today I'm learning to be assertive and not feel guilty when I get angry. I need to stand up for what's right today if I want to continue in my recovery. The second type of anger I have is shame-based anger. I always felt I needed a lot of attention. I felt unlovable and unworthy. I would lash out at the ones I loved the most even when my anger wasn't directed at them. But anger can keep you stuck in a place where you don't want to be. It can cause mistrust of others, paranoia, over sensitivity, and even feelings of being out of control. So we must begin to recognize our anger, and for some of us we need to realize that it's okay to be angry. Pray for God's guidance in your life, to help you deal with your anger, so it won't hinder your recovery. Let Go and let God.

WHO WAS SHE, REALLY?

I've been in Marysville Penitentiary for about a week now. It's Dec. 21st, 2004 just 4 days before Christmas. I can't stop crying. I see a picture of my children and cry. I saw a puppy in the sergeant's office, and I cried. I think I'm crying not only because I miss my family, but also because it's Christmas. I truly know who I am now. I know the true importance of family. I know now what the word blessed means. Without the pills now for over a month, I can feel again. I have true feelings. Feelings of love, fear, friendships and love for Jesus that I never had before. I've heard people say that they go to a certain place to find themselves and I always just laughed. Find yourself, where did you go? But I have found the real me - the inner me. I have found a beauty within myself that I've never felt before. I am a good woman. I am beautiful. I am one of God's children, and I am so blessed that he loved me enough to send me to Marysville so I could find myself, the real me, the person who was lost for many years.

WHY AM I DIFFERENT?
BECAUSE HE LOVED ME

He made my eyes to finally see. He gave me new ears, so that I could hear. He changed my walk, my heart, my soul. He gave me wings that I could fly, to soar through this world, for He is now my guide. He gave me strength, to carry the burdens of this life and to know that they are not too heavy to carry. He changed my voice, to speak of His love, to tell of my joy, to praise Him every day. He gave me friends to soar with me, in times of need. To lift me up when I am down. To show me that I am not alone. That I don't have to do this all alone, like before. He gave me knees to withstand the trials in life, to kneel down on and pray, to cry out to Him, to ask for His strength, to praise His name, to soak up His love and peace. He has changed my all. That is why I am different. And it's only because He loved me. He healed me. He changed me. He has given me the armor of God. I suit up each day. I feel different. I am different. Yes, it does come from within. But it must begin with Him. I cannot do it alone. I am asking for your help. Yes, you, my family. My family on the Hill. I need your arms to lift me up when I am down. I need your eyes to see me through. I need your ears to hear my cup. I need your wings to help me fly. I need your strength when I am down. I am different because today I am not alone. Today I am different because He loved me. He loved you, and together, we will make it. You will make it. We will make it together, because we were chosen.

WHY WON'T YOU LET ME DIE?

"Why didn't he just let me die? I don't have anything to live for. My husband was murdered, my mom died of an overdose and my father was killed in an accident. I have no one. I have nothing to live for. I took twenty Oxycontin and I still didn't die. I took twenty Valium and He still wouldn't let me die. Why? Why Jesus? Why won't you just let me die?" These are the words of a friend of mine that ended up in prison with me. She said that she tried to overdose three times but for some reason, God wouldn't let her die. She told me of her husband's murder and how her parents died. She felt like she had nothing to live for. Then she met a man named Jesus. She had prayed to Jesus many times before. But all of her prayers were for Jesus to let her die. But, Jesus had other plans. Jesus wanted to give her life, not death. She was no longer alone. She might not have any family on the outside of these walls but she has Jesus on the inside. In her heart, she accepted Jesus as her Savior before she came into prison. She no longer had a desire to die, but now she had a desire to live. To live for Jesus. To tell others of what He had done for her. He saved her life. He saved her from a life in Hell. He gave a freedom that she'd never had before. Even though she's unable to be free physically, she's now able to be free from her past. She's no longer alone, because Jesus is with her. He gave her life and a life more abundant. He gave her a reason to live, and the reason is Eternity with Him.

WICKEDNESS WILL NOT PREVAIL
BEHIND THESE PRISON WALLS

God uses even the activities of the wicked to fulfill His good purposes. We must believe that God is not the cause of evil. Evil is just a temporary condition on this earth. Today has been a confusing day for me. I went downstairs, like usual at 6:00 a.m. to get my mail. Receiving mail in prison is the most exciting thing to do all day. But today was different. When I picked up my mail I noticed that this letter was different from all of the other letters that I have received before. It had no return address and the handwriting was messy, written like a 5 year old child would have done it. When I got ready to open it, I read what was written on the back of the envelope, which said, "Live today as it is your last." I knew then that it had to be a death threat. Once I opened the letter to read it, tears filled my eyes. The letter was typed and not signed. It talked of watching my children in church. It went on to say that my husband and children will suffer the rest of their lives for my mistakes. They said that they knew the type of mother that I really was and that I was a fake. The letter went on to say much more, but the rest is not important. What is important is that through this death threat, God was still in control. God will prevail. I am an over comer now, and today I am strong enough to withstand the wickedness in this world. If I had not ended up behind these prison walls, I would have never been the person that I am today, a strong, courageous, and faithful woman of God. Always know that God is in control in any situation, even when you're behind prison walls.

WITH GOD'S HELP, ANY SITUATION CAN BE USED FOR GOOD

Joseph was betrayed and deserted by his own family. Nevertheless, God allowed Joseph to survive and prosper where most would have failed. His ten older brothers, due to his confidence and pride, conspired against Joseph, Jacob's favorite son. Joseph was a man of personal integrity and spiritual sensitivity. Due to this he rose in power from a slave to ruler of Egypt. Joseph was betrayed by his family, exposed to sexual temptation, and punished for doing the right thing. But with God's help, any situation can be used for good, even when others intend it for evil. I have met many women here in prison, in the same situation as Joseph. They were betrayed and deserted by their own families. Some were sold into sexual sin, and were conspired against by their own parents. They strived to do good but the temptation was too overpowering. Today they sit in this prison alone, deserted and betrayed. But, with God's help, they have overcome. They sit here with pride, personal integrity, and spiritual blessings. They are no longer alone because of what others intended for evil, because God used it for good. Today they use their past for good. They spread God's word behind these prison walls. They speak of how God has used their past for His glory.

WITHSTANDING THE STORMS OF LIFE

What kind of foundation have you built your life on? Can it withstand the storms of life, or will your house sink in the "sands" of trials and tribulations? When the rain descends, and the flood flows, and the wind beats at the doors of your heart, will you withstand it? Can you withstand and not crumble and fall? You can, if your foundation is built upon the rock. You can if your foundation is solid. We must practice our obedience to Jesus, because this will become our solid foundation to weather the storms of life. A fool's life crumbles. Many don't deliberately seek to build on an inferior foundation, they just don't think about the real purpose of life. They're headed for destruction, not out of stubbornness but out of thoughtlessness. We must pass on to them Christ's message. We must share with them the true meaning of life, and that is to serve our loving God with all of our heart and soul.

WORKER'S COMPENSATION

I think back to a time in my life when I was a registered nurse, working with children. One day I was at the home of an 11 year old boy with cerebral palsy. His mother asked for my assistance in lifting him back into his wheelchair, so we both bent down to lift him and immediately I felt a sharp pain in my neck. Well, because of the pain and injury on the job, I received workers' compensation. But there is another workers' compensation that we can receive from God. If you get hurt on a job, you get paid for the pain and suffering. The same goes for God's children, because if you get hurt on the job while working for God, he repays you for your pain and suffering. You are rewarded. I know that while I am here in prison, the work I am doing for the Lord, will not go unnoticed. I will receive my workers' compensation. But it will be in His love, peace, and joy unspeakable. God is able to bless your life so much, to the point where you can't even believe that it's possible to feel so good, and still be behind prison walls.

YOU CAN MAKE A SMILE
OUT OF NOTHING

Yesterday when I went into the Rec room, I noticed one of the older sisters in the house crying. It was her daughter's Graduation Day from high school, a day that she never dreamed of missing. She was overwhelmed with grief and pain for not being there when her daughter walked across that stage. Since prison doesn't allow you to give to other people, or even at times show affection, we really had to pull some strings. We went to the officer on duty and asked if we could give something to another sister. We explained the situation and he felt that it was well needed, so we were off. The C.O. distracted her by asking her to go downstairs for a few minutes, so we could get everything ready. About 20 minutes later she walked into her cell. A cell that 20 minutes prior was drab and dreary. But when she looked inside, she began to cry. We had cut balloons out of construction paper with thumbtacks. We made streamers out of toilet paper, and on her bed was a graduation hat and diploma made of paper and toothpaste (for tape). The diploma was written out just as her daughter's would have looked, as she marched across the stage. It would really be something so small to someone on the outside, but to this sister in prison, it changed a day in her life forever. We helped her smile, when all we had was nothing.

YOU CAN'T JUDGE A CONVICT BY HER LOOKS

If you were put in a church house with all of the women in this penitentiary, would you be able to tell the convicts from the other members? Probably not, because I can't tell the difference and I'm in here with thousands of them. They look just like everyday people. Why? It's because they are. I can't look at these women and guess what they have done. If they put a uniform on I couldn't tell if they were a captain or a convict. I have actually sat and wondered why some of these women were here. I have actually tried to guess their crime. I was floored when one of the girls told me that the young woman down the bay killed her two young children by setting her house on fire, then blaming her five year old son for it. She told the young child to tell the police that he accidentally set the fire, but the child told the police that mommy did it. I would have never guessed that she was the one that would murder her own children. That's because we can only see what's on the outside, not the inside. The only way to do that is to show and share God's love. Sometimes as hard as that may be, you have to look past a person's past and to get to their heart. As Christians, we all must be able and willing to have a forgiving heart. A heart to look within, not on the outside.

YOUR THOUGHTS SET THE DIRECTION FOR YOUR LIFE

Success or failure? Your thoughts set the direction for your life. I'm growing weary in this prison. My thoughts are running wild. My thoughts are becoming so negative. I've been setting myself up for failure and didn't even realize it. My mind has been so focused on the negative direction in my life right now that I set myself up for disappointment and despair. My negative thinking has limited my ability to carry out and fulfill God's plan for what He wants for my life. I allowed the devil to build strongholds and to become a stumbling block in my mind. But, today I am in control again. I control my thoughts, and my positive thoughts are about to change my life. Today I submitted my inner thoughts to God. Today, if I speak positive, then my life will change. My thoughts have become His thoughts. Not my will, but His will, because where my mind goes, my heart will follow. As my thoughts are changing, my words are now changing. I will overcome and I will be home soon. How do I know? Because it is God's will and He is in control.

CPSIA information can be obtained at www.ICGtesting.com
Printed in the USA
LVOW11s1107210115

423753LV00001B/70/P